Anonymus

Report of the proceedings in the case of Fitzgerald v. Northcote and another

Anonymus

Report of the proceedings in the case of Fitzgerald v. Northcote and another

ISBN/EAN: 9783741139925

Manufactured in Europe, USA, Canada, Australia, Japa

Cover: Foto ©Thomas Meinert / pixelio.de

Manufactured and distributed by brebook publishing software
(www.brebook.com)

Anonymus

Report of the proceedings in the case of Fitzgerald v. Northcote and another

REPORT OF THE PROCEEDINGS

IN THE CASE OF

FITZGERALD *v.* NORTHCOTE

AND ANOTHER.

TOGETHER WITH

AN INTRODUCTORY NARRATIVE AND OTHER DOCUMENTS.

LONDON:

BURNS, LAMBERT, AND OATES.

DUBLIN: DUFFY. BIRMINGHAM: MAHER.

MDCCCLXVI.

THE following Letter from the Bishop of the Diocese to Dr. Northcote sufficiently explains the circumstances under which this Report is published. It is taken from the short-hand notes of Messrs. GEORGE WALSH and Sons, 3 Little George Street, Westminster; and only such foot-notes have been added as are necessary to correct either manifest errors or misunderstandings, which could scarcely fail to arise out of the evidence, if unexplained.

The Introductory Narrative is composed only of authentic documents, or extracts from such documents, and requires no explanation.

EDMUND J. KNIGHT,
Vice-President.

St. Mary's, Oscott,
March 1, 1866.

Birmingham, Feb. 10, 1866.

DEAR DR. NORTHCOTE,

Having only returned late last night from assisting at Bishop Hogarth's funeral, I had not till to-day an opportunity of reading through the proceedings in the case of Fitzgerald *v.* Northcote. It was after young Fitzgerald had left the College that you informed me of what had passed with respect to him, and I then expressed the fullest approval of the course you had taken; and the facts that have come out on the trial have but strengthened the motives for the approval to which I then gave utterance. I wish completely to identify myself with the position in which that trial may have placed you, and to share with you whatever annoyance it may occasion: although I am disposed to believe that from all thinking men and persons of honourable mind the verdict will be in your favour.

In my opinion you will do well to print the whole proceedings of the trial, from the best report obtainable; for the facts that come out, and the remarks of the Chief-Justice as to what may be rightly done by the Head of an establishment such as that you preside over, will always stand for the complete vindication both of yourself and of the College. As the Chief-Justice observed, "Beyond all doubt, young Fitzgerald had certainly shown symptoms of a mutinous disposition, and had given considerable trouble. He ought to have shown a good example to the boys; but, nevertheless, he had contrived to get into as many scrapes as he could possibly have fallen into." As to these being "of a venial character," morally, and in the abstract, they might be so, but most certainly not as bearing on the discipline of the College, and the preservation of harmony within it. As the Judge remarked, "It was to be borne in mind that in so large an establishment it was most important to keep up discipline and regular habits." Precisely for this reason, that discipline, where large numbers of boyish spirits have to be kept under control, is most important, its open and frequent violation by one whose age and position rendered his conduct influential cannot be considered as venial,—that is to say, such as may be easily overlooked or pardoned.

Speaking in detail of this conduct, the Chief-Justice says, "As to going to public-houses, it was most fit that there should be a rule against it;" indeed, there are more things than beer or any other beverage to which youths are exposed in drinking-houses; and the Judge himself drew the distinction between going for refreshment and seeking diversion in public-houses. And again, as his Lordship remarked, "it was most reasonable that there should be a general rule against the use of fire-arms by the boys in the school. And on the occasion in question the answer of Fitzgerald as to the discovery of the pistol was, to say the least, not satisfactory."

In the circumstances which form the main point in this case—viz. the young man's expulsion, consequent upon his final act—you acted yourself on the principle which the Chief-Justice has laid down. His words are these: "Now, if the fact really was that young Fitzgerald, after the ill-feeling which had existed in former times between the lay and the clerical students, really did organise a confederacy among the students for the purpose of renewing that unhappy and discreditable feud, and making the position of the clerical students of inferior birth uncomfortable and unpleasant, there could be no doubt that it was a most unjustifiable, dangerous, and improper course of proceeding, and one which, if it did in fact exist, would call for the intervention of the President and other authorities of the institution in some marked and conspicuous manner, to crush the attempt before it had reached a head, and thus to preserve the peace and comfort of the establishment." But you, the President, had evidence of the reappearance of this spirit before you knew who was its originator or promoter; and the book, while it confirmed what you had already learnt from other sources, served to point out the originator. We may appeal to any unprejudiced man of ordinary common-sense whether a youth under accusation saying "It is all nonsense," can render null such proof of his acts and of their natural tendency; his very style of speech is an admission of the truth of the charge.

But alas for prejudices! Although I advised you to accept of no compromise, such as implied admission of error,—a compromise of such a character as was offered, and even pressed upon you,—yet I had pretty well calculated that the verdict of your so-called peers would be against you. We Catholics live in an atmosphere of prejudice; foregone conclusions follow us like our shadows. Whenever a case affects the Catholic clergy, these prejudices have to be taken into calculation. The lawyers refer to them by expressions quite proverbial; and in this, as in previous cases, the adverse Counsel played upon them. Nor does the Court seem to have power to protect us from them. Here, however, they came out into the light of day, when, before a word of the Defendants' case had been heard, the Jury expressed their readiness to decide, with the intention of giving their verdict in favour of the Plaintiff.

We may accept the dicta of the Judge, that "the Prefect of Discipline, Mr. Stone, had shown no symptoms of arbitrary temper;" and that "it was impossible for any candid mind to object to what was said by Dr. Northcote to the youth on occasion of pointing out to him the serious character of his persistent disregard of discipline, and warning him that his next offence must be punished by expulsion." And, notwithstanding the remarks that followed, as to what might or might not have been done, and what was to be regretted as not having been done, the moral rectitude and propriety of what you did have full testimony borne to them by the Judge.

For, indeed, it was your extreme kindness and consideration for the youth himself, and your solicitude to save his reputation with his father, that left open for him a way beyond all calculation to enter on "a course of proceeding," to use the Judge's words, "most unjustifiable, dangerous, and improper," and which you were called upon "in some marked and conspicuous manner to crush." But the only marked and conspicuous manner in which, under the circumstances, this could be done was by expulsion, for you had already exhausted all other means of punishment in dealing with this youth. And it must be remembered, as you yourself distinctly stated in your first letter to Mr. Justice Fitzgerald, that you dismissed him not for this last offence of his only, or even principally, but for that taken in connection with all his previous offences of the half-year. Your words are: "Even if this had been his first offence, I should have felt it my duty to mark my sense of such conduct by some very serious penalty; but after all his antecedents of this half-year, I had no alternative but to dismiss him immediately." I do not observe this point any where brought out in the course of the trial as it should have been. Indeed, the Plaintiff's Counsel allowed himself to say the direct contrary; viz. that you had condoned all his previous offences, and attached no importance to them whatever, and sent him away solely on account of the A. B. C.; and this he said while professing to comment on the very letter from which I have quoted.

Justice to the College requires me to notice that the details embodied in this case do not fairly represent the habitual spirit of the establishment. They are exceptional, arising out of an exceptional course of conduct. Oscott has always allowed as much freedom to its students as is consistent with control, and with the responsibility of protecting their moral character. Nor do I believe that a greater frankness or more manly openness of character than prevails there is to be found in any public school.

Praying Almighty God to bless you, and to prosper the establishment over which you have so successfully presided, and over which I hope you will long preside,

I remain, dear Dr. Northcote,

Your faithful servant and friend,

✠ W. B. Ullathorne.

INTRODUCTORY STATEMENT OF FACTS.

EARLY in the year 1793, a "plan of Oscott Seminary" was published, under the sanction of the Hon. and Right Rev. Thomas Talbot, Vicar-Apostolic of the Midland District; the Right Rev. Charles Berington, his coadjutor; with the Hon. Charles Dormer (afterwards Lord Dormer), and Thomas Clifford, Esq. (afterwards Sir Thomas Clifford Constable, Bart.), as joint trustees. In this "plan" it is stated that "the end of the Institution is to supply one priest yearly to the Mission; and that, as the course of education is limited to six years, it is necessary that the Seminary be established for the education of six students."*

In the month of November of the same year, "some Catholic noblemen and gentlemen, finding the necessity of an establishment at home for the education of the Catholic laity, determined to found a public school or college in England, to be under the inspection of a certain number of governors; and a subscription was opened to defray the expense of such an undertaking."†

Amongst the subscribers were the Lords Petre and Stourton, Sir William Jerningham, Sir John Throckmorton, Mr. Towneley, Mr. Hornyold, Mr. Wheble, Mr. Bernard Howard (afterwards Duke of Norfolk), and the Hon.

* Printed document in the archives of Oscott.

† Printed document in the archives of Oscott, signed "By order of the Governors, William Cruise, Secretary."

Charles Dormer, one of the trustees of the Oscott Seminary.

In the following year these two plans were combined; and in October 1794, a prospectus* was published "of the plan of education for the Catholic College at Oscott," "in consequence of the union which has been formed by the Governors with the Bishop and Trustees of the Seminary;" and it was announced that the house would be "ready for the reception of students on the first day of November next."

In 1808 "the College of Oscott, under the direction of Dr. Bew and certain noblemen, &c., being dissolved as a losing concern, the property on the premises was offered to the Vicar-Apostolic, on condition of his paying the debts of the former establishment to the amount of about 600*l.*, which was accordingly done; and a new establishment was formed at once as a college and a seminary,—seven ecclesiastical students, about thirty lay students."†

In 1835 it became necessary to provide more extensive accommodation. A farm was purchased in the neighbourhood of the old college, and a new building begun, which in 1838 was fit for occupation. On the opening of the chapel (May 31, 1838) Dr. Weedall preached "on the origin, object, and influence of Church Seminaries;" and the new college was conducted, as the old one had been, "on the plan of a seminary for ecclesiastics and a college for lay students both together."‡

In the beginning of 1865 there were one hundred and twenty-three boys in the house, of whom twelve only were being educated for the ecclesiastical state; and amongst the lay students were David, John, and Gerald Fitzgerald,

* Now in the archives of Oscott.

† Dr. Milner's Ms. Journal.

‡ Dr. Husenbeth's *Life of Dr. Milner*, p. 158.

sons of the Right Hon. Mr. Justice Fitzgerald, of Dublin, and David, Martin, and James Fitzgerald, sons of Mr. Thomas Fitzgerald, the judge's brother.

On Monday, March 13th, Dr. Northcote, the President of Oscott, wrote the following letter to Mr. Justice Fitzgerald:

"St. Mary's, Oscott, March 13, 1865.

"My dear Judge,—How shall I break to you the very sad news I have to communicate? I hope and suppose David will already have done this for me. He will have given you his own account of what has happened to oblige me to send him away from amongst us this morning. I must now give you mine. I will confine myself to the last circumstance which has forced upon me so grave a measure. I pass over the breaches of discipline and offensive conduct to his superiors, which by degrees led to my having a serious conversation with him, and inflicting a severe punishment, on Shrove Tuesday, scarcely a fortnight ago. After depriving him of his 'privileges' to the utmost, I said, 'There is only one thing which remains in the way of degrading you, and that is to deprive you of your room, and put you into the dormitory. I do not inflict this punishment because it would destroy the only end and object for which you are here, study for your University examination, and I shall not inflict this therefore, happen what may. If you commit any fresh offence, nothing remains but to send you away. With senior boys like you I have no other remedy.' He assured me very solemnly, and more than once, that he would not offend in any way again. I said I hoped he would not, but that, by way of precaution, lest he should, I must write to you and acquaint you with the exact state of things. 'I have never written to your father,' I said, 'any thing but good of you. If I were to dismiss you from the college without warning, he would have a right to complain. He would think I had lost my temper, and been unreasonably harsh with you for a first offence. To protect myself, therefore, I must make him informed of all that has happened.' And with this I dismissed him. He returned to me at 9.30 P.M. to beg that I would not write to you. I repeated the reasons for which I considered myself obliged to do so, and he again and again promised that he would be most careful not to offend again in any way, so that I should be running no risk. 'It comes to this, David; I am risking my character for prudence and moderation and justice against your word of honour that you will not give any fresh cause of offence. Is this safe?' He immediately gave his word of honour, and I accepted it, but not without distinctly setting before him again the two sides of the balance as they appeared to me.

"This conversation took place on the last day of last month; and although I now find he has given frequent cause of complaint to his superiors by breaches of discipline since that time, I had not been told of them, out of a consideration for him, until this morning, when I was informed of the discovery of an association amongst the boys, got up by David, against the Church students of the college. He had prepared lists of all Church students of the last few years, their places of residence, 'with all particulars' (I quote from his Ms., now lying before me) 'as to birth, parentage, qualifications, patrons, &c.' By making all sorts of inquiries, he had discovered, or imagined he had discovered, that 'A. B.'s brother or uncle keeps a small grocery establishment; D. C.'s father is a general inspector of canal-locks, &c.;' and he had persuaded some ten or twelve of his companions to join in this association. Any thing more ungentlemanly in itself, or more mischievous in its probable consequences, I have rarely, I may say never, met with, since my connection with the college. Even if it had been his first offence, I should have felt it my duty to mark my sense of such conduct by some very serious penalty. But, after all his antecedents of this half year, I had no alternative but to dismiss him immediately. I need not say how much it has cost me to have recourse to so extreme a measure with a boy of his promise, and after so many years' residence amongst us. But it is his extravagant conceit which has brought this disgrace upon him; and sad as it is, I only trust it may be the means of sparing him worse falls hereafter, and be some warning also to his brothers, who show symptoms of a similar disposition.

"I write in haste, but I think I ought to send you as early information as I can. He left us at three o'clock this afternoon for Dublin.—I remain, my dear Sir, yours very sincerely, J. SPENCER NORTHCOTE."

On Tuesday evening Dr. Northcote received the following telegrams—from Mr. Justice Fitzgerald: "Let John and Gerald Fitzgerald return home by the early train tomorrow morning;" and from Mr. Thomas Fitzgerald: "I wish my sons David and James to come home by the tomorrow morning's train."

On Thursday evening Dr. Northcote received the following letter from Mr. Justice Fitzgerald:

"March 15, 1865.

"DEAR SIR,—I received your letter of the 13th on my arrival in Dublin yesterday. In order to enable me to form a correct judgment of the course pursued towards David, I desire to be informed of the details of 'the breaches of discipline and offensive conduct towards his superiors,' the antecedents of this half year to which you allude now for the first time. I also desire to see the Mss. from which you wrote. In addition, I think I am not unreasonable in asking you whether it was with your sanction that Mr. Stone, the prefect, took from David's person, by superior force, a note-book containing some papers, and amongst them the Mss. in question; and also, whether it is true that his private room had been previously searched, and this note-book and Mss. secretly inspected? When I have received your reply, which I hope for by return of post, I will be in a position to form an opinion, and will write further to you on the subject.—Your faithful servant, J. D. FITZGERALD."

Dr. Northcote replied:

"St. Mary's, Oscott, March 17, 1865.

"DEAR SIR,—Your note of the 15th inst. reached me last night too late to be answered by return of post, and I confess I was somewhat surprised at the request for information 'to enable you to form a correct judgment on the course pursued towards David.' Two days before, I had received a telegram ordering the immediate removal of the whole family from college; a course of proceeding which seemed to indicate in no doubtful manner a judgment already formed. I will add, also, that your note does not inspire me with confidence as to the correctness of the judgment likely to be formed upon information I may give as to matters in which your own judgment has been already so strongly committed to one side. You will excuse me, therefore, if I write more briefly, perhaps, than you might wish, and than my own inclination would have otherwise prompted me to do.

"I will answer your inquiries in order.

"I. The catalogue of David's offences during the three months before Shrove Tuesday comprises (*inter alia*)—1. Smuggling into college a bottle of spirits, and entertaining his friends, two of whom drank to excess (this came to my knowledge only a few weeks since). 2. Borrowing from the prefect a pass-key, and taking a rubbing and a wax impression of it before he returned it. 3. Going to an inn at Erdington; and this, too, at a time when he was already under penance for minor breaches of discipline. 4. Three days after, being put in penance by myself for the last offence, disregarding that penance altogether, and enticing a companion into the plantations, and shooting there. 5. Equivocating, and otherwise misbehaving himself when detected, and then preferring a complaint to me against the prefect, by way of forestalling the prefect's report against himself.

"The sequel to these acts, and the immediate occasion of his leaving, you are already in possession of; and further details connected with it will come out in the course of this letter.

"II. I cannot consent at present to part with the Mss. asked for; but I enclose a copy of each page that concerns the matter in hand, only omitting lists of names, which David himself can supply.

"III. His room had been searched, and his note-book examined the day before he left us, not by any express sanction of mine—for this was not required—but upon hearing of its contents, I desired the prefect to ask David for it; and, if he refused to give it up, to take it from him, and bring it to me. And this was done in accordance with the practice of this, and I suppose every other society, in proceeding against those who are known to be conspiring against its rights. It had been known to the authorities for the past week that mischief was being concocted in the house against a certain class of its members. One of these, in conversation with a superior about the evil spirit on this subject in 'the bounds,' had been asked who were the chief offenders; and after naming one boy, he added, that perhaps D. F. might have something to do with it, but that he was so careful in all he did that there was no finding him out. On Sunday evening the whole history of the association was laid before the prefect by one of the divines, who had received it from a lay student, and who felt bound at once to denounce it. In this denunciation David's name was given as the originator and life of the movement.

"On this information the prefect immediately proceeded to his room, opened his pocket-book, and found the papers I have quoted, and then for the first time laid the matter before me. The sequel you already know, and painful as it is, it was inevitable.—Yours truly, J. Spencer Northcote."

Extracts from D. F.'s pocket-book, made March 17, 1865:

Page 1. "L. B. C. S., one dozen."

[Here follow the names of all Church students in the house, with the names of the Bishops who send those who do not belong to the diocese of Birmingham, the places of birth of several, and some initials appended to other names, the meaning of which I don't know; therefore, I don't think it worth while to copy.—S. N.]

Page 2. "Uncle or brother keeps a small grocery establishment in Wednesfield Heath. Father, a general inspector of canal-locks. Authority, honorary secretary, A. B. C."

[N.B. Examine Henry Walter of Fred about C * * * (one of the Church students) of Dudley.—S. N.]

Page 3. "A. B. C."

[Here follow the names of the members.—S. N.]

"Governor Moody, elected March 6th, for his magnanimous sentiment about Sedgely Park."

"F* * †—N.B. Consult hon. secretary for information about this 'gentleman' [a former Church student of the house, now and for the last year or more a priest in this diocese.—S. N.]

Page 4. [Contains nothing that concerns the matter in hand.—S. N.]

Page 5. "List of members of A.B. Society."

Page 6. "We want all particulars about the under-mentioned, as to birth, parentage, qualifications, patrons."

[Two loose papers contain a list of all Church students who have come into the college in and since '59, with names of patrons, previous places of education, time of entering the college, &c.—S. N.]

On the 19th March Mr. Justice Fitzgerald wrote to Dr. Northcote as follows:

"19th March 1865.

"REVEREND SIR,—I have received your letter of the 17th, in answer to mine of the 15th. There was nothing in my letter, nor in the subject to which it related, to call for or warrant a sneering or offensive reply. You complain that my judgment stands committed on one side by the removal of my second and third sons.

"I ordered their return as, in consideration of your letter of the 13th inst., I considered they were no longer safe at Oscott.

"The course you have pursued has been to me cruel—nay, inhuman; but I pass over the deep wound inflicted on me, although I might, perhaps, have put also to you the question, was there no consideration due to me? Since the receipt of your first communication I have learned from my sons and nephew a matter not alluded to by you—viz. that immediately after turning my eldest son out on the roadside you addressed to the assembled members and pupils a harangue, in which you endeavoured by poisonous slanders to complete the moral ruin you had so recklessly begun.

"I cannot permit my son to enter life—to join a high and honourable profession—with the stain you have thus fixed on his name; and I will, therefore, endeavour to procure for him an opportunity for public investigation. In doing so I will be actuated solely by a desire to perform my duty to him and to the public, in seeing that truth and justice shall prevail.—Your faithful servant, J. D. FITZGERALD."

Two or three weeks after the receipt of this letter the usual legal notice of action was served on Dr. Northcote and the Rev. W. Stone, Prefect of Discipline at Oscott.*

As soon as the rumours of these legal proceedings got abroad, friends of both parties were anxious to interpose their good offices, to obtain some other settlement of the dispute. Before the end of April a friend of Dr. Northcote wrote the following letter to a friend of Mr. Justice Fitzgerald:

"27th April 1865.

"MY DEAR ——,—I am very glad that you are willing to communicate with me on the subject of the question between David Fitzgerald and Oscott College. It seems to me very desirable for all parties that some settlement should be arrived at out of a court of law; and it would be a great kindness if you would act with me as a medium towards getting a reference of the question.

"I suppose that Judge Fitzgerald considers that his son has been unfairly treated, and that imputations have been thrown on his character undeservedly, which the action he has commenced may serve to remove. On the other hand, I am sure that Dr. Northcote would not object to the adoption of means that would bring the matter before the consideration of an impartial tribunal, in which Judge Fitzgerald would also have confidence.

"I would therefore propose that the question should be submitted to two referees, one to be chosen on each side, with power to choose a third if they do not agree. The question to be submitted cannot be—whether it was necessary or not that D. Fitzgerald should leave the college, as Dr. Northcote would not consent to such a point being referred to any one; nor

* Mr. Stone had been ordained priest in March 1864, and was made Prefect in January 1865. His predecessor, Mr. Martin, was ordained priest, and appointed to the office of Prefect, in March 1860.

indeed could it come in that shape into any court. But the questions might be the same as those that would come before the jury, with the same power to the referees to award the damages. Or, as those questions turn on rather technical points, the case referred, if Judge Fitzgerald so wished it, might be drawn in such a way as to bear directly on the moral and social aspects of it; that is to say—whether in the mode in which the removal was effected, and the circumstances that accompanied it, David Fitzgerald was unjustly or illegally treated, considering his age and standing and antecedents.

"Of course, in making such a proposal I must not be taken as admitting that such was the case, but merely that the question should be put in such a way as to lead to a full inquiry into the facts. The decision when given may be made public, if it should be considered desirable on either side.

"Any thing you can do towards obtaining such a solution will be a kindness.—I remain, &c.

"E. E. Estcourt."

On the 5th or 6th of May Dr. Northcote had in London an interview with the gentleman to whom this letter had been addressed, and who then communicated to him Mr. Justice Fitzgerald's refusal to accept the proposed reference.

Not long afterwards Canon Estcourt had an interview with Mr. Justice Fitzgerald himself, in which the Judge proposed to abandon all legal proceedings if Mr. Stone were dismissed from his office (of Prefect of Discipline) at St. Mary's College. Mr. Estcourt did not think it necessary to communicate this proposal to Dr. Northcote, but declined it at once.

On the 15th of June a mutual friend of both parties wrote, on his own mere motion, to Dr. Northcote, suggesting whether it would not be possible to leave the whole matter to a distinguished Irish ecclesiastic, who should have the legal assistance of an eminent Irish barrister. Dr. Northcote declined this offer, as not being so just and reasonable as that which had been made before and declined by the Judge; but he added that if that proposal could be again renewed, he considered the settlement of the affair "might still be open to negotiation on such a basis." No further communications passed upon the subject, and the trial was expected to come on in November. It was postponed, however, on the application of Mr. Justice Fitzgerald, who was unable to leave Dublin in consequence of the Special Commission for the Fenian trials. Finally, the cause was heard before Lord Chief-Justice Cockburn and a Special Jury in the Court of Queen's Bench on the 5th, 6th, and 7th February 1866.

WESTMINSTER HALL,
February 5th, 1866.

In the Court of Queen's Bench.

Ten Special Jurors answered to their names.

A *Tales* is prayed by Mr. Coleridge, and two Common Jurors having been added, the Jury are sworn. The pleadings are opened by Mr. Philbrick.

Mr. Coleridge: May it please your Lordship, Gentlemen of the Jury,—You will have gathered probably from the statement of my friend Mr. Philbrick, that this is a case a little out of the common way, depending upon circumstances not of every-day occurrence, and which will therefore require at your hands some patient attention, whilst I endeavour to make plain the grounds upon which the action is brought, and what it is that is sought by the Plaintiff in this action before you.

The Plaintiff on the record is the eldest son of the Right Honourable John David Fitzgerald, one of the Judges of the Court of Queen's Bench in Ireland, who was for a good many years Attorney-General for Ireland, and in the Parliament of this country. The two Defendants are Dr. Northcote, the President of a Roman Catholic College at Oscott, and Mr. William Stone, one of the assistants in the tuition at that place.

Young Mr. Fitzgerald, the Plaintiff, is, I think, just nineteen years of age. He is not therefore of age himself to be a plaintiff, and the action is therefore brought by his father as his next friend, under circumstances which I will mention to you in a moment. It is brought for the purpose of recovering damages for what Mr. Justice Fitzgerald and his son allege to be excessive violence towards him on the part of Dr. Northcote and Mr. Stone, the President and Master at Oscott, expelling him from the school under circumstances of great ignominy, as I think you will see, and with a view of establishing to the satisfaction of those who may hereafter be unfavourably affected by the conduct to which Mr. Fitzgerald has been exposed, that there was no foundation whatever for the treatment to which he was subjected, and that those who have so treated him are answerable in point of law in damages to him and to Mr. Justice Fitzgerald.

Now, gentlemen, having mentioned the word "damages," I may say at once that this is an action which the Judge could not bring to put money into his pocket; nor is money the object for which Mr. Justice Fitzgerald appears in this Court. He appears in this Court because he conceives that he has a legal ground of action against the two Defendants; but he certainly would not have made use of that legal ground of action, and you would not have been here empanelled to try this case, if it were not that interests far dearer to him than any amount of money can represent are involved in the issue in this case, and that it is brought, as he does not hesitate to avow, upon a legal ground, but for the vindication of the character of his son, in whom his best hopes in life were centred.

Now, gentlemen, young Mr. Fitzgerald went to Oscott a good many years ago, when he was about eleven years of age, and he was at the time of the transactions which have led to this action there with his two brothers. I have stated to you his age. He is about nineteen now, and his two brothers are considerably younger. When he first went to Oscott, the College was under the Principalship of Dr. Weedall, who was President of it, and who died in 1859; and on his death a gentleman of the name of Morgan succeeded to the Principalship of Oscott. He died in 1860, and in 1861* Dr. Northcote was appointed to the Presidentship of Oscott. Now, I desire to say at once, that throughout this inquiry on the part of Mr. Justice Fitzgerald no imputation is to be made, so far as I am concerned, upon the personal or moral character either of Dr. Northcote or of Mr. Stone. I have no right certainly to claim to be a friend of Dr. Northcote's, but I am a very old acquaintance of his, for we were at Oxford together before he became a Roman Catholic; and I may say that he is a most distinguished man, of whom I never heard any thing but good, and against

* Dr. Northcote was made President of Oscott in July 1860.

whom certainly I do not desire to say a syllable of evil. Dr. Northcote, who was a very great loss to the Church which he left, and is a very great ornament to the Church which he joined, was made the Principal of Oscott in 1861; and certainly in a great many respects the Roman Catholic Communion could not have selected a better person to put at the head of a great institution than Dr. Northcote was. Dr. Northcote, however, was a person who found the discipline of Oscott more lax than he thought that it should be; as soon as he joined it, and when he became Principal, he enforced a very much severer code of discipline than had up to that time obtained. The President of Oscott, I understand, is appointed by the Roman Catholic Bishops, and is responsible to the Roman Catholic Bishops, and to them alone. He appoints and removes all the officers in the Institution. He is, in fact, subject to the control of the Bishops of his Communion, the autocrat of the place; and no doubt it is very right that the head of a great establishment of that kind should be absolutely at liberty to enforce what he thinks right for the discipline of the school. The various officers—the Prefects of Discipline, the Prefects of Studies, and other details of the Institution will appear by and by, when I come to explain to you more particularly how these matters arose; but originally, I ought to tell you that as I understand it, the College at Oscott had been a seminary chiefly for the instruction of priests;* but inasmuch as there was a difficulty in maintaining it for want of funds, it had for a great length of time become a lay college, where the sons of some of the leading Roman Catholic families in this country and in Ireland were educated; and the fact was that at the time when young Mr. Fitzgerald was sent there it was a great place for lay education for some of the first Roman Catholic families in the country. Mr. Fitzgerald was sent there for the purpose of being amongst those with whom he would in afterlife have to associate, and in order that he might obtain the best education that a Roman Catholic institution can afford to such persons.

The fact, however, of a large number of lay people being sent there, and it being for such an institution rather an expensive place of education, did not take away from it the character

* See Introduction, p. 3.

of having priests there to be educated still. And the Bishops were in the habit of sending (the expenses of their education being defrayed out of the large fund which the lay gentlemen paid*) young persons from various other seminaries in the country to Oscott for the purpose of finishing their priestly education. They usually came, I think, about the age of sixteen, and they were drafted from time to time into the various classes at Oscott which their state of preparation enabled them to join with effect. When they had passed through a certain course of instruction at Oscott, they became what were called "Divines." They were removed from the more stringent portion of the discipline of the College. They were ordained priests; some of them were ordained for missions at home, and some abroad; and a good many of them were used for the purpose of the education in the College itself. They had classes put under them; part of the discipline of the College was intrusted to them; and thus it would often happen that young men would come there from other colleges, and for the purpose of being ordained priests they would at a very early age be turned into masters of the College, and be placed over the heads and in authority over young men not inferior to them in any respect, and very little inferior to them in age.

If the necessities of the case require it, of course that is an answer; but any body at all acquainted with education must know that such a system must be very difficult to work, and it must in given cases occasion considerable inconvenience and considerable ill-feeling. Such, however, was the way in which the discipline at Oscott was carried on. I think I told you that the priests were there as free students, the expense of their education being paid out of the profits which accrued to the institution from the presence of the lay boys who were educated there; and no doubt an ill-feeling had sprung up, such as will spring up, and such as exists very often where two classes of boys are brought together under one roof and educated in the same school. A bad feeling, I say, sprung up, and broke out from time to time, as such feelings will, between the clerical and the lay element in this College.

Now, the discipline at Oscott, as I understand, was exceed-

* See Dr. Northcote's evidence.

ingly severe and strict. I do not know whether there was flogging in the form with which I was familiar at an early period of my life; but corporal punishment was undoubtedly practised there to a considerable extent; and the officers of the institution being the President, Vice-President, a Prefect of Studies, and a Prefect and a Sub-Prefect of Discipline, this personal part of the discipline of the College was in the hands of the Prefect of Discipline, and he was the public executioner, so to say, as I understand, with respect to the pupils at Oscott. There were certain written rules as to how the discipline of the College was to be carried on; but at this College, if it was worth any thing—and I daresay it is worth a great deal—of course written rules were the least part of the governing authority in the place; and I presume that at Oscott, as at every great public school with which I have any acquaintance, what really governs is not the written rule, or the local act of parliament, or any thing of that sort, but the great unascertained but perfectly well-known conditions of the place, which every body who has ever been at a public school even for a little while knows, and which really guide his conduct. In such institutions boys are governed by this unwritten code of laws, rather than by any thing definite that a man could put his hands upon; and just as there are traditions at Eton, Winchester, the Charter-House, and other great places of education, so no doubt there were traditions at Oscott by which the boys were governed.

Mr. Stone, the second defendant on the record, it seems, was a very young man. I believe that now he is only twenty-three or twenty-four.* Mr. Stone at a very early age, having been what they called a "Divine" at Oscott, was made Prefect of Discipline. He was therefore put over the heads of all his contemporaries, or boys who were very little younger than himself. He was placed in a position of very great responsibility in the College; and what was still more, he was allowed to exercise a direct and personal control over all the boys, whether they were older or younger than himself. Of course we cannot bring an action for a mistake in point of judgment; but although

* He is in his twenty-sixth year; and few boys, if any, in the College would have been older than David Fitzgerald himself, who in March 1865 had entered on his nineteenth year.

Dr. Northcote is a most excellent and admirable person, at the same time it seems to me that it was a mistake in judgment to put so very young a man in the particular position of Prefect of Discipline, who was to have the power of life and death, in school language, over every other member in the school. That was the condition of Mr. Stone, and that was the condition of Dr. Northcote.

Now young Mr. Fitzgerald was the eldest son of Mr. Justice Fitzgerald. He was a young man of very great ability and very great promise. He had passed through the course at Oscott with the highest possible distinction. He had never been subjected, I believe, to any thing like corporal punishment at all, and he had time after time carried away prizes upon the examinations at Oscott; and his future was looked forward to both by Mr. Justice Fitzgerald and by Dr. Northcote, as I will show from extracts from letters which I will read, with the greatest possible hope and expectation. He had passed through the College, and was to have left at the Christmas vacation in 1863. At that time, I think, Mr. Justice Fitzgerald had some idea of sending him to Oxford; but there were difficulties about sending him to Oxford, and about sending him to other places. Unfortunately it is not an easy matter for a Roman Catholic to get educated at any place, except a place expressly belonging to his own communion; and Mr. Justice Fitzgerald, although he was anxious, as I have said, that his son should have the advantage of the best English education, found that there were difficulties about it; and so matters stood in September 1863. Now on the 16th of September 1863 Dr. Northcote had written to Mr. Justice Fitzgerald about his son, and about his leaving, and what he wished him to do. He wrote to him in these terms:

"My dear Judge,—I have just read your letter of the 14th inst., as well as your first of last week; and I have studied all the points referred to in the Dublin Calendar, and sit down to write my impressions at once whilst they are fresh. I was reading a few days ago the article in the new *Dublin Review* on Catholic wants, &c., especially that portion of it which treats of our need of university education."

Then he goes on and describes what his view of university education is, and the great want of it among Roman Catholics. He says:

"If there were a number of good young Catholics under proper care in Oxford, my love for the more ancient University and my own Alma Mater would make me lean towards it in preference to Dublin. But there is no such system of protection, and home would be far removed. I take it for granted, then, that he will go to Trinity, as you have decided; and the only question now is as to how and where he can be best prepared for it. For mere cramming, it would be strange indeed if a private tutor could not do more than the regular course of a college embracing pupils aiming at many various ends; and if this test is to be too rigidly applied, I can scarcely hope you will approve of D.'s return to us after Christmas. Yet on the whole, and for his real general good, I can conscientiously say that I believe he would do better to stay with us—"

and so on. The rest of the letter is not material.

Then he writes to him also at Christmas, and says:

"I hope your three sons reached you in safety on Wednesday, and that they gave you the same satisfaction as they have given here during the past half-year. You will see by the accompanying reports the high average of marks obtained by John in all subjects, and by Gerald in all but French. David, too, carried the report of his marks with him, which were eminently satisfactory. I shall be anxious to hear your decision as to his destiny for the next four months. I very much wish to see him return myself for many reasons, of which, however, I will only mention one; viz. that I am anxious to finish with him the reading of one of my favourite books, Aristotle's *Rhetoric*, which I believe to be of very real service to one destined for public speaking."

Dr. Northcote has not had much experience of public speaking, I should suppose; however Aristotle's *Rhetoric* shows that he must have known something about Greek, Aristotle's *Rhetoric* being a pretty stiffish book.

"In my day it was very popular in Oxford,"

I do not know what he means by "popular;" in my time we had to read it, but we certainly did not much like it.

"and I studied it well; and when I wrote the other day to one of the Oxford tutors on a subject connected with it, he said in his answer, 'I am glad to see from your letter that Oscott is wiser than Oxford, and is studying Aristotle's *Rhetoric*. Some of our best mental training was founded on that and the *Ethics*; but latterly it has gone out of fashion here, and we are none the better for it.' Whether or not we are doing the very best that could be done for David's making a display at Trinity College, 'this deponent sayeth not;' but I feel sure we are doing real good for his education, and I only wish I could continue it for another couple of years, instead of a few months only. It is a pleasure to teach two such pupils as David and Redington, and to teach them *together*;

for although Redington steadily keeps the lead, he cannot afford to stumble without running a good chance of being overtaken. If David goes, R. may grow careless. Hoping, then, to see the whole triumvirate in good health and spirits, or at least in good working order, on Thursday the 14th proximo, and wishing you all the blessings of this festal season,

"I remain, my dear Judge,
"Yours very sincerely,
"J. SPENCER NORTHCOTE."

It is quite plain that at that time (it is Christmas 1863) young Mr. Fitzgerald was a boy of great promise and ability, and that Dr. Northcote was very fond of him, very reluctant to let him go, and very anxious to have him back; among other things, for the purpose of his reading Aristotle's *Rhetoric*.

Now, in accordance with that wish so expressed by Dr. Northcote, Mr. Fitzgerald did stay; and he stayed after Christmas, and up to July 1864. In July 1864 the regular Oscott course would have been completed by him, and he would have been ready for Dublin or for Oxford, if to Dublin or to Oxford Mr. Justice Fitzgerald could have contrived to send him. On the 23d July 1864 Mr. Northcote wrote again to the Judge as to the state of preparation, and as to what his son David was about at that time, in these terms:

"MY DEAR JUDGE,—I trust your sons reached you in safety on Thursday last. I send the usual half-yearly Report of their places in class and marks for examination, all of which are eminently satisfactory. Indeed, the fact that they all return with double prizes almost supersedes the necessity of a detailed report. David's translation of the speech of Pericles in *Thucydides* would not have disgraced a first-class man's final examination at Oxford, and his examination in Aristotle's *Rhetoric* was scarcely inferior to it. I do not know how he may fare in his competitive examination at Trinity, but I believe his faculties to have been well trained, and to be in thoroughly good working order for any discipline that may now be required of him. John's knowledge of history—"

and so on. That is not material. He says,

"I was sorry not to have seen David before he went off, to have said a parting word to him. But I hope when next he comes to England he will pay us a visit. I shall expect to hear of him in afterlife at least, even if we don't hear of his achieving success at College, which I look for also."

Then there are some private letters, which I do not read. It seems that young Mr. Fitzgerald was really anxious not to go to

Dublin. Dublin, you know, is a Protestant University. Of course in Ireland the sharp distinction between Roman Catholics and Protestants is much stronger than it is in almost any other country in the world. I daresay that a Roman Catholic student in Dublin is at greater disadvantages than a Roman Catholic student in any other Protestant University. Mr. Fitzgerald was extremely anxious not to go to Dublin, and his father yielded to him. For reasons not now material to go into, he could not manage to send him to Oxford, and he determined to send him to the London University. He had heard the highest account of the discipline and the teaching there; and so to London it was agreed he should go; and Mr. Northcote wrote a letter on the subject, in September 1864, in these terms:

"MY DEAR JUDGE,—After Mr. Rowley's advice, I do not quite see what you can do but conform to David's wishes, and send him through the London University course, beginning with matriculation at Christmas; and for this I think he might just as well come here as any where else."

He had left the regular course at Oscott at that time, but he wished him to come back to prepare himself for the London University:

"We shall not have a class preparing for it, and David must depend in a very great measure upon himself for the preparation. But then he is quite equal to this. I will undertake to get him all needful assistance in each branch; and of course we are well accustomed to this sort of thing, so that you need not fear failure of any kind by intrusting him to us for the purpose. It will give you time to think about the future consequent on this change, whether residence in London is advisable and can be arranged here or elsewhere. I write in great haste. But if you approve of the suggestion, David can come as soon as he pleases; and, indeed, should lose no time, as one or two of the non-classical branches of the examination would require regular going through to see that there are no weak points in the harness.

"Yours very truly,

"J. SPENCER NORTHCOTE."

Then there is a postscript:

"I have not told David that I recommend this; only that we shall be ready to receive him if you consent, and I have put before him the disadvantages."

And there is a letter of the same date to young Mr. Fitzgerald himself:

"MY DEAR DAVID,—Twenty-five 'new boys' do not leave me much

time for writing or thinking; but I must write a few lines just to say, in answer to yours received last night, that we shall be quite ready to receive you, if your father determines on sending you to the London University; and we will undertake to get you through without fail for the Christmas matriculation of course. But not having any class going up at that time, and having made our masters' arrangements for this half-year, you would not have the ordinary advantages of a regular preparation. I should be obliged to treat you as a sort of exceptional case, trusting to your own getting up of most subjects, and only going over its difficulties with you. It is for you to consider whether the advantages of having distinct tutors for each branch (which I suppose you could easily secure in Dublin), and the probable consequence of gaining a more distinguished place among the 'honours,' counterbalance the pleasure of a return to Alma Mater, who will be very glad to receive you. I have no doubt that, with your industry, you will here secure for yourself a higher place than" (some gentleman I need not name) "who stood No. 25, you remember, among 200 matriculated. I think that if you had had full time and advantages of preparation, you could have secured one of the first half-dozen places, if not the first, and that you need not be far below it now. But now you must think this matter over, weigh the pros and cons, talk it over with your father, and come to a decision speedily, because it would be a pity to lose any more time for the special preparation always desirable for every examination—"

and so on. Then he says:

"As nobody expected you to return, and it is still so uncertain, I have not interfered with 'so-and-so's' taking possession of the first Philosopher's Room, and some divine has claimed yours; but we would find you a decent room as an exceptional case altogether till Christmas; and by that time something definite will be settled about your future residence."

That was written in September 1864.

Mr. Fitzgerald came back in consequence of these letters, and he came back having already passed through the special Oscott course. He came back, you see, as an exceptional guest altogether; and Mr. Northcote himself puts it both in the letter to the Judge and to the young man, apart from the general system of the college, as a sort of private pupil to receive instruction, when Mr. Northcote could give him time, in these more special subjects for which there was no definite class; and therefore he was not there in the position of an ordinary pupil, but he was there as a kind of private pupil, as an act of grace on the part of Dr. Northcote, if you please, in order that he might have the advantage of his abilities and his scholarship in training for his matriculation at the London University. Under those circumstances Mr. Fitzgerald goes back. He is fit to go to Oxford or to Dublin. If he had gone there, he would have been in a position in which young men are free from personal control, subject of course to that moral discipline which every well-regulated college enforces on all its members; but as to being struck, or as to his being treated otherwise than as a young gentleman ought to be treated, with perfect courtesy and respect by those above him, that would have been out of the question in any college or in any university that I ever heard of. That was the condition under which he went back. The letter I have read was written in September. There was a long vacation, I suppose, and the Michaelmas Term would be from September to Christmas. That was the state of things when he went back.

Now between that time and Christmas nothing seems to have happened to interfere with the thoroughly satisfactory course of Mr. Fitzgerald's life at Oscott. He worked hard. He got such assistance from Dr. Northcote as Dr. Northcote was able to give him. They were on the best possible terms. There are many letters which I do not trouble you by reading, because the tone of them you will have gathered from those I have already read, showing that there was the most friendly feeling on the part of Dr. Northcote towards him; and that feeling continued, and the same pleasant relations existed between them down to Christmas 1864. At Christmas 1864 Mr. Fitzgerald went up for his matriculation at the London University. He was highly distinguished there; I think he was fourth or fifth in honours. I am told that it is a very stiff examination. The result of his examination of course highly gratified him, and highly gratified his father also, who looked forward to his success and distinction. This was the case at Christmas 1864.

There was still the period of time to be covered between the matriculation and the examination for the Bachelor-of-Arts degree, which would take place about nine months or a year after the matriculation. Now, of course, you are aware that the London University is a university, you may say, in idea only, because there are no university buildings. It has no "local habitation," although it has "a name;" and as I remember hearing (I protest that I do not know this myself, but only state *ex rela-*

tione), the only place in which you can find the London University is a place where it is painted up in Somerset House on the third floor—at Burlington House, I understand—but it used to be at Somerset House. It has a Board of Examiners, and it exists for the purpose of conducting, as I believe, an exceedingly stiff system of classical, mathematical, and scientific studies. There are large colleges all over the country and of very different sorts; some of them Protestant, some Roman Catholic, and some Dissenting—all being affiliated to this London University, which only existing in idea has a Board of Examiners appointed, who examine from time to time students who come up to London from all parts of the kingdom. I believe that King's College, London, is one; University College is another; Ushaw another; and Oscott another. Besides which, there are a great many Roman Catholic and Dissenting Colleges all affiliated to this London University, and forming part of it; and the students who come up from time to time to this Board in London to be examined belong in a certain idea to this University; and when they have been examined, and when they have passed to the satisfaction of the Examiners, they have a right to put those emblematical letters "B.A." after their names. And when the London University gets, as in the fulness of time no doubt it will get, a right to return a Member to Parliament, they will be entitled to a vote. It is a system, as I understand, of examinations for the purpose of giving to persons who do not belong to the Church of England, and to many who do, the advantage of examinations which they cannot get or do not wish to get at Oxford, Cambridge, or Dublin, or at other universities in the country. As I have told you, young Mr. Fitzgerald was very much distinguished; and the question was, what was to become of him between Christmas and the time when he was to go up for his Bachelor-of-Arts degree. Dr. Northcote suggested that he had better return to Oscott and continue the course of study which had been found so successful before. Young Mr. Fitzgerald and the Judge were both well inclined that this should be done, and that Mr. Fitzgerald should go back to a place where he had been so happy and so distinguished, where he knew the Principal, where he had made friends, and, in short, where many of those associations of pleasure were around him which were excessively gratifying to him, and that did not in the least interfere with his studies. Well, he went back to Oscott soon after Christmas, and he was to continue there till July 1865.

Now I think I have told you generally the nature of Oscott: that it had been a priestly seminary; that it was found necessary to turn it into a large lay school, and out of the funds produced by lay pupils the priests' education was carried on. Out of the priests many of the ushers and persons who conducted the discipline of the school were from time to time taken. There had been, as I have told you, this feeling, which does and will break out from time to time between different classes of persons when they are associated under one head together; and I really do not know whether it is a mystical word of Fenian origin or what it is, but it seems that the priests, or young people who were to become priests, went by a name which is very emphatic, though I do not know that it is very euphonious. The clerical students went by the name of "Bunkers." At many places there are names given to different classes of persons which it is not very wise to give; but boys have been boys for a great many thousands of years, and if the world lasts they will remain boys till the end of time. The lay boys called these clerical gentlemen "Bunkers." I suppose if a man was a Bunker he did not like to be called so; but they were so denominated; and one of these Bunkers was Mr. Stone. When Mr. Fitzgerald came back he found Mr. Stone promoted from the rank of Bunkers* into the chair of the Prefect of Discipline. A gentleman named Martin had been prefect before; and Mr. Martin and Mr. Fitzgerald had always carried on all necessary correspondence on the best possible terms and with great felicity on both sides. Whether Mr. Stone thought it necessary or desirable, because he was young, that he should hold the reins tight, I do not know. There may have been that natural mesmeric antipathy which we sometimes see between people, like the man who did not like Dr. Fell, and could give no particular reason for it. Whether that was so or not, I cannot tell; but certainly, as soon as Mr. Stone and Mr. Fitzgerald came into the relation of Prefect of Discipline and special private pupil, they did

* It is only the Church students in "the Bounds" who are called Bunkers. Mr. Stone had left the Bounds more than five years before this time, and had been a priest for nearly a year.

not (to use a vulgar but colloquial expression) exactly hit it off. One may have been possibly a little too lofty, and the other may have been a little too severe; but certain it is that Mr. Stone and Mr. Fitzgerald did not at all agree, and it was not a happy relation that existed between them. Mr. Stone was Prefect of Discipline; and Dr. Northcote being President, and having, as president, of course a thousand things to attend to, was obliged to see things very much through the eyes of Mr. Stone. And I do not complain of that. Dr. Northcote, naturally enough, was inclined to take the view which Mr. Stone took and laid before him as president. I suppose it is always right for a commander-in-chief to stand by his *sub* if he can; and it was quite natural that Dr. Northcote should be inclined to take the report of a man in Mr. Stone's position. From the first moment of Mr. Fitzgerald coming back Mr. Stone seemed to delight in putting the very worst possible construction upon his conduct; and it appears that very early in the matter, as soon almost as he got back, he used to tell him to take care of himself; that his position in the house was very fickle, and that a very little on his (Mr. Stone's) part would send him away; and that Dr. Northcote had told him that he was there for his own purposes, and not for the College's, and that a very slight provocation would cause him to be sent away from the College. That was not likely to be very acceptable to a gentleman so highly distinguished as Mr. Fitzgerald was, and the son of a Fitzgerald who had within him the spirit of a gentleman, and who would therefore not like to have his coat perpetually brushed the wrong way—that being certainly not a very pleasant process for any body, and which was not pleasant to this young gentleman of seventeen or eighteen years of age. I daresay he may have resented it, and may have shown Mr. Stone that he did not like it; and he may even have told him so, for aught I know; but the result was that this distinguished young man, having been allowed to walk by himself, and to take his diversions abroad whenever he thought fit,—under proper restrictions, of course,—was literally reduced to the ranks. Of course he did not like that; but I agree that that is not actionable.

There were letters written from time to time by Dr. Northcote, all of them being in the kindest possible tone. No hint was given to the Judge that any thing was going wrong. The boy naturally did not like to worry his father about the quarrels that took place between himself and this Mr. Stone. The Judge was in entire ignorance that there was any thing going on other than had always gone on, and he believed that the relations between his son and the authorities in the College were of the most pleasant kind possible. His son was working hard, and was likely to be extremely distinguished, and was patronised and petted by every body. I think the last letter was a letter written in January 1865—the expressions in that letter being of the kindest possible description. There was not a word to suggest that there was any change of feeling; and Mr. Justice Fitzgerald went his circuit with the full belief that he should soon see his son back with flying colours.

He was excessively surprised one morning when he came to his house in Dublin to find, without the smallest warning or any thing having happened to prepare his mind for it, his son at his breakfast-table; and on inquiring how he came so suddenly to appear in Dublin without warning, he found that he had been expelled from Oscott under circumstances of the most cruel ignominy; after treatment to which criminals are subjected, but to which persons short of criminals are hardly ever subjected in this country—that he had been locked up in his room for hours; that his meals had been handed to him by the servant through the door; that no opportunity had been given to him by Dr. Northcote of defending himself; and that he had been put into a fly and sent off by train to Birmingham, with directions to go at once to his father, without the slightest warning or notice to his father of any kind. Mr. Justice Fitzgerald naturally makes inquiries, and learns what the cause has been. It appears that there were these "Bunkers"—and it really is a sad thing that such serious consequences should have followed from such an absurd vagary—it seems that there were these "Bunkers," and that some boys in the school did not like them, and they got up, or thought that they were getting up, an A. B. C., which represented "Anti-Bunker Confederation" or "Club"—I do not know that the C. ever got finally developed into a "Club." It was, however, either "Club" or "Confederation." It was something beginning with a C. My friend suggests that it was a

"Conspiracy." It was something very dreadful and revolutionary, no doubt; and it appears that they passed resolutions. There was a Mr. Moody, who was one of the tutors of the place, a man of my own age. I remember him perfectly well. He was at Eton and Oxford, and is now carrying on tuition at Oscott. It seems that he had said something which they approved; and it appears from a note that they had a meeting, and that "Governor Moody" was elected a member of the "A. B. C., in consequence of his magnanimous sentiments." This is the sort of way in which the Anti-Bunker Confederation or Club carried on its proceedings; and Governor Moody, one of the Jesuit fathers of the place, was elected at once into the Club because he had said something which pleased them, and that was the way in which they testified their satisfaction. Mr. Stone had risen from the ranks of a Bunker into the throne of the Prefect of Discipline. He felt excessively annoyed at this; and it appears, according to Mr. Fitzgerald's account, that one morning he found Mr. Stone in his room; there was a pocket-book upon the table and some letters, and he found Mr. Stone at the table. He will not be able to say that Mr. Stone was reading his pocket-book; but it is obvious—and Mr. Stone, I am sure, will not deny it—that he did read his pocket-book, and that he read his letters.* Mr. Stone gave him a rough sort of shake, and said, "What are you about? You must come to the President." Mr. Fitzgerald got up and put his pocket-book, with all the explosive papers belonging to the Anti-Bunker Confederation, into his pocket. He goes down and sees Mr. Stone, who uses very strong language, and finally demands this pocket-book. There were other names in the pocket-book besides his own. Mr. Fitzgerald did not like delivering it up, and he refused to do so; then Mr. Stone and he came to a struggle. Twenty-four is stronger than seventeen, *cæteris paribus*, and twenty-four succeeded in getting the book out of young Mr. Fitzgerald's pocket. Mr. Fitzgerald was considerably roughly handled. He was knocked about a good deal, and he was shut up, as I understand, in Mr. Stone's room while he went to the President. Shortly afterwards Dr. Northcote sent for him. But Dr. Northcote would not hear him. He told him that from information which he had derived

* See Mr. Stone's evidence.

from his letters*—(it appeared that his letters had been read, but that Dr. Northcote would have read them I do not believe, and the contents had been communicated to him)—he told him that it was necessary he should instantly go away and leave the College.

Mr. Fitzgerald in vain attempted to explain matters, and asked to be heard; no hearing was allowed him. He had committed this gross offence against the laws and discipline of the College. He had joined this terrible Anti-Bunker Confederation, and he had offended the clerical element of the College too deeply to allow him to remain at all, and he was told that he must go at once. He was sent to his room, and there he was locked up. He asked whether he could see his brothers before he went; and I believe that his brothers were allowed to see him, but not out of the presence of Mr. Stone, who, I believe, was present the whole time that the two young Mr. Fitzgeralds were there. He was locked up and kept in his room for two or three hours. His dinner, or whatever meal he had, was sent up, as it would be to a man confined in prison; and there he was left to eat his dinner by himself. Then Mr. Stone comes and either locks or bolts the door. Mr. Stone makes him pack up his portmanteau and bag and so forth, and hurries him away, telling him that any thing he leaves behind will be sent after him. He takes hold of him, takes him downstairs with his luggage, shows him into the carriage, and sends him off, saying, "Get along with you out of Oscott."

And then Dr. Northcote addresses the school—very well, I daresay, in point of language, but using language exceedingly vituperating the character of Mr. Fitzgerald. The pocket-book was kept and all the papers and letters;† and with all this utter ignominy young Mr. Fitzgerald was expelled from the school.

The object of this action, as I told you frankly in the beginning, and as I do not seek to disguise now, is not to put money into Mr. Fitzgerald's pocket—Mr. Fitzgerald not for one moment saying that as a matter of money-compensation what has happened is to be considered.

The question is—Has there, or has there not, been conduct

* See Mr. Stone's evidence.

† No letters were kept, and only those papers which concerned the A. B. C.

pursued towards him which justifies Mr. Justice Fitzgerald in bringing this action? Has there, or has there not, been a legal cause of action? and if there has, is he not perfectly justified in bringing this case into court, and in challenging Dr. Northcote and Mr. Stone, if they can meet that challenge, to explain under what circumstances they dared to treat a gentleman in the position of young Mr. Fitzgerald as they did treat him, and what their defence is to be to the action which he brings?

I admit, of course, as every lawyer and as every man of common sense must admit, that it is uncommonly difficult to define what are the precise limits of authority which the head of every educational institution ought to have over the property and the persons of pupils who are domiciled therein. I suppose that in the case of an indecent book, or I suppose that, in a Christian place, the case of an openly infidel book, would be a case in which the laws of property would disappear, and no pupil, of whatever age, would have any right to say, "I have a property in that." The master would have a perfect right to say, "I insist on its being given up; and if you choose to defy me, you must get out of the place, for you must not stop here with your abominable contaminating books, doing mischief to the rest of the pupils." I admit that there are cases in which it is essential for the general benefit of an institution of this sort that the rights of property and the legal strictness of things should not be viewed with too critical an eye, and that a man who has the general benefit of the place in his mind and heart must act for the best; and no judge and no jury would let the consequences fall heavily upon him.

But the question is, whether there are not reasonable limits to that, and whether the limits which are prescribed by the law to the authority of the head of an educational place are not that he must do nothing inconsistent with the liberty and with the property of those who are intrusted to his care, which is not reasonably necessary for the well-being of the institution over which he presides? and whether this or that particular act is an act reasonably necessary for the well-being of an educational institution is a question of fact which a jury must decide. And the question in this case, as I humbly conceive, is whether those reasonable limits have or have not been exceeded?

Lord Chief-Justice Cockburn: There is this to be said, that there is an obvious distinction between the case of a schoolboy and a young man finishing his education in the position of a private pupil. The one may be reasonably subjected to personal restraint or punishment to a much greater degree than would be proper in the case of the other.

Mr. Coleridge: Certainly. I am much obliged to your Lordship. I was going to point out that there are obvious limits. Let us, for the sake of humanity, hope that the story is not founded in truth; but let me take such a case as the school described by Mr. Dickens in *Nicholas Nickleby.* Who can doubt that if the atrocious cruelties which are described in that novel had been practised in reality, an action would have lain at the suit of those pupils against Mr. Squeers? It is quite plain that an action would lie, because the cruelty which he practised was not reasonably necessary in the case of the boys at Dotheboys' Hall. And certainly if I had been counsel for the father of any one of the boys, I should have addressed the jury with the greatest possible confidence.

In all cases there are limits which the law will not allow to be exceeded, and those limits are what is reasonably necessary for the proper education of the children.

Then, again, my Lord has suggested another qualification; that what is reasonably necessary for a child of six or seven years of age is not reasonably necessary in the case of a young man of eighteen or nineteen. You may treat one in a very different way from the other. This young gentleman was a matriculated student in the London University. He was at Oscott, that being one of the affiliated colleges of the London University; and it is absurd, as I conceive, to say that what might have been perfectly legitimate treatment, such as no father would complain of, if he had been a boy of nine or ten, when he first went to Oscott, is treatment to which he ought properly to be subjected when he comes to be seventeen, eighteen, or nineteen years of age, and when he is entering on his career of usefulness.

I need hardly point out to you that the consequences of his expulsion must in this case be excessively serious to young Mr. Fitzgerald. Just make the case your own, and consider what would necessarily be the consequence of a stigma such as this cast upon a young man if left utterly unexplained. Here is a lad of high promise, and of admirable character up to this time, who suddenly finds himself collared, locked up in his room, treated like a criminal, his things taken from him, and himself ignominiously expelled from the college at a few hours' notice, as a person utterly unfit for the society of those with whom he has been associated, because it is considered that he is likely to contaminate the rest of the inmates of the college. Not one single complaint was made to the Judge. Not a syllable was written to him to say, "Your son David is not going on very well; you had better come and see him, and take him away;" but instantly, with a word and a blow, the boy is ignominiously expelled, and all for a few youthful follies such as all young men will commit, and which all the wisest and best teachers of young men perpetually overlook. Can you doubt that a few kindly and generous words spoken by Dr. Northcote to Mr. Fitzgerald, pointing out to him the probable mischief that would result from the course he was taking—pointing out the want of consideration that he showed for the feelings of others, and (if he will excuse me for saying so) his want of good breeding in insisting on the difference of rank between himself and others;—if that had been pointed out by a generous man to an ingenuous youth, who can doubt what the result would have been? The fact would appear to be that this youth had set himself sportively against the clerical element in the college, and the clerical body had resolved to ruin him. It is a sad instance of that sort of spirit of clerical exclusiveness and domination which did mischief enough in the Church itself 400 years ago, and which, whenever it reappears in Protestant or Catholic countries, reappears to the breaking up of the comfort of families, and to the threatening of the fabric of society itself. And although I do not for a moment say that these two gentlemen, the defendants, may not be most excellent people as divines, and although I daresay they are most amiable and agreeable persons as scholars, it is manifest that they do not comprehend the character of boys, and that they do not comprehend how to deal with them as gentlemen should be dealt with.

EVIDENCE FOR THE PLAINTIFF.

DAVID FITZGERALD *sworn*. *Examined by* MR. BROWN.

Q. Are you the son of Mr. Justice Fitzgerald?

A. I am.

Q. His eldest son, I believe?

A. Yes.

Q. He is one of the Judges of the Court of Queen's Bench in Ireland?

A. Yes.

Q. And I believe he was Attorney-General for Ireland, under Lord Palmerston?

A. Yes.

Q. What is your age?

A. I was nineteen on the 14th of January last.

Q. I believe you went to Oscott College when you were eleven years of age?

A. Yes.

Q. That college, I believe, is for the education of Roman Catholic boys?

A. It is.

Q. Do you know under whose authority the college is placed?

A. It is placed under the authority of the President, who, I believe, is appointed by four Roman Catholic Bishops.

Q. I believe there is a Vice-President?

A. There is.

Q. And two Prefects?

A. Yes; there is a Prefect of Studies, and a Prefect of Discipline.

Q. Does the President appoint the Vice-President and the Prefects?

A. He does.

Q. When you entered the college I believe Dr. Weedall was President?

A. He was.

Q. And on his death, in 1859, who succeeded him?

A. Dr. Morgan.

Q. And when did Dr. Northcote become President?

A. In July 1860.

Q. When you joined the college did you make any inquiry of Dr. Weedall about opening letters?

A. Yes.

Q. What was the inquiry that you made of him?

Mr. Karslake: You cannot ask that.

Mr. Brown: Dr. Weedall was President at that time.

Mr. Karslake: I could not stop my friend in his opening of the case, but this is an action which is brought for imprisonment and for the taking of a book. My friend has gone very far afield. Of course, I could not stop him. Unless what Dr. Weedall said was communicated to Dr. Northcote afterwards, what was said by him years ago cannot affect the defendants in this case.

Mr. Brown: I will not persist in my right to put the question, as my friend objects to it.

Q. After Dr. Northcote became President was a change made in the discipline of the college?

A. The discipline became somewhat stricter—a new system of impositions was introduced.

Q. I believe that corporal punishment was always practised in the college.

A. Always.

Q. But on the younger boys only, I believe.

A. Yes; until they were about sixteen or seventeen.

Lord Chief-Justice Cockburn: Boys as old as that?

A. Yes, sometimes.

Mr. Brown: I believe that you never incurred that kind of chastisement?

A. Never.

Q. About how many students were there in the college?

A. When I first entered, there were 140; they afterwards declined, and the number was about 120.

Q. Were there two classes of students?

A. There were.

Q. Clerical students?

A. Clerical students and lay students.

Q. About how many clerical students were there?

A. There were about twelve.

Q. Do you know by whom the clerical students were sent there?

A. They were sent there by certain Catholic Bishops.

Q. Did the clerical students after they had finished their studies become what are called Divines?

A. They did.

Q. And were they then placed as masters over some of the lay classes.

A. They were.

Q. When the clerical students became Divines did they wear a distinguishing dress?

A. They wore a cassock and a biretta.

Lord Chief-Justice Cockburn: What is a biretta?

A. A sort of cap; and they also wore a Roman collar.

Mr. Brown: Did they take their meals apart from the other boys?

A. They did.

Q. And had a separate room, I believe?

A. Yes, a separate room.

Q. Were the lay pupils obliged to address them in any particular way?

A. They were obliged to address them as Mr. So-and-So, or Sir.*

Q. Was there any distinction between them and the lay pupils?

A. They were masters over all the junior pupils.†

Lord Chief-Justice Cockburn: How many were there?

A. About twenty Divines.

Mr. Brown: You were at the college, I think, six or seven years altogether?

A. I was; seven years altogether.

Q. When clerical pupils joined the college, did you generally find them as well educated as the others?

A. No, I think not.

Q. Was there any impression prevailing, or was there any

* *i.e.* if they held any post of authority.

† *i.e.* some of them were so employed.

conversation among the boys, as to the clerical students acting as spies over the others?

Mr. Karslake: I must object to that.

Mr. Brown: It is really connected with this subject.

Lord Chief-Justice Cockburn: At all events, we have not come to that part of the case yet.

Mr. Brown: Were the lay or clerical students separated in playing or not?

A. No; they took their play together.

Lord Chief-Justice Cockburn: Do you mean the clerical students or the Divines?

A. The clerical students before they became Divines.

Mr. Brown: I suppose, when they became Divines they did not play with the others?

A. They did not, except occasionally; some of them would sometimes join in the games.

Q. About what age used they to become Divines?

A. From twenty to twenty-two, or sometimes younger.

Q. When you joined the college, did you find that the clerical students went by any familiar name?

A. Yes; they were called "Bunkers."

Q. Did you invent that name?

A. No.

Q. You found it in use when you got there?

A. I found it in use.

Q. Do you know what it meant?

A. No; I had no idea what it meant.

Q. I suppose that in point of fact it had no meaning.

Mr. Karslake: Do not assume that; you will find that it had a meaning.

Mr. Brown: Perhaps my friend knows what the meaning was. If so, he knows more than I do.

Q. During the whole time you were at the college was there really any annoyance practised by the lay students on the clerical students?

A. Never.

Q. I believe that among the lay students there were several classes.

A. There were nine or ten.

Q. Was the highest class that which was called the "Philosophers"?

A. Yes, that was the highest.

Q. When did you enter that class?

A. At Midsummer 1863.

Q. You became what is called a Philosopher, I believe?

A. Yes.

Q. Had the Philosophers some peculiar privileges over the others?

A. They had great privileges.

Q. Among other privileges, had they liberty if they pleased to go outside the college bounds and walk about the neighbourhood in parties of about three?

A. They had the privilege of walking about the neighbourhood in parties of not less than three.

Q. Unaccompanied by any master?

A. Yes.

Q. I must ask you whether one of the privileges of the Philosophers was going to a public-house for a little beer, if they wanted it?

A. It was not a privilege; but they used to do so.

Q. Was that in the time when Mr. Martin was Prefect?

A. Yes.

Q. He was Prefect, I think, down to the end of 1864?

A. Till January 1865.

Q. I suppose the Philosophers could not get on without a little beer sometimes; was that so?

A. Yes.

Q. Did you remain in the Philosophers' class till Midsummer 1864?

A. I did.

Q. Did you then finish the course of education at the college?

A. I finished then.

Q. During the time you were there, from 1859 to 1864, had you taken several prizes?

A. I had taken several.

Q. I believe as many as eight or nine?

A. Yes.

Q. For proficiency in classics and mathematics, and in the Philosophers' examination?

A. Yes.

Q. At Midsummer 1864 did you leave the college with the intention of entering Trinity College, Dublin?

A. I did.

Q. I believe that your father changed his mind about that, and decided on sending you to the London University?

A. He did.

Q. And in consequence of that did you return to Oscott about September 1864?

A. I did.

Mr. Brown: I will now, my Lord, put in two letters. The first is a letter dated the 10th of September 1864, from Dr. Northcote to the witness, and the other is a letter of the same date from Dr. Northcote to the father.

[*The letters are put in.*]

Lord Chief-Justice Cockburn: Do you wish them to be read?

Mr. Brown: I think not, my Lord. They were read by my friend in his opening.

Mr. Karslake: Perhaps they had better be read, because my friend and I differ entirely as to his having gone there in the capacity merely of a private pupil.

The Associate: The first letter is dated 10th September 1864;* the other letter is of the same date.

Mr. Brown: I daresay that is all my friend wishes to be read.

Mr. Karslake: Yes.

Mr. Brown: There is one letter that my friend Mr. Coleridge read of the 16th; we will put that letter in, but it is unnecessary that it should be read again.

[*The letter is put in.*]

Q. On your return in September 1864, were you attached to any class at all?

A. I was not.

Q. As regards your studies, were you left pretty much to yourself?

* See p. 22.

A. I was.

Q. Dr. Northcote, I believe, personally superintended your studies?

A. He superintended my classical studies.

Q. Had you a room to yourself?

A. Yes.

Q. Your studies, I believe, differed from those of the other boys in the highest class?

A. They did.

Q. I believe that Mr. Martin was Prefect at that time?

A. He was.

Q. Were you allowed to take your books and go out of bounds and in the plantations, and so on?

A. I was allowed to study in the grounds, but not in the plantations;—in the play-ground.

Mr. Karslake: In the bounds?

A. Yes.

Mr. Brown: Were your studies there and your privileges different from those of any other boys?

A. They were.

Q. I believe that you remained at Oscott until the 1st of January 1865.

A. I did.

Q. And then you left for the purpose of matriculating at the London University?

A. I went to Ireland for a few days first, and then I went to London to matriculate.

Q. Did you matriculate at the London University about the 14th of January 1865?

A. I finished my matriculation on that day.

Q. I believe that you obtained the twelfth place out of 200 candidates?

A. I did.

Q. And several of those candidates, I believe, were above twenty-one years of age?

A. Five of them were.

Q. After you had matriculated at the London University, did you, about the last day of January 1865, return to Oscott?

A. I did.

Q. To prepare for your first Bachelor-of-Arts examination?

A. Yes.

Q. You have, I believe, since been up, and have obtained your Bachelor-of-Arts degree, with honours?

A. I have.

Mr. Brown: We will put in a letter from Dr. Northcote, dated 12th of December.

The Associate: It is a letter from the Defendant to the Judge:

"MY DEAR JUDGE,—I think you do wisely in leaving David here for the Christmas vacation certainly, and we will take care that he does not lose his time. You are of course aware that we must send his name with baptismal certificate to the Registrar of the University two or three weeks before the examination; so that it would be well if you would kindly send it me at once, that it may not be overlooked or delayed too long. With regard to the future, I have just spent an hour on the study of the Calendar you sent me, and my impression is strong that David will get more direct assistance for his first B.A. examination in July here than he would in University College. If I understand the programme of their studies aright, he will read there but a very small portion of the subject-matter for the Honours' Examination in July—only the Histories of Tacitus. We shall read here Terence and Plautus, Lucretius and Cicero, as well as Tacitus; and I think it is essential for his object that he should read these here, or with some private tutor. In other words, having a class of three candidates for honours, we shall do our best to prepare a class directly for the examination. I do not profess to be A 1* in any thing; but I think this direct preparation under Professors B. will be more likely to attain the end aimed at than indirect preparation under Professors A.; to say nothing of what I should also set a high value on, the continuance for six months longer *in statu pupillari* and under quiet Catholic discipline. In London University the discipline depends wholly on the individual: I am told a student may run into all kinds of excess. After the July examination I should recommend a change. Then he will have more than a year before him preparatory to the next examination; and this year I think he would do well to spend under one of the University Professors.

"I remain, my dear Judge,

"Yours very sincerely,

"J. S. NORTHCOTE."

Mr. Brown (to the Witness): On your return in January

* This was in answer to Judge Fitzgerald's letter to Dr. Northcote, in which he had spoken of the Professor of Mathematics at University College, London, as standing A 1.

1865, did you find that Mr. Stone had become Prefect of Discipline?

A. I did.

Q. Had he been one of the clerical students before?

A. He had.

Q. He had been at the college some years, I suppose?

A. He had.

Lord Chief-Justice Cockburn: When did you return?

A. On the last day of January 1865.

Mr. Brown: He had been a clerical student, and then he became a Divine?

A. He did.

Q. Was he three or four years older than you?

A. He was more.

Q. Had he taught the class of which you were a member some of the minor branches?

A. He had.

Q. Had you, down to January 1865, had any quarrel or any unpleasantness with him?

A. Never.

Q. Within a day or two after your arrival, had you a few words with Mr. Stone about the key of your chamber?

A. The night of my arrival I found my door locked when I went.

Lord Cf.-Justice Cockburn: That was on going to your room?

A. Yes.

Mr. Brown: And you got the key from Mr. Stone, I think?

A. I did.

Q. A day or two afterwards, did Mr. Stone say something to you about your having taken an impression in wax of the key?

A. He did.

Q. Just explain that, if you please. He made some complaint to you about your having made an impression of the key in wax?

A. Yes.

Q. What explanation did you give him?

A. I told him how it had occurred; that I was in the Philosophers' room, after dinner, on the day after my arrival.

Q. You were with the Philosophers, I suppose?

A. With the Philosophers. One of the Philosophers asked me for a knife; and I, in taking the knife out of my pocket, took the key with it. The key was then looked at by some of the Philosophers. I took the key out of my pocket and looked at the Philosophers, and said, "By Jove, I must give this key back to Stone." The key was then looked at by some of the Philosophers, and some conversation took place among them about the desirability of having another. This key, it was supposed by them, would open all the boys' rooms in the passage in which my room was situated.

Lord Chief-Justice Cockburn: Something was said about the desirability of having another?

A. One of the Philosophers, named * * * proposed that it should be taken to the blacksmith at Erdington, and that another one should be made like it. I said, "You do not suppose that a blacksmith could make a key? I will show you a simpler way." I then asked had any one any wax?

Mr. Brown: You got a wax-candle, I believe?

A. Nobody had any wax; I went and got a candle.

Q. What did you do with it?

A. I melted it at the fire and made an impression of the wards of the key; and I also made a drawing either from the wax or from the key,—I forget which.

Q. A drawing on a piece of paper?

A. Yes, on a piece of paper. I showed this to them. I then went out of the room; and just outside I met Stone, and gave him the key. He looked at it, and saw a lot of wax sticking to it, and said, "What have you been doing with this key? have you been putting it in the fire?" I said, "No." He then said, "Have you been putting oil upon it?" I said, "No." He then said, "Well, what have you been doing with it?" I said, "I cannot tell," and I ran up stairs. This was all said in a joking, pleasant sort of manner. I ran up to my room. I had left the impression and drawing on the table, and forgot all about them.

Q. Did you do any thing with them?

A. No, nothing whatever.

Q. And then Mr. Stone found them, I think, and called on you for an explanation?

A. Yes, he found them, and came to my room one night and produced them out of his pocket, and he said, "Did you make this?" and I said, "Yes, I did."

Q. Did you give him an explanation about it?

A. Yes, I did.

Q. Did you tell him in substance what you have told us?

A. I told him exactly the same.

Q. How did it end?

A. It ended in his saying that he saw there was no harm in the matter, and that he would say nothing more about it. It was not in my room that this took place, it was in the cloisters.

Q. I believe that in the course of the explanation which you gave him some angry words passed?

A. Yes.

Q. But he was calmed down towards the end of it?

A. He was calmed down. I did not give the explanation then, but I did afterwards in the cloisters.

Q. Did he come to your room on the night of the 22d of February, as you were going to bed?

A. He did.

Q. What did he say to you then?

A. He looked in.

Lord Chief-Justice Cockburn: What day was this?

A. The 22d.

Mr. Brown: You were going to bed, you say?

A. Yes, he looked in and said, "I take away your privileges for the next three days," naming the days, Thursday, Friday, and Saturday.

Q. Had he before that time used any angry expressions towards you?

A. Not before that time.

Q. It was after that time, was it?

A. It was after that time. I had been up till past 10 o'clock that night and the night before, and I am not quite sure whether it was that night or the night before.

Lord Chief-Justice Cockburn: Was it after the usual time for going to bed?

A. It was not in my case, but it was for the general body of the students; 10 was the hour for them.

Mr. Brown: That was the offence, was it?

A. That was the offence.

Q. During the time of the previous Prefect, Mr. Martin, did you often sit up until that time?

A. Frequently.

Q. With his knowledge?

A. With his knowledge.

Q. What were you doing when you were up at these late hours?

A. I stopped up generally for the purpose of studying and preparing for my examination; sometimes I wrote letters.

Q. Did Mr. Stone frequently come to your bedroom about 10 o'clock at night?

A. Very frequently.

Q. For what purpose?

A. To see if I was in bed.

Q. Had that been usual with Mr. Martin?

A. No; most unusual.

Q. On these occasions when he came to your bedroom in the night, had he made use of any warning expressions of any kind?

A. He had several times told me to take care of myself,—that my position in the house was very fickle.

Lord Chief-Justice Cockburn: Was that his word?

A. Yes, that was his expression.

Mr. Brown: Did he say any thing about Dr. Northcote?

A. Not on these occasions.

Q. Did he say any thing about keeping a strict watch?

A. He told me once or twice, "I am keeping a strict watch over you, young man."

Q. Sometime in February, I believe, Mr. Stone found you and three of the Philosophers in a little country inn; is that so?

A. He did.

Q. What were you and the Philosophers doing there?

A. We were playing bagatelle.

Q. I believe that was an inn that was patronised by the college,—where you used to have cabs and so on?

A. Yes, to a certain extent. The proprietor kopt a couple of cabs, and whenever they wanted a cab at the college they used to send there for it.

Q. Was it against the rules for you to be in that country inn?

A. It was against the rules for Philosophers to be there, but at that time I did not consider myself a Philosopher.

Q. I believe there were some Divines there, were there not, —two of them were Divines?

A. Three of them were Church students.

Lord Chief-Justice Cockburn: Church students?

A. Yes, clerical students.

Mr. Brown: For doing this, I believe, Dr. Northcote gave you and the other students a lecture?

A. He did; he sent for us the next day but one, and gave us a lecture, and then he sent me out of the room and continued the lecture to the other three.

Q. I am afraid that on the 27th of February you got into trouble again about a pistol; is that so?

A. Yes; on the 27th I went to shoot in a remote part of the plantations, which went by the name of "Hell," with another boy named * * *.

Q. You had this little article with you, I believe (showing witness a small pistol)?

A. That is the pistol.

Q. Were you shooting birds, or what were you doing there?

A. We were practising on the stump of a tree, against a high bank, at the back there. Whilst we were shooting, * * * suddenly exclaimed, "There is Stone." I said, "Did he see us?" * * * said, "I do not know; I think he did;" and I said, "O, then, cut;" and we ran away.

Q. And what did you do with the pistol?

A. We ran along the hedge-row, and I flung it into the hedge, and Stone ran after us.

Q. When he came up to you, what did he say?

A. He said, "Which of you owns the pistol?"

Q. Well; go on.

A. I said, "I do." He then said, "Give me up that pistol at once." I said, "Can't—hav'n't got it." He said, "Where is it?" I said, "I flung it into that hedge; beyond that I do not know." He said, "That is a lie." I said, "It is not a lie." He repeated, "It is a lie, sir." I said, "It is not." He then said, "I will box your ears." I said, "No, you sha'n't." He threatened several times to box my ears.

Q. What then?

A. He again asked me for the pistol, and I repeated the statement that I had flung it into the hedge; and he said, "Unless you find that pistol immediately, you shall leave the house to-night." We then all three began looking for the pistol; after some search I found it. Stone came and took it, and said, "It is well for you you have found it; for if you had not, you should not have slept another night in the house or under the roof."

Q. He then ordered you back to the college, I believe?

A. We then all three walked to the college, and after a bit he sent * * * to the bounds. He told me to walk in front of him, and I refused to do so. He told me to walk faster, and I said I would take my time.

Q. What then?

A. He then took out his watch, and said that if I was not in my room within five minutes, I should leave the house that night. He told me to leave the cartridges for the pistol in his room, which I did. He said to me, "Dr. Northcote told me that you were here for your own purposes, and not for the college's, and a very slight provocation would procure your dismissal."

Q. When you got back to the college, did you go to Dr. Northcote and make a complaint to him?

A. I went to Dr. Northcote to make a complaint, but he was not at home.

Q. You saw him, however, the same evening, I believe?

A. I did.

Q. Did you complain to him?

A. I complained to him of Stone calling me a liar, and threatening to box my ears; and I also made another complaint of Stone, as to a conversation of his, part of which I had overheard, in which he said he knew lots and lots of things against me, any one of which would be enough to get me expelled,—that I had never done any thing good that he knew of, but that he knew lots of bad things.

Q. Did Dr. Northcote promise to see Mr. Stone about it?

A. He said he would see him about it.

Q. On the evening of the next day did Dr. Northcote send for you?

A. He did.

Q. Just before night-prayers, I think?

A. Just before night-prayers.

Q. What did Dr. Northcote say to you on that occasion?

A. He was very angry with me, and accused me of carrying malicious complaints. He said that Stone was justified in calling me a liar,—in imputing a lie to me.

Lord Chief-Justice Cockburn: Was that what he said?

A. Imputing a lie to me (I think that was what he said), because I had used equivocation amounting to a lie.

Mr. Brown: Did you offer to exculpate yourself?

A. I did.

Q. Did Dr. Northcote hear what you had to say?

A. He would not hear me at all.

Q. Did you make more than one attempt to excuse yourself?

A. I did. He spoke very rapidly and very roughly, and dismissed me as the bell was ringing for night-prayers.

Q. And he put an imposition upon you, I believe?

A. Yes, he did; that I should walk in the ranks, and study in the common studying-place.

Q. After prayers did you go to the Doctor again?

A. I did.

Q. And what did you say to him?

A. I was beginning to excuse myself, and he would not hear me.

Q. Was any thing said about writing to your father?

A. He had said something before; on this occasion he said something about the next day being Ash Wednesday, and that he hoped I should bear my punishment with humility. I asked him if he was going to write to my father, because he had before said that he should have to write a very bad account of me.

Q. What did he say then about writing to your father?

A. He said, "Well, I will tell you what I will do, David. I will not write if you will promise to give no more trouble for the future."

Q. What did you say to that?

A. I said, "Very well, I will promise;" and then I left him.

Q. Do you remember the night of the 12th of March?

A. I do.

Q. Had you then lying on the bedroom table a pocket-book?

A. I had.

Q. With some loose papers in it?

A. I had.

Q. Lying there with some letters of yours?

A. Yes.

Q. Had you ever attempted to conceal them?

A. Never.

Q. On the morning of the 13th of March did Mr. Stone come and call you?

A. He did.

Q. Was he standing by the table where the pocket-book and the letters were?

A. When I awoke I saw him standing by the table.

Q. This was about six in the morning, I think?

A. It was half-past six.

Q. He told you to get up, I think?

A. As soon as he saw me awake he said, "Get up," and went out of the room.

Lord Chief-Justice Cockburn: Was he in the habit of calling you?

A. Yes; he used to call me every morning, but generally he only came to the door, and shook the foot of my bed till I awoke.

Mr. Brown: I believe that about eleven o'clock the same morning he desired you to come into his room?

A. He came to my room, and was rather surprised to see me there. He said, "Come down into my room; I want a few words of private conversation with you;" and I went down into his room.

Q. How did he begin the conversation?

A. He unlocked the door, and we went in together, and my impression is that he bolted the door; but he turned round to me from the door, and said to me with a triumphant sort of smile, "You have ruined yourself." He also said, "Now you cannot help yourself; but you may help others." I was greatly surprised at this, and I asked him what he meant, and he replied, "You have got a pocket-book." I had put it into my pocket some time in the course of the morning, and when he said this I felt to ascertain if it was there, and he noticed the action and said, "Have you got it on your person?" I said, "Yes." He said, "Give me up that book at once." I said, "No, I won't." He said, "If you do not give me up that book immediately, I will tear it from you by main force." I said, "You will do so at your peril."

Q. What then?

A. He then came up to me. I seized hold of the book firmly in both hands, or seized hold of the pocket rather. He caught hold of me, and after a struggle he succeeded in pulling my hands from the pocket, and snatched the book out of my pocket.

Q. What then?

A. He then proceeded to open the book, and was beginning to say something to me, and I said, "I have nothing more to say to you; I will go to the President." He seemed rather amused at this, and said, "O, come along."

Q. And then you both went to the President?

A. Yes, we both went to the President.

Q. I believe that you did not find him in his room, and Mr. Stone went to fetch him?

A. Yes; he went down, and I think he met him on the stairs, and came up with him presently.

Q. And then you all three, I believe, went into the room together?

A. Yes.

Q. And what passed there?

A. As soon as we got in there, Dr. Northcote said to me, "Well, what have you got to say for yourself?" I said, "I should like to know first what I am charged with." He said, "Has not Mr. Stone told you?" I said "No." And then Stone said "Yes," or nodded to Dr. Northcote.

Q. What then?

A. Dr. Northcote said, very sarcastically, "O, I see," implying that Stone had told me, and that I was denying it.

Q. Then did you say something?

A. Dr. Northcote then continued, and said, "Well, I will tell you; you have been conspiring against the peace and welfare of all the Church students in the house." I said, "I have not."

Q. What next took place?

A. He then said something about playing with pitch and not being defiled. He said, "You think you can play with pitch and not be defiled."

Q. What further passed?

A. Stone handed me my pocket-book, and said that he had examined some of the members of the A. B. C., two or three of whom said that they had been forced into it against their will. Stone then left the room.

Q. Did you offer to give Dr. Northcote an explanation about this A. B. C.?

A. He asked me some questions about it, which I answered. I began explaining it, and he would not hear me.

Q. What did he say?

A. He sat down in a chair and looked out of the window, and pretended not to hear what I said. I then said that I was not ashamed of any thing that I had done, and that I had told my father about it. He looked as if he disbelieved this; and I offered to show him a letter from my father, in which the subject was jocularly mentioned. I did produce the letter, but he refused to look at it, unless I would let him read the whole of it; and this I refused to do.

Q. Why would you not allow him to read the whole of it?

A. Because it was a private letter. I offered to show the whole of that part of the letter which referred to this matter, but he would not look at it unless I would let him see the whole of it. It was a private letter, and there was nothing more about that matter in it.

Q. Did Dr. Northcote give you any order?

A. He then said, "You had better go to your room till I send for you again."

Q. And then you went to your room, I suppose?

A. I went to my room.

Q. In consequence of something that you heard from one of the boys—

A. I left my room afterwards for a short time, and on coming back I found the door locked; and I then went and sat in the neighbouring room. In consequence of something I heard from one of the Philosophers, I went down to Dr. Northcote's room. I had heard that there had been a meeting of the whole college about me. I went down to Dr. Northcote's room, and met him at the door of the room. He asked me where I had been, and I told him, and he said, "I really thought you had taken yourself off; and under the circumstances it would have been the best thing you could have done."

Q. What reply did you make?

A. I said, "What have you done?" He said, "I have publicly expelled you,—that is what I have done." He then took me into his room with him, and began to tell me what he had said at the meeting. He said that he began by reading some extracts from the works of Dr. Newman. He also abused me a good deal, and said I was most conceited.

Lord Chief-Justice Cockburn: What was it that he read from the works of Dr. Newman?

A. It was some definition of a gentleman.

Mr. Brown: You cannot recollect which of Dr. Newman's works it was?

A. No; I do not remember.

Q. Continue the conversation, if you please.

A. He said that my conceit had proved the ruin of me, and would do so afterwards; that I was not to be trusted; that I was not a gentleman; and he said a great deal more, the substance of which I do not remember. And then Stone came in with some money, which Dr. Northcote took and put into my hands, and said, "Really I have nothing more to say to you."

Lord Chief-Justice Cockburn: That was money to enable you to go home.

A. Yes; to go home.

Mr. Brown: Did he then order you to go to your bedroom?

A. He then dismissed me. I went out with Stone, and Stone followed me up to my room. As soon as I went into the room, Stone locked the door on the outside. When I found this,

I went to the door and kicked it till Stone came back. He had only just gone a few paces, and came back immediately. He unlocked the door. I protested strongly against his locking it, saying, "You have no business to lock me up like a felon;" to which he replied, "Who would trust you?" and immediately pulled the door to and locked it again.

Q. I believe that after that some dinner was brought to you?

A. Some dinner was brought to me by a servant on a tray, and Stone left me and went away.

Q. About how long altogether were you locked up?

A. I was locked up altogether nearly two hours.

Q. During this time did Mr. Stone come and look at you three or four times?

A. He came and looked at me once or twice, and when he came I said, "I should like to see my brothers and cousins."

Lord Chief-Justice Cockburn: Did he say any thing when he came in on these one or two occasions?

A. No; he only opened the door and looked at me, and then locked it again. At first he said that, as I was expelled, I could not see them; to which I replied that I would not leave the house before I saw them. He then said he would see about it, and went away; and he presently came up with my two brothers and let them in; and then one of them went and fetched my cousins. He stayed in the room with them while they were there. I asked him to leave the room for a few minutes, that I might talk privately with them; to which he replied, in a very insulting way, that although he did not fear any actual contamination, still an expelled person was an expelled person, and could not be permitted to have any communication with those who were not so.

Mr. Brown: And you had to speak to them in his presence, I suppose?

A. Yes; I was packing up some letters in my desk, and Stone told me not to mind, that they would be sent after me. I said, "You do not think I am going to leave my letters behind me?" to which he said sneeringly, "Suspicion haunts the guilty mind."

Q. From that time, I believe, he did not leave you till you left the college?

A. No; he sent them away than, and did not leave the room till I left the college.

Q. What passed while you were packing your things?

A. He hurried me a good deal, constantly saying, "Make haste, make haste," and took out his watch, and said that if I was not ready within so many minutes (I forget how many he said), he would bundle me out, and send my things after me. He said, "You had better not wait till three o'clock" (three o'clock was the time when the boys came in from the bounds); "for if any of them meet you, they will be disposed to handle you roughly." I replied that I knew better.

Q. Did any thing more pass while you were packing your things?

A. He pushed me several times towards the door, saying, "Come, get along, now; I cannot allow you any more time." He pushed me very roughly, and once very nearly knocked me down. He would not let me lock my portmanteau, saying that I could do that in the cab. I did lock it, however.

Q. You found a cab waiting downstairs?

A. I did.

Q. And in that cab you set off to Birmingham?

A. I set off to Birmingham.

Q. And from thence you went to Dublin?

A. Yes.

Mr. Brown: Now, my Lord, we will put in Dr. Northcote's letter of the 13th of March 1865.

Mr. Coleridge: There are a great many other letters that I did not open; but if my friend thinks that any of the earlier letters should be produced, he is very welcome to have them in. The first letter I read is a letter of the 13th of March 1865 from the defendant to the Judge.*

Q. You have seen that letter of Dr. Northcote's of the 17th of March, in which he gives a catalogue of your offences?

A. Yes.

Q. The first in order stands "Smuggling into the college a bottle of spirits, and entertaining his friends, two of whom drank to excess." Will you state, if you please, what that was?

A. On the night of the 21st of December 1864, that being

* See Letter, p. 5.

the night before the boys went home for the Christmas vacation, I gave a small party to my brothers and two other students. What we had at this party consisted of what we call "prog," cakes and biscuits purchased in the house. I also procured in the course of the day from the inn about a pint of whisky and brandy, with sugar and lemon. I had asked three or four other fellows, who did not come; we boiled water, and made punch.

Lord Chief-Justice Cockburn: Was this after the boys had gone to bed?

A. After most of the boys had gone to bed. We sat up rather late; we separated about twelve o'clock, and up to this time no one had drunk to excess.

Mr. Brown: Were either of you at all tipsy?

A. No, certainly not; none of us were.

Q. Did you drink up all the spirits?

A. We drank up all, except a small quantity that was spilt.

Lord Chief-Justice Cockburn: A libation on the occasion.

A. One of the boys was sick in the course of the night and the next day, and the doctor who saw him said it was the change of the weather.

Q. This was the breaking-up night, as I understand?

A. Yes; the boys all went off the next day, except a few who stayed for the vacation.

Q. The next offence I see was "Borrowing from the Prefect a pass-key, and taking a rubbing and wax impression of it before he returned it." That you have explained.

A. Yes.

Q. Had any complaint been made to you about getting this bottle of spirits?

A. Not till long afterwards. No one knew any thing about it till after the vacation; not for more than a month or six weeks afterwards.

Q. The second offence about the key you have explained. The third is about going to the inn—that you have explained; the fourth offence is about the pistol, and that you have also explained; the fifth is "equivocating, and otherwise misbehaving himself when detected," about the pistol: you have explained that.

A. Yes.

Q. Now as to this charge about the A. B. C.; what did the A. B. C. mean?

A. The A. B. C. meant Anti-Bunker Confederation; L. B. meant List of Bunkers; C. S. meant clerical students; C. M. meant Churchmen; S. P. meant Sedgely Park; N. S. M. meant national schoolmen. I do not remember what the other initials were.

Q. Is this the pocket-book in question (showing a pocket-book)?

A. Yes; that is the book in question.

Q. I will hand the book up to my Lord, while I ask you a question or two about it (handing the book to the Lord Chief-Justice). I believe the first page contains a list of clerical students.

A. It does.

Q. With the places from which some of them are supposed to have come?

A. Yes.

Q. What did you make that list for?

A. For fun; for a lark.

Q. Was it made before the 28th of February, when Dr. Northcote took away your privileges?

A. It was. All that is in ink was made at the same date; it was made before the 28th of February. There were two loose papers, which were also made at the same date.

Q. Did you tell Dr. Northcote that, when you were with him?

A. I told him that part had been made before that conversation, and part afterwards.

Q. I see in the second page there is this: "Uncle or brother keeps a small grocery establishment in Wodnesfield Heath; father a general inspector of canal locks." What was that for?

A. That was told me by the Honorary Secretary, who saw me scribble it down in pencil; I do not remember now to whom it referred.

Q. Who was the Honorary Secretary?

A. His name was * * *.

Q. Who appointed him?

A. I appointed him.

Q. Had he a very laborious office to perform?

A. No.

Q. Had he any duties at all?

A. Not that I know of.

Lord Chief-Justice Cockburn: Had he any salary?

A. No.

Mr. Brown: The third page, I see, begins in this way—"A. B. C." What does that mean?

A. Anti-Bunker Confederation.

Q. Then it contains your name, and * * *'s, and two or three more.

A. A good many more.

Q. Then there is this: "Governor Moody, elected March 6th." Who was Governor Moody?

A. He was a master in the college.

Q. "Elected March 6th, for his magnanimous sentiment about Sedgely Park." What is the meaning of that?

A. He was supposed to have a great dislike to Sedgely Park; but the particular thing that is there referred to is, that one day a boy was laughing very loud in class, and he said, "Silence, So-and-so, one would think you were at Sedgely Park."

Q. What is Sedgely Park?

A. It is a sort of preparatory school, where Church students came from.

Q. In consequence of that you voted him a member?

A. Immediately.

Q. I believe that you had not asked Governor Moody's consent?

A. No. And a great many of those whose names are put down there knew nothing about it; and I also told that to Dr. Northcote.

Q. What are the boys whose names appear down under the A. B. C.?

A. Some of them knew something about it, and some of them knew nothing about it.

Q. Was this confederation any thing serious?

A. Certainly not.

Q. What object had it in view?

A. It had no object.

Q. Had you ever a meeting together?

A. Never a meeting; never a convened meeting.

Q. Had you agreed upon any design at all of any kind?

A. We had not.

Q. Was there any design at all contemplated by you or by the boys whose names were put down in this book against the clerical students?

A. There was not.

Q. Or against the rights of the house?

A. No; nor against the rights of the house.

Q. Did you tell Dr. Northcote as much?

A. Yes, I told him that there was nothing serious in it whatever. What I said was, that it was a bit of humbug and nonsense, and that he ought not to take any notice of it; that it had already died out, and that no entries had been made for several days.

Q. Had you any plan of action of any kind for this confederation?

A. We had not.

Q. When did the book come back to you?

A. It came back to me about a fortnight after my expulsion.

Q. By post?

A. It came by post in a cover, directed in a handwriting that I do not know.

Q. Did it come in that cover? (showing a paper to the witness.)

A. Yes.

Q. Has it a date upon it?

A. April the 9th.

Cross-examined by Mr. Karslake.

Q. You went to Oscott, I think you say, when you were eleven years old?

A. I did.

Q. Oscott is one large college, the whole of the masters, the boys, the Divines, and every body are under one roof, are they not?

A. They are.

Q. I may take it that the boys and the students and others who are under the control of the President of the College number more than 200, may I not?

A. No, I think not.

Q. When you went there were 140?

A. There were 144 boys and Philosophers.

Q. Those were students?

A. Yes; at that time there were, I should think, about 200.

Q. And when you went away there were 120, I think you say, students and Philosophers?

A. Yes.

Q. Then there are Divines?

A. Yes.

Q. And masters?

A. And priests.

Lord Chief-Justice Cockburn: What is the distinction between Philosophers and students? I suppose the Philosophers are the upper class?

A. That is the upper class: they have certain privileges,—they are still students.

Mr. Karslake: All the students in Oscott College, whether they were lay or clerical students, belonged to the different classes, I suppose?

A. They did.

Q. All mixed up together?

A. All mixed up together.

Q. I do not know whether it was the same there as it was in the school I was at,—were there forms?

A. No, no forms, but there were ten classes.

Lord Chief-Justice Cockburn: It is the same thing under another name.

Mr. Karslake: First of all there were Philosophers,—they were the head class?

A. Yes.

Q. And Poets?

A. And Poets and Rhetoricians.

Q. Those were the three classes, and the Philosophers were the highest of those?

A. The Philosophers were the highest of those.

Q. When you first went there, were there a great number of clerical students?

A. I think not; I did not know very well then.

Q. But when you saw a boy going along the cloister, you heard him called after as a Bunker, did you not?

A. No, never.

Q. When did the name "Bunker" first arise in your time?

A. I heard it before I had been in the college a week.

Q. When you first went?

A. When I first went.

Q. To whom was that term applied at that time?

A. To Church students.

Q. And the Church students in almost every instance came, I believe, upon funds provided by charitable institutions or by the diocese they belonged to?

A. I understood so.

Q. You say there was no combination at all formed against them?

A. There was not.

Q. Not at that time?

A. Not at that time.

Q. The philosophy class you got through quickly, did you not?

A. I was a year in it.

Q. Very often there are two years, are there not?

A. Not now.

Q. But there used to be at that time?

A. No.

Q. Never more than a year?

A. Sometimes a Church student, if he was not fit to go into philosophy, was kept half a year, or it might be a year longer.

Q. If he were going to become a priest, he would go into the divinity class after he had finished the philosophy class?

A. He would become a Divine.

Q. You left in July for good, did you not?

A. Yes.

Q. In what year?

A. 1864.

Q. As a Philosopher, you had your private room, I suppose?

A. I had.

Q. Which the Philosophers had?

A. In common with the Rhetoricians and Poets.

Lord Chief-Justice Cockburn: All these had private rooms?

A. Yes.

Mr. Karslake: They were a sort of upper school, I presume, and had their private rooms?

A. Yes.

Q. The others used the dormitory?

A. Yes.

Q. And I believe that, in addition, the Philosophers had a sort of public room in which they studied, had they not?

A. They had a room called the Philosophers' room.

Q. Was it a punishment to a Philosopher to be degraded sometimes from his room and to be sent to the dormitory?

A. That was never done.

Q. Did no instance of that kind occur while you were there?

A. No.

Q. Did it ever occur to a Poet or a Rhetorician?

A. Yes.

Q. To be degraded and sent to his room?

A. Yes.

Lord Chief-Justice Cockburn: Which is the highest stage?

A. Rhetoric; and below that, poetry.

Mr. Karslake: I believe that Philosophers were sent sometimes to the common room to study as penance, were they not?

A. I never remember an instance of that except my own.

Q. When you went back in September, did you attend different classes?

A. No; I studied privately by myself.

Q. Do you mean that you attended none?

A. I did attend the philosophy class in one thing; they were reading an author whose work would be useful to me.

Q. And so you attended that class?

A. I attended that class in that particular thing.

Q. Did you attend the classical class?

A. That was the one that I did attend.

Lord Chief-Justice Cockburn: For that one thing?

A. Yes; the Georgics of Virgil.

Mr. Karslake: Your great object at that time was to improve yourself in the classics?

A. Yes.

Q. So, when that class was going on, you used to attend it?

A. I used.

Q. Did you attend to all the other rules of the house?—did you rise at the same time as the other Philosophers?

A. No, I did not.

Q. What time did you rise?

A. I rose at varying times, but generally at half-past six.

Q. Did you attend the morning prayers, and so on?

A. There was half an hour's meditation in the morning, and I did not attend that; after that there was Mass, and I usually attended that, but not always.

Q. In September, when you went back, were the rules read out loud.

A. In September 1864?

Q. Yes.

A. No.

Q. In your presence?

A. No.

Q. Was it the practice to read the rules?

A. It was the practice to read the rules at the beginning of each half-year; that is, the boys' rules.

Q. And the Philosophers'?

A. No.

Q. Was that never the practice?

A. The year I was a Philosopher they were not read; I cannot say what was done before.

Q. You knew them before?

A. Only by hearsay.

Q. Did you never hear them read?

A. Not while I was a Philosopher.

Q. Before you were a Philosopher did you?

A. No.

Q. Did you know that one of the rules for the Philosophers was that they were allowed to go out in parties of three with the permission of the Prefect?

A. Certainly.

Q. A list was to be given to the President or to the Prefect?

A. No.

Q. You do not know that?

A. It was to be put in the Prefect's room.

Q. Did you know that no Philosophers were allowed to go into the town or village without express permission, or to go to places of public amusement and such like?

A. I heard that afterwards.

Q. How far is Oscott from Birmingham?

A. Six miles; it is considered five miles and a half.

Q. And Erdington, how far is that?

A. About a mile.

Q. Beyond the bounds?

A. Certainly, beyond the bounds.

Q. In December 1864, just before you went away, there was this wine or spirit party which you gave, and you were going to say, as I understood you, but you were stopped, that at the time when you left nobody was drunk?

A. No.

Q. Did nobody get drunk afterwards?

A. No.

Q. Was nobody at all the worse for it?

A. I did not say that nobody was at all the worse for it.

Q. You may make a fine distinction, perhaps, between getting drunk and being intoxicated.

A. I say one fellow was sick.

Q. And the doctor attributed it to the change of the weather?

A. Yes.

Q. I suppose you did not think much of that doctor, you knowing what you did about it?

A. I thought it rather funny.

Q. I will not mention boys' names, but I will ask you whether, with these spirits which you had brought in, there were not two boys intoxicated?

A. Certainly not.

Q. Of course it was entirely against the rules of the college to bring spirits in?

A. There was no rule against it.

Q. But tradition?

A. No, nor tradition either.

Q. Did you consider that it was according to the rules of the house to get in spirits, and to drink them at night?

A. No. I do not say that; it was against the customs.

Q. Did you ever know an instance of half-a-dozen young men sitting down together and drinking?

A. I have known instances of it.

Q. And of their being caught by the President?

A. No; I never knew an instance of that.

Q. They managed it too well for that?

A. They did.

Q. Did Mr. Stone speak to you about this in January when you returned?

A. I think he had heard of it.

Q. Did he speak to you about it?

A. I am not quite sure; I remember Dr. Northcote did.

Q. Was it mentioned to you, and were you begged not to do any thing of that sort again?

A. Yes.

Q. How came it to be mentioned to you?

A. Dr. Northcote said that if he had known it at the time, he would not have let me come back.

Q. I suppose you promised never to do it again?

A. I did not.

Q. Did you do it again?

A. Not after that; certainly not.

Q. Dr. Northcote said that he would not have let you come back, to go on with your studies for matriculation at the London University, if he had known of this before?

A. He said, "If I had known of it, I should have thought it my duty not to let you come back."

Q. You did come back?

A. I did.

Q. About the end of February?

A. The end of January,—the last day of January.

Q. Was there more than one occasion, or were there several occasions, on which Mr. Stone came and said, "You must abide by the regulations of the college, and must not stay up after ten at night"?

A. I do not remember his saying that at all.

Q. Did he come to your room to tell you to go to bed?

A. He came to me once when I was in the Philosophers' room, and told me to go to bed.

Q. He called you every morning, you say?

A. Yes.

Q. It was his practice to do so?

A. Yes.

Q. On the 23d of February you were actually under penance, were you not?

A. I was not.

Q. Were you confined to bounds?

A. Stone had told me that he took away my privileges, but he had no power to do so.

Q. The Divines were called "Mr."?

A. Yes.

Q. Was it the custom to call the Prefects "Mr."?

A. Yes.

Q. Because I observe that in your evidence you continually speak of Mr. Stone as "Stone." When you addressed Mr. Stone did you address him as "Mr. Stone," or "Stone"?

A. "Mr. Stone."

Q. He exercised authority over you, as Prefect of Discipline?

A. He did.

Q. Was it on the occasion of your coming back after your matriculation that you borrowed the key of him?

A. Yes; he offered to lend it to me.

Q. Your own key of your room was lost?

A. No; he lent me his key.

Lord Chief-Justice Cockburn: The key of your room?

A. A key that opened my room. I asked him to open my room, and he gave me the key, and said, "Give it to me back to-morrow."

Mr. Karslake: What time next morning was it that you took an impression of it in wax?

A. About one o'clock in the day.

Q. Did you make a rubbing of the key also?

A. No; I do not know what a rubbing is.

Q. Did you make an impression of it on paper with a view to get the shape of the key or the wards?

A. No.

Q. Did any body else, to your knowledge?

A. Not that I know of.

Q. When the key was given back did not Mr. Stone tell you that he had had brought to him an impression of the key?

A. He did not.

Q. And did he not ask you for the key back again?

A. He did not.

Q. Did you tell him, or did he intimate to you, that he knew that an impression had been taken for the purpose of having a duplicate key made?

A. He did not.

Q. Did you know that that key was a master key, which opened the masters' rooms and several other rooms?

A. I did not.

Q. Did Mr. Stone tell you so?

A. He did not.

Q. Now I will ask you whether, when Mr. Stone received that key back from you, and commented on the wax upon it, you did not admit to him that it was a dishonourable thing that you had been guilty of, and did you not beg him not to mention it to the President?

A. I did not.

Q. Nothing of the sort?

A. Nothing of the sort.

Q. Did you not say that you ought not to have done it; and did you not beg Mr. Stone to keep it secret, and not to mention it to the President?

A. I did not.

Q. Nothing of the sort?

A. I said I ought not to have done it, but I never begged him to keep it secret.

Q. You did say that you ought not to have done it?

A. I said it was only done in humbug.

Q. Was that the expression that you used,—that it was only done in humbug?

A. Yes.

Q. I must put to you again my version of it. Did you not say that you ought not to have done it, and did you not beg Mr. Stone not to mention it to the President?

A. I did not.

Q. You seem to have taken some interest in keys. What is the meaning of the memorandum in the pocket-book, "Key of the bakehouse opens the paint-shop"?

A. I suppose it does.

Q. What made you curious to ascertain that?

A. I do not know that I was.

Q. You have not the least notion?

A. No.

Q. All humbug. Just look at your own handwriting in your pocket-book. Had you access to the bakehouse or paint-shop?

A. Yes.

Q. How?

A. Through the door.

Q. How could you get through that door if you had not got a key?

A. The door was very frequently open; or if not, the key was hung up on the outside.

Q. Did the same key open the bakehouse and the paint-shop?

A. I suppose it did.

Q. How came you to be so curious about keys?

A. I have had that pocket-book a great many years, and I do not know what entries there are in it.

Q. Was not that the key that it was desirable to have a duplicate made of?

A. I certainly was not going to have a duplicate made of it; certainly not.

Q. What was the object of having a duplicate? The students thought it was desirable to have a duplicate?

A. Because it opened their rooms, or they thought so.

Q. That was why it was thought desirable to take it to Erdington to have a duplicate made?

A. Yes.

Q. Had you ever made impressions of keys before?

A. Never.

Q. You showed them the way to do it?

Mr. Coleridge: What is written is this, "Mem. To get note-book for logic; key of bakehouse opens paint-shop. Mem. Got off natural philosophy. Postage stamps, 5*s.* 6*d.*"

Mr. Karslake: Then it was to open the doors of the other students that they thought it desirable to have a duplicate?

A. No; to open their own doors.

Q. Did that key open all the doors in one gallery?

A. I do not know; I never tried.

Q. But that was thought to be the case?

A. That was thought to be the case.

Q. On the 22d February something happened, you told us?

A. Yes.

Q. What was that?

A. Stone came to me as I was going to bed, and looked in and said, "I take away your privileges for three days," naming the days.

Q. Was it the next day that you were at Erdington?

A. Yes.

Q. Who was with you on that occasion?

A. Three Church students.

Q. There were three with you playing at bagatelle in the public-house?

A. Yes.

Q. Did you go before Dr. Northcote the day after?

A. We did.

Q. What punishment was inflicted for that?

A. We were docked of our privileges,—that is, we were obliged to keep within bounds.

Q. For how long?

A. Till Easter.

Q. You were not allowed to go out in walking parties?

A. No.

Q. There are two sets of bounds in the college, are there not?

A. Yes; big bounds and little bounds.

Q. Senior bounds they are called sometimes, are they not?

A. Big bounds.

Q. Is that where the head boys play?

A. Yes.

Q. And the little bounds are where the smaller schoolboys play?

A. Yes.

Q. Where did you play?

A. In the big bounds.

Q. Was that what you were confined to?

A. Yes.

Q. Was it while that was going on that you were in the plantation with a pistol?

A. Yes.

Q. Who was the boy you had taken with you there?

A. A boy named * * *.

Q. A small boy?

A. No; I do not know his age, but he was the same size as myself. I expect he was a couple of years younger.

Q. Do you know what punishment he got for it?

A. He got licked.

Q. You say that on that occasion Mr. Stone found you there?

A. Yes.

Q. And you ran away, did you not?

A. Yes; we did.

Q. Did you deny to him having a pistol.

A. Certainly not.

Q. Do you mean to say that you did not deny to him having the pistol or knowing where it was?

A. I did not.

Q. Did Mr. Northcote tell you that he considered you had been equivocating?

A. He did.

Q. When you saw Mr. Northcote upon that subject, had he a considerable conversation with you about your conduct?

A. He had not a conversation with me. He gave me a very harsh lecture.

Q. At that time, I believe that, in consequence of this former offence against the discipline of the college, you were made to study in the study-place, were you not?

A. I was.

Q. Did Mr. Northcote tell you that there was no other punishment that he could inflict upon you but to deprive you of your room and make you study in the study-place?

A. He did.

Q. Did he say that he was sorry to do that, and that it was almost better that you should go home than have your studies interfered with by having to study in the study-place?

A. No; he did not.

Q. You had your room still, but you had to study in the study-place?

A. He said he would not deprive me of my room: I used my room for studying except during study-hours.

Q. Did he say that if he had to deprive you of your room, it would be better for you to leave the place at once, because it was necessary for you to have a private room for you to study in?

A. He did not.

Q. Did he tell you at that time that if you committed any fresh offence he should be obliged to send you away, as he had exhausted all the punishment that was applicable to a person in your position?

A. He said something to that effect.

Q. He did not say those very words?

A. No; not those very words.

Q. But it was to that effect?

A. Yes; to that effect.

Q. Did he tell you that he should write to your father and say how precarious your position was in the college?

A. No, he did not; he said something about writing, but he did not say that he would write. He said he thought he must write, or something to that effect; he did not say it categorically.

Q. Did he not expressly tell you that he should write and tell your father how precarious your position in the college was?

A. He did not.

Q. Did he dismiss you from him after having given you this harsh lecture?

A. He did. The bell was ringing for night-prayers, and he went out of the room.

Q. Did you come back to him yourself and beg him not to report you to your father?

A. No.

Q. Did you ask him at all that day not to write to your father?

A. I did not.

Q. Did Mr. Northcote tell you that he certainly must write; for that if any fresh offence should occur, your father might justly suspect him of having dealt harshly and unjustly by you?

A. He said something like that, but not those words. He did not say certainly that he must write.

Q. Did he not say that unless he did write, your father might consider he was acting harshly towards you if you were sent away afterwards without notice?

A. Yes, he said that.

Q. Did you say there was no danger, as you would commit no fresh offence or transgression of the discipline of the college?

A. I did not.

Q. What did you say?

A. He asked me would I promise to behave myself—to "give no more trouble," was the expression he used, I think; and I said I would promise.

Q. Did he say to you, "David, I am risking my character with your father for justice, prudence, and moderation, against your word of honour. Is that safe?"

A. He said that just before I left him.

Q. On that occasion?

A. On the second interview I had with him.

Q. About the pistol?

A. About the pistol.

Q. The one after prayers?

A. The one after prayers. That was the last thing he said as I was leaving the room.

Q. Did you say to him, "Your confidence shall not be abused"?

A. I never said any such thing.

Q. Did you intend to do something afterwards, then?

A. I did not.

Q. Did you give him your word of honour that you would not do any thing, if your father was not written to?

A. I promised to give no more trouble.

Q. I asked whether, when you went back after prayers, it was for the express purpose of asking him not to write to your father?

A. It was not.

Q. What did you go back, then, for?

A. To excuse myself for the injustice which had been put upon me, and also to ask if he was going to write. I at that time intended to write to my father, saying I had been very unjustly treated, and asking him to remove me from the college. In my conversation with Dr. Northcote, he promised that he would not write, if I would promise to give no more trouble. I intended to write myself, but I changed my mind. Easter was near, and I thought I would not write.

Q. On the morning after that interview was the punishment which Mr. Northcote said he should inflict carried out?

A. It was. I voluntarily submitted to it.

Q. Did Mr. Stone come to you and tell you that it was to be carried out?

A. No; I went into the ranks of myself, and went into the study-place.

Q. Did not Mr. Stone come to you that morning and say "that the punishment was to be carried out, and that you must go to the study-place"?

A. I do not remember it.

Q. But you went to the study-place and studied there?

A. I did, and I went to the ranks.

Q. When first had you any conversation with other boys or students about the Anti-Bunker Confederation?

A. I cannot say when.

Q. Was it after you came back in January?

A. It was.

Q. When were these names written that you have in your pocket-book? Were they written at different times?

A. At different times.

Q. There are among you boys who are the sons of tradesmen and professional men and others?

A. Yes.

Q. What is the meaning of this which I find here, "Uncle or brother keeps a small grocery establishment"? Did you believe it at the time you made this memorandum?

A. I do not believe it.

Q. Did you believe it then?

A. I did.

Q. Was an inquiry to be made whether some boy's uncle or brother did keep a small grocery establishment?

A. It was not.

Q. Why, then, was this written down?

A. It was written down because it amused the honorary secretary, and amused me too.

Q. You were a Philosopher, you know.

A. I was.

Q. Were you writing down this wholly for your amusement?

A. Yes.

Q. "Uncle or brother keeps a small grocery establishment in Wednesfield Heath. Father a general inspector of canal locks." Where did you get this information from?

A. The honorary secretary.

Q. What were you?

A. I was nothing at all.

Q. There are five Fitzgeralds who are members of the Confederation?

A. No.

Q. They are put down here as such. "A. B. C. Fitzgerald 5." What does that mean?

A. That there were five Fitzgeralds in the house, but not five Fitzgeralds A. B. C.'s.

Q. Just look at this—"A. B. C. Fitzgerald, 5;" and tell me whether that did not mean that five Fitzgeralds in the college should be members of the Anti-Bunker Confederation?

A. I did not mean it so.

Q. "* 1?"

A. One * * *.

Q. "* 2; * 2; * 1; * 1;" and so on—fourteen in all?

A. Yes.

Q. What are those fourteen?

A. They were not all members of the A. B. C.

Q. I ask you what they were?

A. Boys at Oscott.

Q. So you put their names down and cast the numbers up, and made the whole number fourteen?

A. Yes.

Q. The "A.B.C.," at all events, we know means "Anti-Bunker Confederation"?

A. Yes.

Q. Then underneath I see, "Governor Moody elected March 6th, for his magnanimous sentiments about Sedgely Park." Then it was going on, at all events, between January, when you came back, and the 6th of March?

A. No; not in January.

Q. How soon after January?—February?

A. I do not think any thing was done before the 26th of February.

Q. What was done then?

A. All the entries in ink were made on the 26th of February by myself, singly, in my own room, and the entries on the two loose scraps of paper.

Q. You had a conversation with other boys about this, had you not?

A. I showed the entries to some of the boys.

Q. To what boys?

A. To W., for one.

Q. Did you speak to him about being secretary?

A. Yes.

Q. You appointed him, you say?

A. Yes. I said, "Will you be honorary secretary?"

Q. Was it his duty as honorary secretary to make inquiries about these boys?

A. No.

Q. What were his duties, then?

A. He had no duties.

Q. Did he live in the locality?

A. I do not know where he lived.

Q. Sedgely Park was a proprietary school, you say, from which a great many of these boys came?

A. Yes.

Q. Were all the boys that came from Sedgely Park called "Bunkers"?

A. Most of them were.

Q. If they came upon charitable funds they were called "Bunkers"?

A. If they were Church students, they were called "Bunkers." I do not know what funds they came on.

Q. About how many of the Sedgely boys do you think were in the college altogether as Church students?

A. At that time there were about six or seven or eight Church students, and a great many of the "Divines" had come from Sedgely Park.

Q. Did the "Divines" play in the upper bounds?

A. They did sometimes, but not often.

Q. I suppose that some of these Sedgely students were in such a position that they played there too?

A. Decidedly.

Q. Where else did they chiefly come from, those who came as Church students?

A. They chiefly came from Sedgely Park.

Q. But there were others besides?

A. There were.

Q. Why did you want "all particulars about any of the under-mentioned as to birth, parentage, qualifications, and patrons"?

A. There were no qualifications.

Q. That was written merely as a piece of idle amusement?

A. Entirely.

Q. "Humbug?"

A. Yes.

Q. Was this also "humbug"—"Consult honorary secretary for information about this 'gentleman,'" with inverted commas?

A. Yes.

Q. "Humbug?"

A. Yes.

Q. Was the gentleman's name F * * *?

A. Yes.

Q. Was there such a person at the college?

A. No.

Q. Who was F * * * then?

A. He had been at the college.

Q. And I suppose he was a "Bunker" when he was there?

A. Yes.

Q. And was the honorary secretary to inquire about F * * *?

A. No; the honorary secretary came to me one day and told me to write that. I do not say those very words, but something to that effect.

Q. It was on the 6th of March that "Governor Moody" was elected for his magnanimous sentiments about Sedgely Park? Did you know, or were you told by Mr. Stone or by Mr. Northcote, that there had been complaints about the confederation?

A. Never.

Q. Were you told by Mr. Northcote that it had come to his ears that there was a confederation of this sort formed?

A. No.

Q. Did you tell Mr. Northcote that it was all "humbug" at first?

A. I did.

Q. Or nonsense?

A. I did.

Q. Did you tell him afterwards that you admitted——

Mr. Coleridge: Ask him what he said.

Mr. Karslake: Did you say to him that this society or confederation was on foot, and that this had been done by you in a fit of spleen or spite?

A. No; but I said that one of the entries was written when I was in a very splenetic mood.

Q. Which of the entries was that?

A. The first entries of all.

Q. Which are those?

A. The entries in ink.

Q. That is the names of certain persons with the letters "S. P." against them and "P. P."?

A. The entries in ink in the book and on those two loose scraps of paper.

Q. It begins first of all with "L. B. C. S. (one dozen)." I do not know what that means.

A. List of Bunkers, one dozen.

Q. "F. M * * *, S. P." Is that Sedgely Park?

A. Yes.

Q. "J. R * * *, S. P.," the same place; "E. S * * *," "M.D * * *," "Dr. Amherst,"—is that right?

A. Yes.

Q. What is Dr. Amherst?

A. The Catholic Bishop of Northampton.

Q. Was he the patron of Mr. * * *?

A. Yes; I believe he was.

Q. "S. A * * *, S. P.?"

A. Yes.

Q. Then there are two more, "* * * *," and "Dr. Clifford," after them?

A. He is the Bishop of Clifton.

Q. He was a patron, I suppose?

A. He was, I believe.

Q. "M * * *, S. P." "J. B * * *, S. P. Query, Irish?" Surely you did not object to him on the score of his being Irish?

A. London Irish.

Q. That is a bad form of Bunker, is it? He ranks before "J. C——, of Stourbridge Potteries"?

A. Yes, he does.

Q. The London Irishman is better than the Potteries' man?

A. Decidedly.

Q. "C * * *?"

A. He was not there at the time. He had left, I think.

Q. "A. D * * *, of the Bell Inn, Stourbridge." That is another objectionable form of "Bunker," is it?

A. Yes.

Q. How many men had you spoken to yourself about being members of this society?

A. About three or four.

Q. Was it to be one of the rules of the society that none of the Bunkers should hold any of the offices which the boys had among them?

A. No.

Q. You say there were no meetings regularly convened?

A. No; nor were there any rules; nor was there any society.

Q. You have an officer that is called "the public man"?

A. We have.

Q. He is the man among you who manages the games, and so on?

A. He is.

Q. And communicates with the President?

A. Yes.

Q. Is there a librarian also?

A. There is.

Q. Were the "Bunkers" to be prohibited from being public men or librarian?

A. No.

Q. You had no arrangement of that kind?

A. I believe that at that time the two librarians were "Bunkers."

Q. But after that time that I am speaking of?

A. There was no such arrangement, and there was no real society at all. It was, in fact, like the mock prospectus.

Q. I understand you to say that there was no prospectus issued, and that no meetings were convened; but that you had talked to two or three men about the "Anti-Bunker Confederation"?

A. I said to some fellows, "Will you be an Anti-Bunker?"

Q. Did they understand what you meant by it?

A. They had a general idea.

Q. What was the general idea that they had?

A. That they were to bear the name of "Anti-Bunkers."

Q. How do you mean?

A. They were to go by the name "Anti-Bunkers," the same as other fellows went by the name of "Bunkers."

Q. You were to exalt yourselves into "Anti-Bunkers"?

A. And were so to be called.

Q. And the "Anti-Bunkers" were to be in opposition to the "Bunkers"?

A. Yes.

Q. How was their opposition to be carried out—in petty annoyance?

A. Certainly not.

Q. How then?

A. In no way.

Q. Then it was "humbug" from beginning to end? When you had this interview with Dr. Northcote, and you talked about it being an absurdity and all that sort of thing, did he tell you that he understood what the character of the society was, and that it was formed for the purpose of annoying these "Bunkers"?

A. No; he said it was a conspiracy against the peace and welfare of all the Church students.

Q. Did he not expressly refer to the Church students who were supported out of charitable funds?

A. I do not know how they were supported.

Q. Did he refer to the Church students as being the objects of the confederation?

A. He did. He said it was against the peace and welfare of all the Church students in the house; those were his very words.

Q. Do you remember his using this expression to you,—"It may be all very good fun for you, but it is death to the frogs"?

A. No.

Q. You do not remember that?

A. No; I remember another expression about pitch.

Q. But did he not say so in that conversation?

A. I do not remember it.

Q. Was not that said by him when you were saying that this was all "humbug"?

A. He said something about pitch; I do not remember that he said any thing about frogs.

Q. Did you not admit that you were a member of that society, and did you not say that you got it up in a fit of spleen, or, as you say, in a splenetic mood?

A. No; I did not say any such thing.

Q. Mr. Stone saw you alone on the morning of the 13th.

A. He did.

Q. Did he tell you later in the day that Mr. Northcote wanted to see you? Was the message brought by him?

A. No.

Q. He did not?

A. He did not.

Q. Did Mr. Northcote send for you?

A. No.

Q. How came you to see Mr. Northcote?

A. I said I would go to him myself, and Stone said, "Come along."

Q. Did he not at 11 o'clock send for you? Did not Mr. Stone come and say he had been sent by Mr. Northcote for you?

A. He did not.

Q. Did you take your book with you to Mr. Northcote?

A. Stone took it.

Q. Was the conversation a long one?

A. It was.

Q. Now I ask you whether the whole of that conversation was not on the subject of the annoyance which this society was going to cause to the boys?

A. No; I think not.

Q. What else was there?

A. I do not remember.

Q. Did Mr. Northcote on that occasion desire you to go to your room and wait until you were sent for?

A. He did.

Q. And you went?

A. I went.

Q. How came you to leave your room after having received that order from him? Were you going down to the boys to see them?

A. No.

Q. Where were you going?

A. I went to chapel.

Q. I suppose all the students were there, were they not?

A. No, they were not.

Q. None of them?

A. No.

Q. Who else was there?

A. Myself.

Q. Only yourself.

A. Yes; only myself.

Q. How long were you there?

A. About a quarter of an hour.

Q. Where did you go to then?

A. Back to my room.

Q. Did you remain in your room?

A. My room was locked.

Q. Mr. Stone let you in, I understand?

A. Afterwards.

Q. Was it about half-past one when you say you saw Mr. Northcote again when you went by his room?

A. No; immediately after one.

Q. How long did that interview last?

A. It lasted a very short time.

Q. Was it at that interview that he said he had seen the boys and explained to them the reason why you were going?

A. Yes; he did not use those words.

Q. He told you what he had said to them?

A. He said, "I have publicly expelled you,—that is what I have done."

Q. Did he refer to what he had said to the boys and to a passage he had read from Dr. Newman's book?

A. Yes.

Q. Was not the passage this? "It is almost a definition of a gentleman to say he is one who never inflicts pain. The true gentleman carefully avoids whatever may cause a jar or a jolt in the minds of those with whom he is cast: he can recollect to whom he is speaking; he guards against unseasonable allusions or topics which may irritate."* Did he read that?

A. I remember the first part.

Q. Did he also read a passage from Fuller's *Worthies* to you?

A. I do not remember. He read some extracts from books.

Q. Did he read this? "If his birth be not, at least his qualities are, generous. He endeavours by his own deserts to ennoble himself. Thus valour makes him son to Cæsar, learning entitles him kinsman to Tully, and piety reports him nephew to godly Constantine. He is not in his youth possessed with the great hopes of his possessions; only his parents acquaint him that he is the next undoubted heir to correction, if misbehaving himself."

A. I do not remember that.

Q. When you left on that occasion did he tell you to go back to your room; that you were dismissed; and that when you went back, a cab would be obtained for you, and you would leave?

A. He said, "Really I have nothing more to say to you."

Q. He had dismissed you before that?

A. Yes.

* Newman's *Lectures on University Education*, p. 328.

Q. And then you never saw him again?

A. I saw him again before I left. I asked him a question.

Q. What did you say?

A. I said I was a member of the Oscotian Society; and I wanted to know whether he expelled me from that too.

Q. What is that society?

A. A society which he has got up among the late students of the college.

Q. Was what you asked him, whether you might come to the Oscotian meeting?

A. He said he would make inquiries; that it was a very difficult case to decide; that he did not see his way to it.

Q. That was the last you saw of him before you left?

A. It was.

Q. At what time did you actually leave?

A. About a quarter-past three.

Q. At what time had you been sent with Mr. Stone to your room?

A. At about a quarter-past one.

Q. When you went to your room, you were to pack up your things and go as soon as you could?

A. I was to have my dinner first.

Q. Was what Mr. Stone did, to urge you to get on with your packing?

A. Yes.

Q. And did he tell you that unless you chose to go on with your packing, your things would be sent after you?

A. He said he would bundle me out, and my things after me.

Q. You did not pack up your things?

A. Yes; I did pack them.

Q. Eventually?

A. Yes.

Q. Were you not delaying the packing, and was not Mr. Stone urging you to pack?

A. He was.

Q. Did he tell you expressly, when you asked about your brothers, that your brothers could come to you, but that you could not see the rest of the students of the college?

A. No.

Q. Did you see your cousins?

A. Yes.

Q. You have been talking about Mr. Stone saying this and that to you. Did Mr. Stone expressly, on more than one occasion, say, at your request, that he would not tell the President?

A. No; never.

Q. I ask you as regards the key, whether you did not ask him not to tell about it, and whether he did not say he would not?

A. I gave him an explanation of it.

Q. Did you not expressly ask him not to tell?

A. No.

Q. Did you not afterwards say that you would release him from the pledge of secrecy?

A. I thought he might tell. He had said that he knew a great many things against me, but he would not say any thing about them. He told Dr. Northcote that he was under a promise not to reveal them. I asked him what they were, and he would give me no particular answer. I then said that if the key matter was one, he might tell about that as soon as he liked. I imagined that he might be under the impression that he was bound not to tell because he had said he would not. He said then he did not care to tell, because he knew it was only a trick.

Q. When was this?

A. This was the 28th of February.

Q. After the pistol affair?

A. It was.

Q. You are a student for the Bar now?

A. Yes.

Q. When did you enter for that?

A. In Easter Term 1865.

Q. Have you finished your University education?

A. No; I am still at the University College.

Q. I must ask you one question. Do you mean that any thing further was done by Mr. Stone as to the pocket-book beyond putting his hand in your pocket and taking it out, when you refused to give it to him?

A. No.

Q. You talked about violence?

A. I did not say there was any violence. He said that if I did not give it to him at once, he would take it by main force.

Lord Chief-Justice Cockburn: You did your best to keep it?

A. I did.

Mr. Karslake: And he took it?

A. Yes, he took it.

Re-examined by Mr. Colleridge.

Q. About this Oscotian Society; did you hear any thing about that, or what made you ask Mr. Northcote any thing about it?

A. I was a member of the Oscotian Society.

Q. Had any thing been said by him to you, when he told you that he had told the boys he had publicly expelled you, as to expelling you from the Oscotian Society?

A. He said so to the boys, but he did not say so to me.

Q. You had heard that?

A. No; I merely asked him the question.

Q. It has been put to you whether you said to Mr. Stone that you had been guilty of a dishonourable act. Did you say any thing of that sort?

A. Certainly not. I gave him an explanation of the matter. He said that he ought not to have been in my room; that I had explained the matter, and that he would say nothing more about it.

Q. If this kind of notice had not been taken of the Confederation, would it have died a natural death?

A. It would have died a natural death. It had collapsed then.

Q. There are fourteen persons mentioned as members of the Anti-Bunker Society. Did you speak to every one of those persons or not?

A. Not to more than four or five.

Q. You never spoke to the others at all?

A. No.

Q. Their names were put down there, then, without their authority, and they knew nothing at all about it?

A. They did not.

Q. And they never would have known, probably?

A. They never would have known.

Q. Had you yourself friends among the Church students?

A. I had personal friends among them.

Mr. JOHN FITZGERALD *sworn.*

A Juror: I think, my Lord, we have heard quite enough; and the jury seem rather to wish to come to a decision.

Lord Chief-Justice Cockburn: You have not heard the other side yet.

Mr. Coleridge: I am sure I do not want to keep the gentlemen of the jury here. I do not know that we need trouble Mr. John Fitzgerald; but I will just call Mr. Justice Fitzgerald.

The Right Hon. JOHN DAVID FITZGERALD *sworn. Examined by* Mr. COLERIDGE.

Q. You are a judge of the Court of Queen's Bench in Ireland?

A. I am.

Q. And a member of the Privy Council?

A. Yes.

Q. For some time you were Attorney-General for Ireland?

A. I was Attorney- and Solicitor-General for five years.

Q. You are the father of the Plaintiff?

A. I am the father of the Plaintiff.

Q. Up to the time at which you found your son in your house in Merrion Spuare; had you any intimation whatever from Mr. Northcote that matters were otherwise than perfectly harmonieus between them?

A. Never. I had repeated communications with Mr. Northcote, both personally and by letter, all the time he was President of the College, and I never heard a word of complaint of my son's conduct. My last letter to him was written on the 6th of February previous, when I remitted him a sum of 176*l.* in advance* for the current half-year—that is, to the end of last Midsummer; and in all that time I never heard a word from Dr. Northcote except of praise. I am wrong. On one occasion, in 1862, I remember there was a complaint that on the breaking up for the summer holidays of 1862, my son, with a young gentleman of the name of * * * and three or four others, had been a

* *i.e.* a portion of this sum was the pension in advance.

little turbulent, insisting on singing in the dormitory, "We will all go home in the morning." During the whole time that my son was there, that was the only complaint that I ever heard of.

Q. Then it was a great surprise to you to see him at your house?

A. It was more than a surprise; it was a great shock to me.

Cross-examined by Mr. Karslake.

Q. Did you know upon any occasion of his having been kept back for some hours after the other boys?

A. That is the occasion I refer to. It was at the time of the Great National Exhibition. I had directed him to come to London. His two brothers came, and he did not; and on my writing, an explanation came from Dr. Northcote to that effect—that is, of the singing in the dormitory.

Q. Knowing that he had been kept back, you telegraphed, did you not, for him to come?

A. Not knowing why he had been kept back.

Q. But he was kept back?

A. Yes; for three or four hours.

Q. You learnt that he had been kept back as a punishment?

A. For singing in the dormitory on a sort of carnival night —the night of the break-up.

Q. You admit that that was a fit matter for the exercise of Dr. Northcote's discretion?

A. Yes; I do not complain of that.

Q. Every letter from Dr. Northcote was written in a spirit of kindness towards the boy—always appearing to take the greatest interest in him?

A. Yes; always taking the greatest interest in him.

Q. Was there not a letter which you received in which he pointed out to you that the fault, and the only fault that he could find with your boys, was that there was a certain amount of grumbling and discontent on their part when they were subjected to punishment?

A. No; not exactly that.

Q. You have the letter I refer to?

A. No, I have not. I do not know whether the attorneys have such a letter. On that occasion, after they had been at home some time for the summer vacation—not at their instance, but collecting from their conversation that they had some causes of complaint about the food of the college, and some about the absence of proper sanitary regulations—I did write about those complaints to Dr. Northcote; and in his reply he complained, I recollect, of their grumbling.

Q. I should be glad to see the letter. May I take it that this is the substance of what he said, that the fault he had to find was, that when they were a little bit rebellious, they would not take their punishment without complaining?

Mr. Coleridge: This is the letter:

"Many thanks for the cheque: and as to the list of grievances which accompany it, I am sure you will allow me to be as plain-spoken as yourself; and if I must say what I really feel about them, it would be this—that they quite come up to the popular English notion of 'Irish grievances;' a notion which, as it is commonly held, I entirely dissent from. They seem to me to savour strongly of what is supposed to be the national characteristic of supporting any thing 'against the Government.' For if there is one thing on which Oscott would more willingly challenge comparison with any college in England than another, it is the matter of eating and drinking. * * * * * * But, joking apart, I am really extremely sorry to find your boys making complaints of this sort. It is one of the principal faults in the characters of the two eldest (I have not heard it spoken of in Gerald) that they seem to think nothing good enough for them, and that it ought to be somebody's duty to shield them from every possible ill or inconvenience."

and so on.

The Witness: I now recollect, my memory having been refreshed by reading that letter, which I have not read since, that the complaints which were made were complaints coming from myself, in consequence of my having overheard the conversation of the boys. The complaints principally referred to rancid butter, and to the tea and sugar being mixed together, and poured from a common vessel. I called Dr. Northcote's attention to that; and I should add that these grievances were removed afterwards, though Dr. Northcote expressed himself so strongly against their existence.*

Mr. Karslake: Your son did not complain of them?

A. I inquired into the matter.

* The tea never had been made in the way supposed; nor was any change whatever made in consequence of these complaints.

Q. Did you receive a letter from Dr. Northcote, in which, among other things, he told you that the fault he found with the boys was grumbling when they were subjected to any sort of punishment?

A. I do not recollect any such thing, except in the letter that has been read.

Q. Was there not a letter in which he said there was a great spirit of pride and petty rebellion?

A. Decidedly there was no such expression in any of his letters. There was neither that expression, nor any thing in substance like it.

Mr. Coleridge: If my friend likes to have all the letters put in, he is exceedingly welcome to them, and, of course, may make any use of them he can.

The Witness: I made a careful search for all letters, and I sent them all across.

Re-examined by Mr. Coleridge.

Q. You say you do not know of any other letters being in existence except those that have been produced here?

A. No.

Q. Do you remember any letter containing such an expression as that which my friend has just put to you?

A. Nothing like it, either in form or in substance.

Q. That the fault he had to find with them was their grumbling and discontent when they were subjected to punishment?

A. No.

Mr. Coleridge: That, my Lord, is the Plaintiff's case.

Mr. Karslake: May it please your Lordship:—Gentlemen of the Jury,—When you say that you have heard enough of the case already, and that you are prepared to come to a decision at once upon it, it is right that I should ask you, at all events, to hear both sides before you come to a decision; because, gentlemen, it is not always that, when a plaintiff comes before you and gives his own evidence, you can make up your minds quite safely as to whether the issues (and they are somewhat complicated ones in this case) ought, or ought not, to be found against the defendants; and I am quite sure that you will suspend your judgment until you have heard the Defendant's evidence, and until you have heard from my Lord what the real question is that you have to decide;—a question, let me say, of very considerable importance to Dr. Northcote, who is the principal defendant here, and who, of course, as President of this College, over which he exercises jurisdiction, has a deep interest in showing that he has not been guilty of that which my friend designated as conduct which ought not to have been exhibited to a youth such as Mr. Fitzgerald, and that he has not been guilty of that cruel and heartless misconduct which he is alleged to have exhibited towards Mr. Fitzgerald's father.

Gentlemen, there is one matter as to which I confess I felt some surprise. My friend, in an amusing and somewhat inflammatory address, with which he occupied some time this morning, called your attention to several letters, and intimated that young David Fitzgerald was sent away from Oscott College without any letter, and without any intimation of any sort or kind having been made to his father of the reason why he was sent away. It may not have occurred to your minds that, although no letter was taken by the hand of David Fitzgerald when he left the college in March 1864, yet that there was a letter written by Dr. Northcote to Mr. Fitzgerald's father, in which the whole history was given as to the reasons which actuated Dr. Northcote in sending him away at once; and I think that my friend, before he closed his address, ought, in justice and fairness to Dr. Northcote to have laid the terms of that letter before you. Gentlemen, that letter was posted on the very day on which David Fitzgerald left, and it reached Judge Fitzgerald the next morning in due course of post immediately after he had seen his son, Mr. David Fitzgerald. From the first, therefore, the Judge knew perfectly well what the charge was which was made against his son; and I think that when my friend was heaping the amount of odium on Mr. Northcote, and Mr. Stone his coadjutor, that he did this morning, he might at least have told you that a letter was written, and sent by the post on the very day on which Mr. David Fitzgerald left, explaining all the circumstances under which Mr. Northcote had found it necessary to order him to leave the college. Let me just call your attention generally to the letter which my friend did *not* read in his opening speech; and I pray your particular attention to it, because it is, in point of fact, the case I am going to set up before you; it is the case I am instructed to set up before you; and by the view you may take of his conduct on that occasion, with the knowledge he then had of the existing state of things, Mr. Northcote is ready to stand or fall to-day.

Gentlemen, I need not call your attention to the difficult position in which Mr. Northcote was placed. He is a gentleman who has been elected for the purpose of acting as President of this College. He is placed there to preside over an establishment in which—including boys and masters—there are about 200 persons, all living under the same roof. Among those there are 120 or 130 students of different grades, some of them being the more privileged class—as the Philosophers and Poets we have heard of—and some of them being comparatively small boys. Over the whole of this establishment Mr. Northcote has to exercise his supervision. The constitution of the college, and the character of the boys who are sent there, and the circumstances under which they are sent, will be explained to you; and you will find that they have a very material bearing indeed on Mr. Northcote's conduct. Gentlemen, my friend is wrong in stating to you that out of the moneys which are paid by the richer students those who are not so well able to afford to pay for their education are maintained. Such is not the case. There are a certain number of students who, like Mr. Fitzgerald, are the children of men of wealth and opulence, who are well able to pay for their education in the college; and there are others who are sent there on charitable funds, or on funds subscribed and obtained from different sources, and those are generally Church students. The whole of those students are mixed up together in the school; and I need not tell you that if the President of that institution were to allow young gentlemen who prided themselves on their high birth and position—like Mr. Fitzgerald—to snub and cold-shoulder those who do not possess the same advantages as they themselves enjoy, the college might as well be at once shut up; for it would be impossible for youths—except in the rank of Mr. Fitzgerald—to go there; or, if Mr. Fitzgerald and his friends were allowed to go there, than the other class of students must be excluded altogether.

Now, gentlemen, I will call your attention to the state of things which existed at the time when Mr. Northcote became President of this College. Mr. Northcote, when he came there, knew perfectly well—as every master and every person there knew—that there had been a strong feeling exhibited by some of the boys in the higher classes in the school against those whom they chose to call "Bunkers." I know that when these things are described before a jury, they are calculated to raise a smile; and you laugh with and sympathise with young Mr. Fitzgerald, who represents that all his acts were of an innocent character, and that he simply did that which is continually done by boys at every school; but you will look a little deeper into the matter by and by, and say whether it was possible for Mr. Northcote,—having regard to the interest of the college of which he was the superior, and having regard to the interests of that class of boys who had to look to him for protection, in the event of their being snubbed or ill-treated by other boys in the school,—to act otherwise than as he did. When he sent David Fitzgerald away from the college, he did so most reluctantly, for he was fond of the boy, and had taken more than ordinary care of him, and felt more than an ordinary interest in him. He had, however, good grounds for believing—or, at all events, he had what he considered good grounds for believing—that there was an improper feeling existing among some of the higher boys in the school, and that measures were being taken for the purpose of degrading those students who, as they considered, were of a lower grade than themselves, and who were not able to afford out of their own or out of their parents' funds the means to pay for their education, and who were maintained out of funds obtained from different sources. Gentlemen, years ago, in this school, or in this college, which was originally established for the benefit—as I believe you will find—of the clergy, or those who had been educated for the Church, it was determined that lay students should be admitted. They were admitted, and the students in the college were then all mixed up together; and I believe that, after the change had been made, a feeling exhibited itself on the part of the lay students against the clerical students, which produced a most disastrous effect. That feeling, however, had died out to a very considerable extent; and when young Mr. Fitzgerald went there, as he told you, although he did not know the name of "Bunker," he found very little distinction was made between the clerical and the lay students; and I believe he is perfectly accurate in saying that until somewhere about February or March 1864 the spirit which had once existed seemed to have died out, and it had never been revived up to that time.

Gentlemen, I appeal to the letters which were written by Mr. Northcote to Judge Fitzgerald, and I ask you to say—looking at the tone in which those letters are written—whether Mr. Northcote had any ill-feeling of any sort or kind towards young David Fitzgerald. I find that in July 1863 (I think that was the date), he had left, and at that time he did not contemplate coming back again. It was upon the suggestion of Mr. Northcote himself, after it had been found that it was not expedient to send young David Fitzgerald to Trinity College, that he came back, mainly for the purpose of being perfected in the classics, he having at that time gone through the course of philosophy, and having obtained the highest position in the college. He came back, as you will find by the letters, not as my friend suggests, as a sort of exceptional pupil, but he was to be bound by the rules of the college and by the discipline of the college, and he was to be under the President and Prefects just the same as any other student in the college might be; but he was to this extent excused from attending lectures, that he attended only those lectures which bore on the particular class of studies that he was anxious to pursue. For that purpose he attended the classical classes, though he did not attend those for mathematics, and so forth. That was the state of things in September 1864. If there were any distinction to be made between young Mr. Fitzgerald and the generality of the boys, I should say that young Mr. Fitzgerald, being received there as an act of kindness rather on the part of Mr. Northcote, ought to have been doubly cautious that his conduct was of such a character as could never give offence to the Principal of the College; and I should have thought also that, coming back to the college in that way, he would have taken the utmost care never to come into collision with a person who, so far as we may judge from his conduct in the box, he seems to have treated with the most profound contempt, calling him "Stone," and speaking of him as a person to whose control and authority he was not bound to submit. What was the first thing that was done? It is all very well for my friend to say that "boys will be boys;" but I ask, was it right or proper for young Mr. Fitzgerald, when he came back, and before he left in 1864, to have in his room a party of boys, and to give them spirits, knowing that it was altogether contrary to the rules of the college to do so, and that if he was caught at it, the consequences would be most serious to him? Was it right or proper that he should induce other boys to join him in doing that which both he and they knew to be wrong? It happened that at the time he was not found out; and having gone away for the vacation, he returned to the college at the end of January, it being intended that he should continue there for some months before going to University College, and before going to London to reside. Before this last occurrence, when, as Mr. Northcote thought, it was utterly impossible, having regard to the interests of the college, and having regard to the welfare of the students, that he should remain any longer in the college; when, having first confined him to his room, he sent him away in consequence of the existence of what he believed to be a dangerous combination, of which young Fitzgerald was the head, and which had been formed for the purpose of annoying a large class of the members of that college,—Mr. Fitzgerald commenced a series of breaches of discipline, to which I will call your attention shortly; because you will find, in the course of the narrative, that they have a very material bearing on the conduct of Mr. Northcote. First of all, we find that, on the 23d of February, he being at that time under punishment, and it being as well known to Mr. Fitzgerald as it was to every other student, that it was entirely against the rules of the college that he should go to any public-house in the neighbourhood, he, being confined to the bounds, broke those bounds, and was found at a public-house, where in the afternoon he was, with other students, playing at bagatelle. I know, when that is stated, and a boy comes and says, "I went there with two other fellows, and I meant no harm by it," one is very apt to say that the best thing is to take no notice of it. But suppose all the boys in a public school are doing the same thing; and suppose the monitors, and those who ought to set a good example to the other boys, are found to be wilfully defying the masters and the authorities, and to be taking the law into their own hands, and going to public-houses, and going out of bounds,—I do not say they may not do it, and do not do it, and that they will not continue to do it; but I do say, that if they are discovered, and if they receive such punishment as the President thinks it proper to inflict upon them for such an offence, neither they nor their fathers ought to turn round and complain that they are hardly used by the President taking such a course as he thinks it essential to take in order to maintain the discipline of the establishment.

Then, gentlemen, you will find that, only a few days afterwards—on the 27th—he does that which again causes in court a smile, and it is said there is no great harm in it. It is difficult from the mere description given by a witness on one side or the other to appreciate exactly the conduct of any boy or young man on any particular occasion when it is detailed some few years afterwards. What was the charge? It appears that he had taken a boy, named * * *, out with him into the plantations, and in defiance of all authority, and contrary to what he perfectly well knew to be the rules of the school, he had done that which, I will venture to say, at the public schools that were mentioned by my friend in his opening speech would in all probability have induced the head-master—especially if the boy had committed other offences against the discipline of the school—to send him away. You find Mr. David Fitzgerald going out into the plantations with a boy who was liable to suffer corporal punishment—which you hear is sometimes inflicted even at Oscott—with a double-barrelled pistol, with which they were amusing themselves. Of course David Fitzgerald knew perfectly well that his being in the plantations with a pistol, when he was under penance, was utterly against the rules of the house and of the institution to which he belonged. But that was not the worst. You will hear from Mr. Stone what occurred; and you will hear whether David Fitzgerald was not on that occasion guilty at least of equivocation, when he was charged by Mr.

Stone with having committed that breach of discipline; and he is degraded by having to study in the common room, instead of in the room that is usually appropriated to the use of the head boys in the establishment. He is told that that penance is to be suffered by him until Easter; and, under the circumstances, Mr. Northcote told him that it would be impossible for him to overlook any future breaches of discipline, because he had at that time done all he could do to punish and degrade him, and that, in the position in which he stood in the college, there was no other punishment that was applicable to his case. Young David Fitzgerald tells you, "I was in such a position that corporal punishment could not be inflicted upon me. I was in such a position, as Mr. Northcote told me, that having, as an ordinary thing, a private room of my own, to which I might go at all times, when I was not required to be at lecture, if that private room was taken away from me, the very object of my being at the college would be defeated." Mr. Northcote said, "I can do nothing further; if you choose to go on setting at naught the rules of this house, the result will be that you will have to leave the place altogether." I beg your particular attention to the warning that was given to him at that time. Mr. Northcote said "Now mind, although I have overlooked other faults, I must write to your father on this subject." That seems to have created some impression on David Fitzgerald's mind, for he came back, and begged Mr. Northcote most earnestly not to write to his father, and gave him his word of honour, that if he would not write, no further breach of discipline should be committed by him, and that no further cause of complaint against him should arise. Mr. Northcote may well regret now that he took that boy's word as he did, though I have no doubt that the boy at the time fully intended to keep it. Mr. Northcote said to him, "You see you place me in a very serious position; because, if I do not write to your father, in consequence of your promise not to offend again, what will be the consequence if your promise should not be kept? If you break your promise, I shall have to dismiss you from the college; and then such treatment of you will be considered harsh and unkind." Young Mr. Fitzgerald upon that gave his most solemn promise to Mr. Northcote that nothing of the kind should occur again;

and upon that promise being given, the young man was allowed to remain in the college without any further notice being taken of what had passed, and without any thing being said to the father on the subject.

Gentlemen, I come now to that which immediately preceded the conduct which caused the dismissal; and I refer to it now particularly, because, when I come to say a few words to you upon the evidence as to Mr. Stone, I shall have to make an observation or two as to the use of the key which was referred to in the course of Mr. Fitzgerald's examination.

Now I have told you that there was—as Mr. David Fitzgerald himself says—a class of students in this college who were peculiarly circumstanced. I daresay I address some gentlemen who have been at schools where a distinction has been made between "full boys"—or "tug muttons" as they used to be called—and others; and although it may sound ridiculous enough in court, yet you may know perfectly well the annoyance to which boys are subjected from other boys, when they do not happen to be in the same class as those who consider themselves the aristocratic members of the school. It happened that in this college there were a great number of clerical students—and I pray your attention to this—that a great many clerical students were boys who came originally from a sort of preparatory school, called Sedgely Park, and they almost all came there for the purpose of receiving such an education as would fit them afterwards for occupying the position of priests. Those were the boys against whom persecution had arisen—many of them not being in the same class or in the same social position as Mr. Fitzgerald and others with whom he combined for the purpose of annoying these young men. I need not tell you that, if it be the fact that there was an association formed, of which Mr. Fitzgerald was a member, the object of which was to cold-shoulder and to insult those who were in the same school, and who used the same playground as they used themselves; if the object was to keep them at arm's-length, and to insult them more by tone and manner than by actual language; if the object was to insult those young men on account of their poverty, or because they came there on funds provided by charitable persons or institutions—you can well imagine that nothing could be more detrimental to the college of which Mr. Northcote was the head; and that nothing could be more cruel towards the young men who were made the objects of that persecution. I shall have to ask you whether you think young Mr. Fitzgerald's statement as to what did occur in March is strictly right or not. Mr. Fitzgerald is a man against whose talents and learning I have nothing on earth to say. Mr. Northcote, as you will find, had the greatest possible pride and pleasure in his pupil, who I hope, and have no doubt, has a distinguished career before him. The simple question that you have to consider is not a question whether Mr. David Fitzgerald was ever guilty of an act of immorality—that is not the question at all. The question is—Was he, or was he not, combining with others for the purpose of annoying these young men, who were not in the same social position as himself? Was he, or was he not, forming a confederacy most dangerous to the interests of the college, and which not only justified but obliged Mr. Northcote to take the step he did take, of dismissing him from the college, in which he was then sowing the seeds of disaffection? It came to the knowledge of Mr. Northcote, or to the knowledge of one of the prefects of the school, some days before the 13th of March, that there was a society in the course of formation which was talked about and commented upon by the Church students in the college—a society to be called the "Anti-Bunker Society;" the objects of which were believed to be, and which I think you will find were, to insult these "Bunkers"—as they chose to call the Church students—who were maintained on charitable funds, and to treat them as persons who were inferior in degree and class to those who combined against them, who called themselves the "Anti-Bunker Confederation;" of which society Mr. Fitzgerald was the head and the prime mover. Before the 12th of March this had been brought to the notice of Mr. Stone and other persons in the college. An investigation was made, and it was found—or there was a widely-spread belief, at all events—that such a combination existed. On the 14th of March Mr. Fitzgerald was mentioned to Mr. Stone as the ruling spirit in that confederation; and Mr. Stone, acting upon his own judgment in the matter, did find that pocket-book of Mr. Fitzgerald's, which, as he considered, bore out to a very considerable extent the statement which had been made to him, that there was such a society in existence, and that it had been formed for the purposes I have mentioned.

Now, gentlemen, let me call your attention to what is put down by Mr. Fitzgerald himself. He says that all this was written down by him merely as humbug, or for amusement. It is a question for you whether that was so or not. As late as the 6th of March we find an entry, written by Mr. Fitzgerald himself, stating that Governor Moody was "elected March 6th, for his magnanimous sentiment about Sedgely Park." What was that magnanimous sentiment? It was, "Do not make such a noise; it is more like Sedgely Park than Oscott." You find that there is an honorary secretary appointed. Then there is "L. B., C. S. (one dozen);" that is said to mean "List of Bunkers;" and then there are the names of a number of students put down, all of whom have been sent from Sedgely Park. Besides those, there are two others, who seem to have left in January 1865. There are two men, named C * * * and D * * *, who seem also to have been put down in the list of these Bunkers who were to be avoided: and besides that there is a Mr. B * *, from Sedgely Park, who seems to have been considered by Mr. Fitzgerald as the lowest pariah because he was "London Irish." Then there is a memorandum that the uncle or brother of some particular person "keeps a small grocery establishment in Wednesfield Heath: father, a general inspector of canal-locks; authority, honorary secretary A. B. C. H * * * W * * * Then there are put down the names of the Anti-Bunker Society, and they consist of fourteen; five Fitzgeralds, one W * * *; and so on. Then we find there is a man named * * *, who seems to have been obnoxious; for there is a note here, "Consult honorary secretary for information about this gentleman;" the word "gentleman" being in inverted commas, as much as to say the "honorary secretary knows why we should not treat him as a gentleman." We then find, "We want all particulars about any of the undermentioned as to birth, qualifications, and patrons." Patrons are the persons who send particular boys to the college, and they are generally Roman Catholic Bishops.

Then, gentlemen, having discovered that there was the existence of this society, and it being known what the effect of it was likely to be, you will hear from Mr. Northcote and Mr. Stone the steps that were taken. Mr. Northcote had young David Fitzgerald before him. It is very well for him to say here that he was expelled from the college without the least opportunity being afforded to him of making his defence; but you will find that he was interrogated upon this subject—that he denied all knowledge of the society—that he treated it as an absurdity or as fun; and that he was told by Mr. Northcote, "It may be very good fun for you, but it is death to the frogs." You will hear from Mr. Northcote that he talked to him upon the subject for some time, and explained to him most fully the reason why he was about to take the step he did; that he told him that a society like this, formed by those who set themselves up as the aristocrats of the college, could not be permitted, and that the only course for him to take was to tell Mr. Fitzgerald that he must leave the college then and there, and no longer be among the boys, among whom he was stirring up a spirit of disaffection. He was sent back to his room. He remained in his room for some time; and after that he was again seen by Mr. Northcote. Mr. Northcote again explained to him why he was to go, and why he could no longer be allowed to continue at the college. He pointed out to him that, if he was a member of such a conspiracy and such a confederation, and still more, if he was the originator of it, it was in his view absolutely necessary, having regard to the interests of the college, that he should at once leave. Upon that, young Mr. Fitzgerald was sent to his room, with instructions to pack up his things as speedily as possible. His door was locked, in order that he might not communicate with any of the boys who had been members of the society, or with other members of the college; and at three o'clock in the afternoon, after having been seen by Mr. Stone, he finally left the place. Mr. Stone will describe to you his own conduct; and he will tell you that on that occasion Mr. Fitzgerald said he would not hurry himself; but upon being told by Mr. Stone, that unless he packed up at once he would be sent off, and his things would be sent after him, he did proceed to pack up his things; and at three o'clock a cab came to the door, in which he went away. He went to Ireland that night: and he was himself followed by the letter to which I am now about to refer; which letter was written on the very evening of the day on which he left.

Before, however, I refer to that letter, I will just say a word with reference to something that was stated by Mr. Justice Fitzgerald himself. You have heard that one of the things that was thought most improper on the part of young Mr. Fitzgerald was this,—that when he came back in January 1865 he behaved wrongly with regard to the use of a key which had been lent to him by Mr. Stone. Mr. Stone had a key which fitted the door of the room to which David Fitzgerald was to go when he came back to the college in January; and he lent him that key, which was a master-key, opening all the doors in that part of the building, with express instructions to give it back to him at once. It was not returned until the next day, when Mr. Stone found that something had been done to it; an impression of the key had been brought to him; and he found that there was a certain amount of wax sticking to the key itself. Mr. Stone spoke to young Mr. Fitzgerald, and asked him what had been done to the key. Mr. Fitzgerald, as was his custom, made light of the matter; but he afterwards stated that the object had been to get a duplicate key made by a man at Erdington. He was spoken to seriously about it by Mr. Stone. He expressed his regret at what he had done; admitted that he had been guilty of dishonourable conduct in wishing to have a duplicate of that key; and expressly asked Mr. Stone not to repeat it to the President. Mr. Stone, as you will find, was most forbearing on that occasion, and on others also, by not reporting things that would operate prejudicially against him with Dr. Northcote.

Now, gentlemen, I will read to you what was written by Mr. Northcote on the 13th of March, after the dismissal.

[*Here was read the letter given in p.* 5.]

That was followed by other letters, which you have heard read; Mr. Justice Fitzgerald having, immediately on the return of his son David, taken away his other boys, and then having written to Mr. Northcote to say that he waited for an explanation of conduct which he considered most improper.

This, gentlemen, is the case which I have to lay before you. As regards the position of this young man in the school, about which so much has been said, I say that he was to all intents and purposes one of the pupils in the school, and was subject to precisely the same discipline as every other boy. It is true he was there mainly for one purpose and with one object, and that object was kept in view. For all other purposes, he was in the highest grade in the school; but he was still *in statu pupillari.*

Let me call your attention to a letter written by Mr. Northcote on the 12th of December. In that very letter we find Mr. Northcote pointing out to him that certain books will be read; and as regards other matters, that it is expedient he should not attend the London University. He says; "In the London University the discipline depends wholly on the individual: I am told that a student may run into all kinds of excess." In December, therefore, it was expressly notified that if he came back, he should remain for six months more *in statu pupillari,* and should be subject to the discipline of the college until the proper time should arrive for his going up to the London University, when—that University having no local habitation—he would have to live either in London or elsewhere, without being in any way subject to the control of the principals. It was under those circumstances that he came back.

You have heard what the breaches of discipline were. The issue for you to determine will be this,—it is an inconvenient one to have raised in this form; it is an inconvenient thing for any head-master to be told that with respect to any punishment he may have inflicted on a boy he is to be liable for it in a court of justice;—the question for you will be, whether, under the authority delegated to Mr. Northcote by the father, and under the authority which he had as ostensible and real head of this college—he being answerable for the discipline of the college, and *bonâ fide* believing, as he did, that there was a scheme on foot which, if carried out, would be extremely detrimental to the interests of the college—he had a right to imprison young David Fitzgerald, as he did, and to inspect his pocket-book, as he did, for the purpose of gaining information as to whether the discipline of the college was being set at naught, and the interests of the college compromised.

Lord Chief-Justice Cockburn: As I understand it, the pocket-book was taken possession of after they had obtained the information.

Mr. Karslake: It was necessary for them to get, if they could, further information.

Lord Chief-Justice Cockburn: Then there is what is alleged to be the imprisonment.

Mr. Karslake: After the pocket-book had been taken from him, he was told to go back to his room and not to leave it; and he was told that he must leave the college at once, without any further communication with any of the boys in the college.

Lord Chief-Justice Cockburn: There still remains the question whether they had a right to shut him up.

Mr. Karslake: That, as I submit, is covered by the justification.

Upon that subject I will just say one word. Mr. Northcote had made up his mind that it was necessary the boy should leave the college; and Mr. Northcote considered that, in the exercise of the large discretion which must be committed to any schoolmaster or person in the position of Mr. Northcote, it was not expedient or right that so long as he remained under the roof of the college he should be allowed to speak to other boys or have any communication with them; and accordingly he directed that he should be sent to his room to pack up his clothes, and that he should not leave it till he went away. If Mr. Northcote found, as he believed he had found, that there was this conspiracy or association, with objects such as those I have described, I submit that he was right in putting this young man in prison, as it is called—that is, in keeping him to his room while he was investigating the matter—and that he was afterwards right in saying, "I shall keep you under my own control until you leave the college, because it is not right or safe that you should mix any longer with those who I believe you have been setting your face against and injuring in the way that has been described." This is the justification that Mr. Northcote sets up.

I shall have an opportunity, after Mr. Northcote and Mr. Stone have been called, of again addressing you. I ask you to give your best attention to the case, because of its great importance, not to Mr. Northcote only, but to all who have children—boys or young men—committed to their charge. Mr. Northcote was acting under a belief, at all events, that he was doing that which he was entitled to do, and which under the circumstances he was bound to do. It is clear, according to my friend's own admission, and according to the view that common-sense would dictate, that where there is a head of a college of this description he must be invested with large authority and with a large discretion. It is equally clear that he can only act on that which he believes to be true. The question for you to consider is not the mere question whether there really was or was not a conspiracy existing, but whether Mr. Northcote was, under the circumstances, warranted in believing that there was a dangerous association existing, and that David Fitzgerald was one of its members, and whether he was justified in coming to the conclusion he did, that it was inexpedient that this young man should be allowed to remain any longer in the college. The question as to the expulsion has nothing whatever to do with the case. The charge against Mr. Northcote is, that in the course of what he did with regard to David Fitzgerald he told him to go to his room, and kept him there. That Mr. Northcote justifies on the ground that what he did was proper and expedient; and I trust that you, gentlemen, will be of opinion that—although I have not a word to say against the great talents of young David Fitzgerald or against his moral character—that had occurred during the last few months of his residence at Oscott College, which obliged Mr. Northcote to do that which he did; or, at all events, that his belief in the existence of the association, and in the part young Mr. Fitzgerald had in it, justified him in what he did, and therefore that he has a clear answer to the charge which is made against him.

Lord Chief-Justice Cockburn: We will go on with this case to-morrow morning.

A Juror: My Lord, if we have really made up our minds, it would seem to be a waste of time to go on any further.

Lord Chief-Justice Cockburn: Gentlemen, you really must hear the case out.

[*Adjourned till to-morrow at* 10 *o'clock.*]

After this manifestation of feeling on the part of the jury, it was easy to see on which side the verdict would be given. And before leaving the court, it was suggested by Plaintiff's Counsel that the case should be allowed to end here; that, by mutual consent, a juror should be withdrawn on the following morning, Defendant having first stated, by his Counsel, that "he had acted on the belief that there was a dangerous association formed, of which Fitzgerald was the head and originator, and that its object was to annoy and insult the Church students; but that, after the statement on oath of the Plaintiff, he was ready to believe that he had been mistaken, and that Plaintiff was not intending to combine with others for the purpose of offering insult or annoyance to the Church students."*

It was urged upon Dr. Northcote that the result of this arrangement would be, that there would be no adverse verdict,—in fact, no verdict at all,—and therefore that each party would have to pay their own costs; whereas if the trial was persevered in, Dr. N. might safely calculate upon having to pay the Plaintiff's costs as well as his own. Dr. Northcote, however, felt that there were higher interests at stake than the costs in question; that not only his own character, but that of the College over which he presides, was altogether forfeited, if he allowed the statements that had been made in court to go forth to the world uncontradicted. If it were true that the Prefect of Discipline at Oscott had behaved with great harshness and injustice to one of the senior students, and that the President had not only upheld him in such conduct, but had on two or three

* These are the terms which were submitted to Dr. Northcote by his own Counsel after conference with Mr. Coleridge.

several occasions refused to listen to what the boy had to say in his defence, and finally had expelled him under a "mistake," what parent could ever be again expected to send his son to a college so grossly misconducted?

Dr. Northcote felt that his true jury were not so much the twelve men empannelled to hear the cause as the educated portion of the whole Catholic body, and especially the parents who had intrusted their sons to his care. For their sakes, then, he deemed it his bounden duty to take no step which should prevent the real facts of the case from being put fully and fairly before the public; and supported in this view of his duty by the advice of those friends whom he was able to consult, he declined the proposed compromise; and the trial was therefore resumed on the following day.

SECOND DAY.

The Very Rev. JAMES SPENCER NORTHCOTE, D.D., *sworn*.
Examined by MR. KARSLAKE.

Q. You are a Doctor of Divinity and a Master of Arts?

A. Yes.

Q. Were you formerly a scholar of Corpus Christi College, Oxford?

A. Yes.

Q. In the summer of 1860 were you appointed President of Oscott College?

A. Yes.

Q. That, as we have heard, was a college of considerable size, with a good number of members belonging to it?

A. Yes.

Q. All under one roof?

A. Yes.

Q. When you were appointed, about what was the whole number of students?

A. I cannot say exactly; but I should say about 120 or 125.

Q. Besides the students, is there a large staff of masters belonging to the college?

A. I think perhaps about ten or twelve clergymen, and about three or four lay professors, and the body of Divines who were spoken of in court yesterday, some of whom were used as teachers.

Q. By whom were you appointed?

A. By the Bishop of Birmingham—the Catholic Bishop of Birmingham.

Q. Were you the responsible head of the college, both of the masters and of the students?

A. Entirely.

Q. For what purpose was the college originally founded?

A. I am hardly antiquarian enough to say, perhaps; but I believe it was originally founded by a committee of Catholic gentlemen and noblemen for the education of their own sons.

Q. Before your time had there been a body of students who were studying for orders?

A. Yes, for many years.

Q. And also lay students?

A. Yes.

Q. Is it the fact that funds which were provided by the lay students, or any part of that which was paid for the lay students, went for the support of other students in the college?

A. Not a farthing.

Q. Were many of the clerical students sent there upon funds provided by charitable institutions or charitable persons?

A. It is the Bishops who send them to me, and they are responsible to me for the pension; and I know nothing of the funds from which the Bishops pay.

Q. I suppose they are what are called patrons of the boys?

A. Yes.

Q. Do many of these clerical students come from Sedgely, the place that we have heard mentioned?

A. Yes.

Q. That is a preparatory school?

A. Yes.

Q. And many of the boys there come to the college afterwards?

A. Yes.

Q. And are many of the Sedgely students students who are sent there by patrons?

A. Yes; I suppose all of them are who come to us. There are not more than two or three in each year from Sedgely.

Q. About what is the number of clerical students in the college at a time?

A. It varies. I should think the number was never more than twelve. In my time and at this moment I think it is not half that number.

Q. Are there always at the college a considerable number of lay students who are men of good birth and social position?

A. Yes.

Q. Have you among the students, and especially among the clerical students, boys who are of humbler birth?

A. Yes.

Q. Some of them, I believe, are the sons of tradesmen?

A. Yes, some of them are.

Q. Is there under you a Vice-President?

A. Yes.

Q. A Prefect of Discipline?

A. Yes.

Q. And other prefects?

A. Yes.

Q. We have heard (and I may go over this shortly) that the higher classes in the college are called Philosophers, Rhetoricians, Poets, and so on.

A. Yes.

Q. Have the Philosophers privileges which the others have not?

A. All those three classes have.

Q. Are there, besides the traditional rules, certain printed rules applying to the college?

A. Not printed; they are written.

Q. Is it the practice to read those rules aloud at the commencement of each quarter or half-year?

A. At the beginning of each half-year.

Q. Then there are certain rules which are peculiarly applicable to the Philosophers, which are read to them alone?

A. Yes.

Q. To the higher classes; I call them Philosophers?

A. Yes.

Q. I believe that that class is allowed more liberty than the lower classes in the school?

A. Yes.

Q. Among other privileges, are they allowed to go out in parties?

Mr. Coleridge: I should like to see the rules.

Mr. Karslake (to the Witness): Have you the rules here?

A. Yes; I have a copy of them.

Mr. Coleridge: I have a reason for wishing to see the original.

Mr. Karslake (to the Witness): We have heard what David Fitzgerald has called the big bounds and the little bounds: are there the upper bounds, where the higher classes have their playground?

A. Yes.

Q. And the lower bounds, to which the lower classes in the school are confined?

A. Yes.

Q. Is it against the rules for the higher classes to be in the lower bounds, or for the lower classes to be in the higher bounds?

A. Quite.

Q. Is it the fact that the Philosophers are, under certain restrictions, allowed to go out in parties?

A. In parties of not less than three.

Q. That is, in the grounds belonging to the college?

A. Yes.

Q. I believe that the grounds themselves are somewhat extensive?

A. Yes.

Q. And the Philosophers are allowed to go into a part of the grounds into which the others are not allowed to go?

A. Yes.

Q. The plantations, among other places?

A. Yes.

Q. We will have the rules read, if necessary, by and by. You went to the college, as you have told us, in 1860?

A. Yes.

Q. When you went there, we understand David Fitzgerald was there?

A. Yes.

Q. And he continued there until March 1865?

A. Yes.

Q. When you came to the college yourself, did you know of there being any feeling manifested towards the students who came from Sedgely, who were sent by patrons?

A. I had often heard before I came to the college that there was a feeling against the clerical students.

Mr. Coleridge: Will you be kind enough to confine yourself to answering the questions put to you?

Mr. Karslake: Did you find that feeling manifested at all yourself when you came there?

A. I cannot remember to have seen it manifested, but I was well aware of its existence.

Lord Chief-Justice Cockburn: You never saw any sign of it yourself?

A. As President, I was hardly likely to come across it: the Prefect has much more to do with the boys than I have; and he would have seen much more of it than I should.

Mr. Karslake: Was it the duty of the prefects to communicate to you from time to time any thing of that sort that they found existing in the school?

A. It was the duty of the Prefect to report to me any thing that was amiss in any way in the school.

Q. I understand you to say that you personally were not brought so much into communication with the boys as the prefects were?

A. No.

Q. But you received reports from those who were under you?

A. Yes.

Q. Was the term "Bunker" a term which was known to you by communication with the prefects at the time you came to Oscott and afterwards?

A. I cannot at all remember when I first heard the word.

Q. Had you heard of it before the year 1865?

A. No doubt.

Q. And did you know to what class it was applied?

A. Yes.

Q. What was the particular class to which you always understood the term was applied?

A. I always understood it was applied to the clerical students.

Q. I am not sure whether I am right; were you Vice-President before you were appointed President?

A. For six months.

Q. You became President in 1860?

A. Yes; at Midsummer.

Q. So far as you know, from the time you became President

till 1865, had there been any annoyance at all given to this class of clerical students in the college?

A. I set myself to work from the first moment of my arriving at the college to abolish all distinctions between the two classes, in order to destroy this feeling as far as possible; and I had reason to believe that I had succeeded almost entirely by Midsummer 1864.

Lord Chief-Justice Cockburn: What were the distinctions?

A. They were small petty distinctions, which I thought did a great deal of harm. At Midsummer the lay boys went home on Midsummer-day, and the clerical students were not permitted to go till the end of the month, and their vacation was only allowed to be a month, whereas I was anxious that they should have seven weeks, the same as the lay boys; in fact, with the permission of the Bishops, I abolished all distinctions.

Mr. Karslake: And as far as you could do so, the clerical students were placed on the same footing as the lay students?

A. Precisely, in every way.

Q. At Midsummer 1864 you say you thought that every thing was right, and that there was no feeling against the clerical students?

A. I do not know whether I am at liberty to mention my reason for thinking so.

Q. Yes, if you please.

A. It was the report of the Prefect to myself. Two days before the end of the half-year, there was a public cricket-match between the boys at the school and old Oscotians; and on that occasion all the boys were in the same bounds—both the junior and senior boys were in the big bounds—and the Prefect gave me to believe that there was not the smallest vestige of feeling against the Church boys in the house. Many of those who were playing in the cricket-match were themselves clerical students.

Q. I believe it happened that all of those who came to the college having been sent by the Bishops from funds provided by them did not succeed in becoming priests.

A. No; they are sifted, in the course of the three or four years that they remain with us, before they become ecclesiastics.

Q. I do not know whether you superintend particularly any class of students?

A. I have always taught the Philosophers certain subjects.

Q. And we understand that David Fitzgerald in his last year was one of that body?

A. He was one of that body.

Q. I believe you found him a very promising boy indeed in that class?

A. Yes.

Q. And he had passed through it—that being, as you say, one of the highest classes—at Midsummer 1864?

A. Yes.

Q. We have heard that there was a correspondence between you and the Judge as to his coming back again?

A. Yes.

Q. And when he came back at Midsummer 1864 (I think in September), he had his separate room, as he had when he was in the philosophy class?

A. Exactly.

Q. We know that he was reading at that time for a particular purpose, in order to matriculate at the London University in London?

A. Yes.

Q. And did he attend some of the classes which were pursuing studies which were useful to him?

A. Several; three sets of classes to my knowledge.

Q. Were any terms made by you, either with him or with the Judge, that he was to come back in any other character than as a student of the college?

Mr. Coleridge: You did not see the Judge personally?

A. No.

Q. Then that would appear from the letters?

A. Yes.

Mr. Karslake: Was any arrangement made between you and David Fitzgerald that he should come on any other terms than as one of the students of the college?

Mr. Coleridge: Whatever arrangement was made between Mr. Fitzgerald, or Mr. Justice Fitzgerald, and you, was made, I presume, before Mr. Fitzgerald came back?

A. There was no arrangement made whatever.

Q. But he came back after some letters had passed?

A. Some letters had passed as to where he could best be prepared for his matriculation.

Q. Whatever had passed between you and Mr. Fitzgerald or Mr. Justice Fitzgerald between the end of the summer vacation and his return in September had passed on paper?

A. Yes.

Mr. Karslake: After he came back, did any thing pass between you and young Mr. Fitzgerald as to his being exempted from the general discipline of the college?

A. Nothing whatever. I should not have received him on any other terms than those on which I received all the other students.

Q. As far as the discipline of the college went, was he under the ordinary control of the Prefect of Discipline?

A. Precisely.

Q. And under the control of yourself and others?

A. Yes.

Q. From September, until he left in December, did he continue to attend the classes you have mentioned?

A. Yes.

Q. When other lectures were being given, he studied, he says, alone?

A. Yes.

Q. Up to the time when he left at Christmas 1864 for the vacation, and afterwards to go up to matriculate, had you had any information whatever of this feeling as to the Church students having broken out at all?

A. I think that between September and Christmas 1864 I heard that this feeling had again shown itself.

Q. However, nothing was done at all up to Christmas 1864?

A. Nothing.

Q. That is, by you.

A. Nothing.

Q. We understand that Mr. David Fitzgerald returned about the end of January 1865?

A. Yes.

Q. And he was to stay until the middle of that year, was he not?

A. Yes.

Q. Did he after his return in January continue to attend classes as before?

A. Certainly, the same.

Q. I mean the classical classes.

A. Yes, and the French.

Q. Was he present at the times when, according to the rules of the college, the other students were required to be present at prayers, and on other occasions?*

A. I cannot swear of my own knowledge that he was; and of course, having heard him swear yesterday that he was not, I believe he was not; but I cannot understand how he could have been absent.

Q. You gave no sanction to it?

A. No, none.

Q. He has told us that it was against the rules to go into public-houses, and so on. I suppose we may take it that there is an express rule upon the subject?

A. Public-houses are not mentioned: they are not at liberty to go into any private house without leave.

Mr. Coleridge: "Private house?"

Mr. Karslake: I will read you the rule.

Mr. Coleridge: A private house is not a public house.

Lord Chief-Justice Cockburn: You had better leave out the epithet, and then it will be no house at all.

Mr. Coleridge: I take it that it is a school very unlike other schools, if they are not forbidden to go to any public-house.

Mr. Karslake: This is the rule—"No Philosopher is allowed to enter any house, town, or village, without express permission; to frequent places of public amusement, and such like."

Q. I need hardly ask whether, as far as you know, any of the students, either of the higher or lower classes, were in the habit of going to this public-house at Erdington?

A. I never heard of it before the occasion when I had to speak of it to David Fitzgerald.

Q. I believe that, according to the rules of the college, no boy in the position of a Philosopher is liable to corporal punishment?

* Dr. Northcote misunderstood this question, if it was really asked as here reported. He understood that he was asked whether Mr. Fitzgerald had been present at the usual reading out of the rules.

A. No.

Q. Would corporal punishment be inflicted in any case except by your orders?

A. The corporal punishment of the ferula is inflicted without any orders from me by the Prefect.

Q. And the flogging?

A. I do not recollect an instance of that, except by directions from myself; and I do not recollect that corporal punishment has been inflicted in more than a very few instances in the course of six years.*

Q. And as to boys about 16 years of age, I believe no corporal punishment is allowed, except by permission of the President?

A. No.

Q. And the Philosophers are entirely exempt?

A. Yes.

Q. After young Mr. Fitzgerald came back in January, did you hear a complaint made of him with regard to something he had done before Christmas?

A. Yes.

Q. That was about having had spirits in the house?

A. Yes.

Q. Of course that was against the rules?

A. Yes.

A Juror: Was the complaint made before he came back, or after?

A. After he came back.

Mr. Karslake: Was the fact of its being stated that he had done so brought to your attention after he came back in January?

A. Yes.

Q. Did you speak to him upon the subject?

A. I cannot recollect the circumstances, but I am quite sure that I did speak to him. I did not send for him specially to speak to him, because it was a thing that had happened in times past, and bygones were bygones; but I have no doubt that I

* This answer is incorrect. What Dr. N. should have said is, that there had been very few of those exceptional cases in which his sanction was necessary for the infliction of corporal punishment. The ordinary punishment is with the ferula; but the Prefect is at liberty to use the cane for graver offences which are of very rare occurrence.

said what Mr. Fitzgerald stated yesterday, that if I had known of it before, I should not have allowed him to return.

Q. With regard to the breaking-up party at Christmas, and so on, is it entirely against the rules of the college to have such a party?

A. Entirely: it was the first time I ever heard of it myself.

Q. On the 25th of February did you receive a complaint from Mr. Stone, the prefect of discipline, of David Fitzgerald and others having been at Erdington at a public-house?

A. Yes.

Q. At that time did you know that Mr. Fitzgerald was under punishment for some other breach of discipline?

A. Yes.

Q. And that he was confined to bounds?

A. Yes.

Q. In consequence of that information, did you have David Fitzgerald before you?

A. Yes.

Q. Just tell us the substance of what passed between you at that time, and what you did?

A. I gave him a lecture, as he said, I have no doubt, upon the subject. I believe that what I said was, that, next to an actual charge of immorality, the fact of being found in a public-house was, to my mind, one of the most grievous offences he could be guilty of; and that in his case it was especially culpable, as he was already under punishment, so that it involved the setting at defiance the authority of the Prefect.

Q. I believe that on that occasion you punished him and the others by confining them within the bounds until Easter.

A. Yes.

Q. That was on the 25th of February: on Monday the 27th of February did David Fitzgerald come to you and make a complaint against the Prefect of Discipline?

A. I think that those dates can hardly be correct, the 25th and 27th of February; I think they can hardly have been so near together.

Q. But do you remember, at all events, his coming to you after this affair at Erdington and making a complaint?

A. Yes; that was on the evening of the 27th of February certainly.

Q. Now just tell us what passed between you when he came to make this complaint.

A. Shall I give you the substance of his complaint?

Q. Yes, if you please.

A. He first reminded me that he had promised me sometime before never to bring any more complaints against his masters, because he had made so many complaints before, and in each case when it came to be examined into by myself—

Lord Chief-Justice Cockburn: This is what passed?

A. Yes; this is what he said to me: he reminded me of this—this was the beginning of the conversation.

Q. You are going now to anterior circumstances?

A. I was only repeating his expression to me; it was his apology for making the complaint. He said that he now must make a complaint against the Prefect; that the Prefect had found him shooting in the plantation, and that in the altercation which ensued between them the Prefect had called him a liar, and had threatened to box his ears. I made no reply but to say that I must hear the Prefect's version of the story before I made any comment whatever. I heard the Prefect's version of the story on the following day, and sent for David Fitzgerald in the evening, and told him that, although he seemed only to have equivocated, his equivocation under the circumstances was equivalent to a lie. I made no comment upon the complaint as to boxing his ears, because I did not wish to comment on the conduct of the Prefect in any way to a student; but I went on to lecture him on the many acts of insubordination which had been brought before me, and upon his manifest purpose to measure strength with the new Prefect; that the authorities of the house must be upheld, and that such insubordination from a boy in his position must be visited by the severest punishment; that I should therefore do what I had never done before—degrade him to the ranks altogether; that he must walk in the ranks and study in the study-place; and that I only did not deprive him of his room altogether and turn him into the dormitory, because the effect of that would be to destroy the very object for which he was here, and that I should not therefore inflict that punishment upon him, whatever fresh offence he might commit, but that I should send him away for the next offence; and that I must also write to his father at once to acquaint him with the state of affairs, because his next offence would certainly be visited by expulsion,—by his being sent away. We then left the room together, because the bell for night-prayers had rung; and on our way I spoke no longer to him as a schoolmaster, but simply as a father and friend. I pointed out to him how his pride and conceit had brought him into trouble so constantly, and that I knew how keenly he would feel the degradation I had just put upon him, but that humiliations were often the means of producing humility; and the next day being Ash-Wednesday, I hoped he would receive this punishment in the spirit in which I had given it to him; and from his manner I gathered and hoped that I had made a favourable impression upon him. That was the whole of that interview.

Mr. Karslake: Did he say any thing at that time about writing to his father himself?

A. No, certainly not.

Q. He says that he offered to exculpate himself, but that you would not hear him at all; is that the fact?

A. Certainly not.

Q. Did you hear all that he had to say?

A. I heard all that he had to say until it was the old story over again—that he was a persecuted man. I do not mean that he used those words, but that it was the old story over again.

Lord Chief-Justice Cockburn: What do you mean by the old story over again?

A. As I was about to say just now, when on former occasions he had made appeals to me from his masters, I always examined into them, and found so incessantly that I had to justify the masters, and never give a verdict in favour of Mr. David Fitzgerald, that I forbade him to bring any further appeals, because I saw that it was his temper, and that his complaints were unreasonable.

Q. When you speak of other appeals, had they been from other prefects of discipline or other masters?

A. Appeals from other masters, ever since I have known him.

Q. In former times?

A. In former times.

Q. After prayers did you see him again?

A. Yes.

Q. Tell us what passed then.

A. He asked me not to write to his father.

Lord Chief-Justice Cockburn: Did he come to you?

A. He came to me. I explained to him the necessity under which I was to write to his father.

Mr. Karslake: Just tell me what was said.

A. I said that I had never written any thing to his father but good reports of him, and that if I sent him home, as I certainly should for his next offence, if he committed it, his father might justly complain of me for want of consideration; he would think that I had lost my temper, and inflicted a harsh sentence upon him for one offence, when, in fact, the sentence would be for an accumulation of offences. He told me that I need not fear, for that he would commit no fresh offence. I said, "You see, David, how the matter stands; I risk my character with your father for justice, prudence, and moderation against your word of honour; is that safe?" and he answered, "It is safe, and your confidence shall not be abused," or words to that effect. I will not positively swear to each word. I said, "I will take your word, David, and will not write to your father to-night;" but I again repeated to him in other words precisely the same thing as I had said before, as to the balance between us of his word of honour against my character which was put into his hands.

Q. Did you refuse to hear what he had to say upon that occasion at all?

A. I do not remember that he offered to say a syllable, and to the best of my belief he did not. I understood him to come to ask for a grace, and not at all to justify himself in any way.

Q. He was under punishment from that time?

A. From that time.

Q. That is, he was put into the ranks, instead of having the privileges of the upper students.

A. Yes.

Q. And he was subjected to that punishment?

A. Yes.

Q. I think he told us yesterday that the dormitory is where the general body of boys sleep who are not in the higher classes?

A. Yes.

Q. And that is the place where they study when they have private studies?

A. No; it is a different room altogether. I am afraid I have not understood your question.

Q. You said you would not send him to the dormitory?

A. Yes; not to sleep there. If I had done so, the effect would have been to deprive him of the opportunity of reading at extra hours, after the others had gone to bed.

Q. What is the rule at Oscott as to the hours at which students go to bed?

A. In the winter they all go to bed after night-prayers, which are at a quarter-past eight o'clock, that is, all those who sleep in the dormitories; but all those who have private rooms have a right to sit up till ten o'clock.

Q. Have they any right to sit up after ten o'clock, except by express permission?

A. Never.

Q. After this occasion, when you had the conversation with him about writing to his father, did you hear between that time and the time when you saw David Fitzgerald about the Anti-Bunker Confederation? Had you heard from the college authorities any thing about a movement taking place in the college?

A. Yes, exactly midway between the two things,—just a week after David Fitzgerald's last interview with me.

Q. Did you hear of that more than once before the time when you saw David Fitzgerald?

A. Before the time I saw David Fitzgerald? Yes.

Q. When was it that any communication was made to you respecting David Fitzgerald?

A. An unofficial communication was made to me on Sunday night the 12th of March, I believe.

Q. That was not in the regular form of a complaint?

A. It came to me from the Vice-President. It was the report of a matter that had been brought before him by the Prefect, I being absent that Sunday afternoon.

Mr. Coleridge: By the Prefect you mean Mr. Stone, I suppose?

A. Yes.

Mr. Karslake: Was that with reference to this same movement?

A. Yes.

Q. I understand you to say that David Fitzgerald's name was mentioned to you in connection with that?

A. It was given to me by the Vice-President.

Q. Had you, between the time when you first heard of that movement and Sunday the 12th of March, when you heard from the Vice-President, had information as to the objects of the movement or the character of it?

A. No; I only heard that there were symptoms of distinction being made; that there were lists afloat in the house of what was called the Aristocracy of the place.

Q. You say that on the Sunday the Vice-President mentioned to you David Fitzgerald's name in connection with this?

A. Yes.

Q. Nothing further took place that night, I suppose?

A. No.

Q. On the Monday did you receive further information with regard to David Fitzgerald?

A. Yes.

Q. From whom?

A. From the Prefect, my co-defendant, Mr. Stone.

Q. In consequence of what Mr. Stone told you, did you give instructions to him to have David Fitzgerald before you?

A. Not immediately.

Q. Before you gave any instructions to have him before you, had you any meeting of the Superiors of the house?

A. The Superiors of the house met in consequence of the information which I had received.

Q. After that meeting did you give any instructions to Mr. Stone as to David Fitzgerald?

A. Not immediately after that meeting. That meeting was held at nine o'clock, and the evidence was laid before me upon which the charge was brought against David Fitzgerald.

Q. Did you yourself, between the time of that meeting and the time when you had David Fitzgerald before you, have further inquiries made with reference to this movement, and with reference to the part which David Fitzgerald had taken in it?

A. There was nobody else of whom to make further inquiries.

Q. Did you, between the time when you had this meeting of the Superiors and the time when you sent for David Fitzgerald, make further inquiries as to the movement, and as to David Fitzgerald being a party to it?

A. We carefully went over the evidence at two meetings of the Superiors before I saw David Fitzgerald.

Q. When you speak of evidence, were statements made to you by the Prefects?

Lord Chief-Justice Cockburn: You had better ask him what the evidence was.

Mr. Coleridge: Was there a minute kept?

A. No.

Lord Chief-Justice Cockburn: What was the evidence that was laid before you?

A. The evidence was, that a lay student of the house had reported to a Divine the existence of a conspiracy against the Church students, known by its members as the A. B. C.; that each member had a list of the other members, and that David Fitzgerald was the prime mover in it; that the Divine said that this matter was too important to be treated as a matter of gossip, and that it must be reported to the authorities, and that this Divine therefore had reported it to Mr. Stone; that Mr. Stone had, therefore, gone to David Fitzgerald's room to look for this list of members; that on his table he found an open pocket-book, and that in this he had found not only a list of members, but many particulars about the birth and parentage of clerical students in the house, which left no doubt whatever upon his mind of the truth of the report he had received as to the conspiracy, and as to David Fitzgerald's part in it.

Mr. Karslake: Up to that time had you known any thing about the Prefect of Discipline having seen the list?

A. Yes; I alluded before to a list of the Aristocracy that was going about.

Q. But did you know, until this interview which you had on the Monday, of the fact of the Prefect of Discipline having seen the list in David Fitzgerald's pocket-book which was referred to?

A. No.

Q. After that information had been received by you, did you send for David Fitzgerald?

A. After our second meeting I did.

Q. Was the same statement which was made to you laid before the Superiors at the meeting?

A. It was laid before us all in common.

Q. And did you act afterwards in consequence of the determination which was come to at the meeting?

A. Yes, I sent for David Fitzgerald.

Q. At the time when you sent for David Fitzgerald after this meeting, did you believe the information which you had received to be true?

A. Certainly.

Q. What time was it when David Fitzgerald came to you in consequence of your sending for him?

A. Just after eleven o'clock.

Q. Did Mr. Stone come with him?

A. Yes.

Q. And was the book which had been referred to brought?

A. Yes.

Q. By your directions?

A. Yes.

Q. Did you give directions to Mr. Stone, when you sent him for Mr. Fitzgerald, also to bring the book?

Lord Chief-Justice Cockburn: Did you send for Mr. Stone?

A. Yes.

Mr. Karslake: Did you give Mr. Stone any directions about the book?

A. Yes.

Q. What did you direct him to do?

A. I desired him to bring the book with David Fitzgerald.

Q. Was it in the regular course of things at the college when a boy was sent for under those circumstances that Mr. Stone should be the person, as Prefect of Discipline, to bring him before you?

A. Certainly.

Q. Just tell us, in your own way, what happened when David Fitzgerald came to you?

A. Mr. Stone and David Fitzgerald came into the room, and the book was at once put into my hand by Mr. Stone. I opened it, and saw the lists and pages that you have seen. I asked David Fitzgerald what he meant by this; and he answered, "Nothing at all."

Q. Lord Chief-Justice Cockburn: Those were his words, were they?

A. As nearly as possible. He answered, "Nothing at all;" and went on to say that it was all nonsense. I said, "It may be all nonsense and fun to you and your companions, but it is death to the frogs." He again repeated that he meant no harm by it; to which I gave the answer which David Fitzgerald himself reported yesterday, that it was impossible to handle pitch without being defiled by it. I pointed to some of the entries in the book, and asked him if he thought it was innocent amusement to ferret out particulars of the birth and parentage of those of his companions who were beneath him in social position, and asked him how he came to do such an ungentlemanly thing; to which he replied, that he had done it in a fit of spleen. I reminded him that spleen had been the cause of many evils, and that I feared his would cost him dear. He then fell back upon the plea that it was all nonsense, and that if I would let him go to his room to fetch a letter he had received from his father, he would satisfy me that there was no harm in it. I told him I should be only too glad to hear any thing he had to say in justification of himself. He fetched the letter, and pointed to two lines at the bottom of a page in it, and said that that was all he could let me see. All I read was, "What is the subscription to the A. B. C.?" I said, "This shows me nothing as to the innocence of your association; it tells me what I am surprised to hear, that you have told your father of it, and I should much like to know what he thinks of it. If, as I cannot but believe, he condemns it as unworthy of your position, it would show me that there was something in it; but this mere question shows me nothing at all." He, however, refused to let me see any thing more.

Mr. Karslake: You saw no more of it?

A. No.

Q. What further happened?

A. I asked him who "Governor Moody" was, because there was a boy in the House, a son of Mr. Moody the Professor, whose nickname I had heard was Governor Moody; and I thought, from my knowledge of his character, that it was impossible he could have joined in such an association. He explained that it meant the father; and he went on to say that there were other names also down in the list without the knowledge or consent of the boys themselves. I asked him to exonerate all he could, that I might not punish the innocent with the guilty; and he said that his brother John had distinctly refused to join the association,—that his youngest cousin knew nothing about it, and some of the other boys also; and I remarked to him that his brother John's refusing to join it did not seem to me to indicate that there was no harm in it. I asked him who the president of the association was, that was alluded to in the paper——

Mr. Coleridge: Just point out, if you please, where the president is alluded to. Look at the pocket-book (*handing it to the Witness*).

A. (*after looking at the pocket-book*) No; I must have put my question in some other way. I asked him distinctly "Who was the president?" I cannot have spoken of the president as being alluded to in the paper; but I will swear that I asked him "Who was the president?" and that he said he himself was.

Mr. Karslake: What else passed at this interview?

A. I asked him for an explanation of these different initials, that I did not know myself.

Q. There is "F. M* * *, S. P.," I see: was any explanation given as to the "S. P."?

A. I believe there was, if I had not already guessed it; which I think probable.

Q. Was any explanation given of the "L. B."?

A. No.

Q. "L. B. C. S. (one dozen)"?

A. I never knew what that meant until I was told yesterday.

Q. List of Bunkers?

A. Yes.

Q. What is "C. S."? was any explanation given of that?

A. No, I think not.

Q. "S. P."? was any explanation given of that?

A. I cannot swear that I asked him for it; I think it probable that I should have guessed it without asking him.

Q. Sedgely Park?

A. Yes.

Q. That, we understand, is a school from which many of these Church students come?

A. Yes.

Q. Were all these, with the exception of C * * and D * * in the school at the time?

A. Certainly, every one of them.

Q. Is it the fact that C * * * and D * * * had left the school in January 1865?

A. They were two boys who had been dismissed during the Christmas vacation.

Q. I see "E. S. * * *, S. P. * * *, N. S. M.": do you know what that meant?

A. Yes; I know what * * * *'s father was; and that enables me to know what was meant.

Q. What was he?

A. A national schoolmaster.

Q. "W. N. * * *, S. P. W. * * *, C. M." Do you know what he was?

A. No.

Q. Was any explanation given to you of the meaning of "C. M."?

A. I do not remember that there was.

Q. In page 3 there is "A. B. C. Fitzgerald, 5," and so on: was the A. B. C. explained to you?

A. Yes.

Q. As what?

A. My memory was, until I heard the statement of Mr. Fitzgerald yesterday, that it was "Anti-Bunker Club." I do not think I ever heard of "Anti-Bunker Confederation" until I heard it yesterday.

Q. Were there five Fitzgeralds in the school?

A. Yes.

Q. One * * *?

A. Yes.

Q. Two * * *?

A. Yes.

Q. Two * * *?

A. Yes.

Q. And one of each of these others,—* * *, * * *, * * *, and * * *?

A. Yes; there were more * * *; but there was only one they could reckon on.

Q. Who was * * *; who is described as a "gentleman," in inverted commas?

A. He was a priest who had left the house, I should think, more than twelve months before. He had been Sub-Prefect in the house, I believe: he had certainly taught in the house, and I think he was Sub-Prefect; but I am not sure of this.

Q. Then there is somebody as to whom it is said, "Uncle, or brother, keeps a small grocery establishment at Wednesfield Heath."

A. From my knowledge of the clerical students I know who that means; but I would rather not mention his name.

Q. Then there is, "father, a general inspector of canal-locks"?

A. I know for certain that there was a clerical student whose father was an inspector of canal-locks.

Q. I see below, "Examine Henry Walter, of Fred, about" (a certain person) "of Dudley."

A. I do not understand to this day what that means: "* * * of Dudley" was a clerical student in the house.

Q. Then I see in a memorandum at the back of p. 3 there is a list of the names of some persons. Did he make you a statement about that list of names?

A. He made a statement that it had no reference whatever to the Anti-Bunker Club.

Q. There are several names there?

A. Yes.

Q. I see, at page 5, there is "a list of the members of the A. B. C." Society, but no names following; and in page 7, "We want all particulars about any of the undermentioned as to birth, parentage, qualifications, and patrons." Was there any explanation of that?

A. No; it spoke for itself.

Q. Was what you have given us the substance of what passed upon that occasion?

A. I think the whole of it.

Q. What did you do upon that?

A. I desired him to go to his room, and to remain there until he was sent for.

Q. We find, from the particulars, that the assault and imprisonment were on the 15th March 1865. Was he had before you on that occasion, and kept in your room, for any other purpose than for the purpose of examining him as to this society?

A. For no other purpose whatever.

Q. And was the book used solely for that purpose?

A. Solely for that purpose.

Q. You say you sent him to his room, and ordered him to remain there until he was sent for, I think you say?

A. Yes.

Q. What did you do upon that?

A. I went to consult with the Vice-President.

Q. And did you consult with the Vice-President?

A. Yes.

Q. And with any body else.

A. I think not in the Vice-President's room. I next saw the Prefect; but I cannot swear whether that was with the Vice-President, or in my own room alone. The Prefect reported that some news of what was going on had oozed out among the boys as to the discovery of this Anti-Bunker Confederation, and that it was causing some excitement. I thought the matter of sufficient importance to summon the whole house together, and I desired that David Fitzgerald should be brought to the meeting.

Q. He did not come, I believe?

A. The Prefect reported that he could not find him.

Q. We understood from him that he had gone to the chapel, I think he said. Was the bell rung, and was the ordinary summons given for the house to assemble?

A. The bell was rung; that was the ordinary summons for all to assemble.

Q. Did you address them about this?

A. Yes.

Q. He was not present; but you afterwards stated to him—as he has told us—some part, at all events, of what you said?

A. Yes.

Q. Did you tell him the substance of what you had said?

A. Every thing, as far as I remember it.

Q. Then we can have it now; and we had better take it now as what you said to the boys?

Lord Chief-Justice Cockburn: It is not necessary to go through that.

Mr. Karslake: I do not wish for it, my Lord; only something was said about the cruelty of making a speech before the boys. This is an action for an assault.

Lord Chief-Justice Cockburn: It is not an action for what was said.

Mr. Karslake: But my friend says that Dr. Northcote went behind the back of Mr. Fitzgerald, and made a speech to the boys; and, of course, on the question of cruelty, and on the question of expulsion, it is material for Dr. Northcote to justify his conduct, which has been impugned.

Q. Perhaps you will have the goodness to state what you did say?

A. I told him that I had explained to the boys my notion of a gentleman, and that I was very sorry to find that there were some boys in the house who had very different notions as to what a gentleman was,—who measured gentility by the length of their fathers' purse, or by any titles that they happened to have; that I thought that "handsome was that handsome did;" and that every boy, once received into the house, should be received into equal companionship with the rest of the inmates; and that they were all to be treated alike, unless by their own misconduct they had shown that they did not deserve to be so treated; and that I found that certain boys had formed an association against others not in an equal social position to their own; that David Fitzgerald was at the head of it, and that I had felt it my duty to expel him in consequence. The main part of my speech was, I believe, on what gentlemanly conduct consisted in, and especially on what I considered further was required of a *Christian* gentleman; and I pointed out how diametrically opposed to these notions was the conduct of Fitzgerald and his companions in this matter. I said that I did not read aloud the names of the members of the association, because David Fitzgerald had himself exonerated some, and there might be some whose participation in guilt was not equal to the others'; that I was very happy to see that there were not the names of boys who held such a position in the house as would disgrace the general character of the house,—that they were boys much junior to Fitzgerald; that the fact of his position had brought them into it, they being so much younger than himself; and I am not sure whether I told him also—I suppose I did not—what I had said about the Osostian Society, because he came to me afterwards about this.

Q. Was that the substance of what you told him?

A. It was the substance. I did not go through all his misdemeanours for which these punishments had been inflicted, but I named several of them; I am not sure whether I named them specifically, but I spoke of his acts of insubordination and setting the authorities at defiance.

Q. You say you mentioned that he was expelled and sent away. Had you told him before you sent him to his room that you should do so?

A. I think my words were, "You know the consequences;" but, from what had passed between us on the last occasion, I knew that he *did* know the consequences.

Q. You had intimated to him what they would be?

A. Yes.

Q. After this meeting had taken place, did you see him again?

A. Yes.

Q. I suppose that it was at that meeting that you read the extracts from Newman and Fuller?

A. Yes.

Q. As to what constituted a gentleman?

A. Yes.

Q. You saw him again, you say?

A. Yes.

Q. What time was that?

A. I think it was about a quarter-past one.

Q. Where did you see him?

A. I found him at my room-door.

Q. What took place then?

A. I told him that I was surprised to see him; that I

thought he had left the house; and that I was not surprised that he should have done so, as I supposed it was only natural that he should desire to avoid the humiliation of being present whilst I publicly expelled him. He said he thought he had been hardly dealt with; and I reminded him of our conversation together, and the terms on which we had parted, on Shrove-Tuesday evening, and that this was the inevitable consequence of what I had then said. I really do not remember much more, or, indeed, any thing more, at this moment, unless my memory is refreshed as to what I did say.

Q. How long was he in your room at that time?

A. I should think about twenty minutes,—or it might be half an hour.

Q. Was Mr. Stone there?

A. Mr. Stone came there; but whether I sent for him or not, I am not quite sure.

Q. And how did it end?

A. It ended in my saying that I had really nothing more to say in the matter; that he was expelled; and that now I handed him over to Mr. Stone, to get him his dinner, and to do all that was necessary for sending him away.

Q. Did you give any instructions that he should go to his room until he did leave?

A. Certainly.

Lord Chief-Justice Cockburn: Till he left?

A. Yes.

Q. Did you give any directions for locking him up?

A. I cannot undertake to swear whether I did or did not. My own belief is that that is the usual course in all cases; but I cannot undertake to swear whether I did or not: probably the Prefect (I have not asked him the question) would be able to say whether I did or not.

Mr. Karslake: Was it at that interview that something was said about the Oscotian meeting?

A. No.

Q. You say you do not recollect whether you gave directions to have him locked up or not; have you had occasion to send boys from Oscott before?

A. I have done so.

Q. Can you speak as to what has been the practice on former occasions?

A. I can only judge as to the practice from the practice that prevailed at the school I was at myself, where, when a boy was expelled, he was locked up, and was not allowed to have any communication with others.

Q. In your judgment, having regard to what you believed Mr. Fitzgerald had done, was it proper or expedient that he should mix with other boys between the time he left you and his leaving the college?

Lord Chief-Justice Cockburn: You cannot ask that.

Mr. Karslake: Then I will only ask you whether you thought it expedient that he should go to his room?

Lord Chief-Justice Cockburn: That is a very different question. It is one thing to say you must leave, and another to put him under lock and key. I mean it is a matter for the jury.

Mr. Karslake: In your judgment was it expedient and proper, under the circumstances, that he should not mix with the other boys before he left?

A. Certainly.

Q. Were there in the same passage in which his private room was a number of rooms belonging to boys of his own class?

A. A great number.

Q. You say you do not know what was done; but was there any thing to prevent the other boys in the house from having access to him, unless some precaution was taken to keep them away from him?

A. Nothing whatever.

Lord Chief-Justice Cockburn: What time of the day was this?

A. About a quarter-past one; by the time he left my room it would be perhaps twenty minutes to two, or half-past one.

Mr. Karslake: Where would the other boys be at that time?

A. They would be just coming out from dinner.

Q. What do they do after dinner? Do they go to their rooms?

A. They play in the play-grounds. There was nothing to prevent their going to their rooms.

Q. You saw him, we understand, once again before he left?

A. Yes.

Q. When was that?

A. I think it was exactly at three o'clock.

Q. Just before he left the house?

A. Yes.

Q. And then it was that he spoke to you about the Oscotian meeting.

A. Yes.

Q. Just tell me what he said about that?

A. He asked me if he would be allowed to come to the Oscotian meeting at Midsummer, as he was a member of the Oscotian Society; and I answered that it was a case that had not occurred before; but that of course he could not come, as he was expelled from the house.

Q. That is the last that you saw of him? He then went from the house, and went home?

A. Yes.

Q. That same evening, in time for the post, did you write a letter to the Judge?

A. Yes.

Q. There was a further correspondence, and the other boys were removed. When were they removed?

A. They were removed by telegram the next day—four of them.

Q. Were they all brothers?

A. No; two brothers and two cousins.

Q. And they were all removed before you received the Judge's letter in answer to yours?

A. Yes.

Q. You say that David Fitzgerald came to you a second time before you sent him back to his room. At that time did you also believe that he was implicated in this Anti-Bunker Society?

A. Certainly.

Q. And was it on that ground, and because you thought him not fit to remain at the college, that you sent him to his room until he should leave?

A. Certainly.

Q. Suppose such a society existed, as you thought at that time did exist, in your judgment would it be very detrimental indeed to the interests of the college?

A. It would be ruinous to the college.

Q. And to the boys who were the objects of dislike to the association?

A. Certainly.

Q. I will ask you this question with reference to the new assignment. You sent back the book after some little time, having kept a copy of that part which has been read, and which you considered contained the evidence against David Fitzgerald?

A. Yes.

Q. Having done that, you sent the book over to Dublin?

A. Yes.

Q. Something has been said about letters. Had you any letters brought to you, or did you see any private letters of David Fitzgerald's?

A. Never.

Cross-examined by Mr. Coleridge.

Q. There was a telegraph between Oscott and Dublin, was there not?

A. Yes; that is, between Birmingham and Dublin.

Q. But you did not communicate with the Judge by telegraph?

A. No.

Q. You did not think that desirable?

A. I did not see any possible use in it.

Q. As to these Church students—you have spoken of their numbers—do you include in the Church students the Divines?

A. No.

Q. But they are another form of Church students, are they?

A. Not necessarily.

Q. They are Church students in the chrysalis state?

A. Rather in the butterfly state; but there are many Divines who have never gone through the chrysalis state.

Q. There are a good many Divines?

A. Yes.

Q. How many Divines would there be?

A. The number varies very much. I have known there to be as few as fourteen, but at present there are about twenty-six.

Q. Those would have to be added to the twelve Church students to make up what I may call the clerical element?

A. I should say not. I do not think that there is any feeling against the Divines.

Q. But they are persons who are about to become priests?

A. Certainly.

Q. It is not common, I suppose, that a Divine relapses into a layman?

A. It is not at all uncommon.

Q. But the object of their being Divines is, that they may become priests and go to missions?

A. Yes; but they are sifted, and some of them fall through, just in the same way as Church students whilst yet in "the bounds" do.

Q. When you speak of there being twelve Church students, that does not include the Divines—that is all I mean?

A. No.

Q. You speak of their being sent by the Bishops, who are answerable to you for the pension: do the pensions that are paid by the Church students or Divines cover their expenses?

A. Entirely.

Q. Could Oscott go on without the assistance of the laity?

A. We could not keep so large an establishment—we should only occupy a twelfth part of the house, and keep a twelfth part of the number of servants.

Q. Could the house go on simply as a seminary for priests, if all the priests were Church students and paid only what the Church students pay?

A. I think so.

Q. Do you mean to say that it could be done at all?

A. I think so.

Q. The lay students are there, I suppose, at a profit?

A. Of course.

Q. And the Church students are not, I suppose?

A. I have never calculated with accuracy, but I should consider that they more than pay their expenses.

Q. Do they go back at Christmas in the same way as the others?

A. No; they have not the liberty of going home at Christmas.

Q. Then the change which you made applies only to Midsummer?

A. Only to Midsummer.

Q. That is the only change you have made, is it?

A. There are some minor changes; that is the only one that has been made with reference to the vacation.

Q. You say that when young Fitzgerald came back, there were certain classes that he attended: do you mean to say that he attended more than one classical book at a time?

A. He attended two classical books at a time at least.

Q. Between September and Christmas?

A. Yes.

Q. Two?

A. Yes.

Q. What were they?

A. Cicero and Virgil.

Q. After Christmas was it Aristotle's *Rhetoric* only?

A. I do not think it was Rhetoric at all—it was the Cicero continued, I think: he also attended the French, and I think German.

Q. Did you give him private instructions as well?

A. In common with his two companions, who were going up for the same examination.

Q. You gave him private instruction?

A. With these other two.

Q. The regular Oscott course, if I understand, had been finished by him at Midsummer 1864.

A. I suppose you may say that it was—most boys would leave then; sometimes we have boys who stay for two years in philosophy. I have one at this moment who intends to do so.

Q. He did not come back and stay for philosophy?

A. No.

Lord Chief-Justice Cockburn: What did the philosophy class comprehend besides classics?

A. Logic and mental philosophy and natural philosophy.

Mr. Coleridge: He had so far completed that course, and he came back for a special purpose: was any special arrangement made, or did the pension go on the same as before?

A. Exactly the same. I think he was charged as other boys would be charged who had any special private lessons in addition to the usual course.

Q. That, I suppose, was arranged between the Judge and you?

A. It was a matter of routine; nothing was written about it at all; it is always done.

Q. He had been a very distinguished boy, had he not?

A. Yes.

Q. And you had never, except in the letter that was referred to yesterday, made any complaint about him to the Judge?

A. No; I think not.

Q. You say that the corporal punishment of the ferula may be inflicted without your knowledge: I am familiar with other forms of punishment, but not with the ferula; what is a ferula?

A. Upon the hand. I do not think I ever saw the instrument myself, but I believe it is a thong of leather applied to the hand.

Q. What is that punishment for which the interposition of the President is required?

A. In graver matters.

Q. I suppose in matters requiring a heavier punishment?

A. Yes.

Q. What is that heavier punishment?

A. With the cane, I should think.

Q. And that is only inflicted by the order of, and upon the special interposition of the head, is it?

A. I cannot say positively, because the discipline of the house is carried on by tradition, and is in the hands of the Prefects so much that my interference is only called for when any special difficulty arises.

Q. As I understand, young Fitzgerald came there from September to December; and then there was this breaking-up party of which you have spoken?

A. Yes.

Q. You have not mentioned what school you were yourself at before you went to Oxford?

A. One of King Edward VI.'s Grammar Schools, which depends for its character entirely on the master at the time being —a school at Ilminster.

Q. Were breaking-up parties altogether unknown at Ilminster?

A. Quite, so far as I ever heard.

Q. Do you know whether in scholastic discipline, as in moral theology, there is a distinction between venial and mortal sins?

A. Yes, I daresay there is.

Q. Should you say that having a breaking-up party is a mortal sin?

A. With spirits introduced into the house, it is. I should consider introducing spirits into the house a mortal sin in any case.

Q. You did not ascertain that that mortal sin had been committed until some time afterwards, and therefore you let it pass?

A. That was not the only reason. There had been a change of Prefects at the time, and the matter was a little complicated in consequence; and therefore I thought it better upon the whole to let it pass.

Q. You say that introducing a little whisky or brandy at a breaking-up supper would be quite intolerable?

A. Quite.

Q. I think you said that you also afterwards heard of his having been in a public-house?

A. Yes.

Q. The house at Edington is not like a public-house in Seven Dials, or any thing of that kind, is it?

A. No.

Q. It is a modest auberge, is it not?

A. It is a small inn.

Q. And that, you thought, was one of the very worst offences that he could be guilty of?

A. If he was in the habit of frequenting the house.

Q. That is, if he was a public-house haunter?

A. This was a case of one of our Philosophers going there.

Q. If he went there once, should you consider that to be one of the worst offences that he could be guilty of?

A. It would depend entirely on circumstances.

Q. If a young man, having taken a long walk, feels thirsty, and goes into an inn to get a glass of beer, would that, in your opinion, be one of the worst offences that he could commit?

A. I should think that he had much better walk home first.

Q. But still you would not think it one of the worst offences of which a man could be guilty?

A. No, I should think not.

Q. I am glad to find that we have still so much in common. You thought, however, that it was peculiarly wrong in him?

A. Yes; because of his being under punishment.

Q. That gave the thing a darker dye, did it?

A. It made it worse certainly.

Q. Then he was to be reduced to the bounds?

A. Yes.

Q. I think you say that you saw an indication in him of a desire to measure strength with the new Prefect?

A. Yes.

Q. It did not occur to you at all that the new Prefect wished to measure strength with him?

A. I should not have thought the cases parallel.

Q. You never heard of a Superior wanting to annoy a boy very little younger than himself?

A. The gentleman I appointed Prefect had been a priest about twelve months before I appointed him.

Q. Then he would be twenty-four, and Mr. Fitzgerald was nineteen?

A. Only eighteen certainly; there was about six years' difference in their ages.

Q. But is it quite a thing unknown for a person in the situation of Prefect to bear a little hard upon those who are under him?

A. Such a case has never come before me in my experience at Oscott.

Q. And probably your mind would not be readily accessible to such an impression?

A. It would not naturally occur to me.

Q. I should suppose so.

Lord Chief-Justice Cockburn: How long was this gentleman a Prefect?

A. He was only appointed in January 1865.

Mr. Coleridge: New brooms, we know, are in the habit of sweeping up rather clean?

A. I think not always.

Q. Had Mr. Fitzgerald ever complained to you before of any body besides Mr. Martin and Mr. Daly?

A. I really cannot undertake to say.

Q. Will you undertake to say that he had?

A. I believe he had; but I cannot undertake to swear it, there are so many masters in the house.

Q. That is why I put two names to you.

A. I can swear as to those two that he has complained; and I believe I can swear that he has complained of another, Mr. Williams.

Q. And in the case of Mr. Daly his sentence was reversed, was it not?

A. There have been so many of those cases, I do not remember.

Q. When did this happen about Mr. Daly?

A. I do not recollect.

Q. You do recollect the fact of an appeal against Mr. Daly?

A. I believe I do.

Q. Do you believe that you upheld Fitzgerald, and reversed the decision of Mr. Daly?

A. No; I think it is extremely improbable.

Q. So do I; but still it was done, was it not?

A. I do not think it was done; I do not remember ever to have reversed a master's sentence in Mr. Fitzgerald's case.

Q. Or in the case of others?

A. Yes.

Q. You say that the authorities of the house must be maintained, and that the discipline must be upheld?

A. Yes.

Q. Your first impression would be, of course, against the boy, and in favour of the master?

A. It would depend entirely on the character of the boy.

Q. And on the character of the master also, would it not?

A. Yes.

Q. Generally we know as a fact that an appeal to the head-master in a public school is not very often successful; is not that your experience?

A. I was not at a public school myself.

Q. In King Edward's school?

A. I do not think there were any appeals at the school I was at; I think that each master there was supreme.

Q. Whenever Fitzgerald had talked to you, you had, in his case, always upheld the master?

A. I believe that I was always obliged to do so.

Q. When this matter occurred about the plantation, you say you did not like the notion of Mr. Stone's having threatened to "box his ears"?

A. I believe it is contrary to the practice.

Q. But *that* you did not say any thing about?

A. Not to him.

Q. That was upholding the authority of the master?

A. It was not lowering his authority.

Q. What is the distinction?

A. There *is* a little difference, I think.

Q. It was, I think you say, about a week after this answer had been made by you about upholding the authorities of the college that you heard of the A. B. C.: from whom did you hear of that?

A. Not of the A. B. C., but of the existence of a feeling.

Q. From whom did you hear it?

A. The Vice-President.

Q. I understood you to say, that the first intimation you had of this movement was about a week after your interview with Mr. David Fitzgerald about the pistol?

A. Yes.

Q. Was that from the Vice-President?

A. We have a meeting every week of the Superiors, and it was mentioned at this meeting; but whether the Prefect of Discipline, the Vice-President, or the Prefect of Studies, mentioned it, I cannot undertake to say.

Q. Was it not Mr. Stone?

A. I cannot undertake to say; it was mentioned at the meeting.

Q. You say that an unofficial communication was made to you by the Vice-President on the subject?

A. Yes.

Q. That was something that had been uttered by Mr. Stone?

A. Yes.

Q. *That*, you say, struck you as very serious?

A. Yes.

Q. So serious that you convened a meeting of the whole house?

A. Much more had happened before the whole house was convened. I convened a meeting of the Superiors first.

Q. At that meeting, you say, the evidence was laid before you?

A. Yes.

Q. And there was a second meeting?

A. Yes.

Q. When was the second meeting?

A. I think half-past ten.

Q. On the same day?

A. Yes.

Q. Was the first meeting at nine o'clock in the morning?

A. Yes.

Q. You say the evidence was gone into, and I think you said it was sifted?

A. I do not think I used that word. We had only the report of the Prefect as to what he had heard and read with his own eyes.

Q. Mr. Stone told you that a Divine had said that a lay student had said that there was this A. B. C.?

A. Yes.

Q. And that young David Fitzgerald was at the head of it?

A. Yes.

Q. A lay student had reported to him the existence of a conspiracy against the Church students, known by its members as the A. B. C.; that each member had a list of the other members, and that the plaintiff was prime mover in it. The evidence was, that Mr. Stone had said that a Divine had said that a lay student had said,—what I will not repeat?

A. Certainly.

Q. And then there was the pocket-book?

A. Yes.

Q. That was the evidence?

A. Yes.

Q. Did it occur to you that it would be well to send for the lay student?

A. No.

Q. Or for the Divine?

A. No.

Q. Did it not occur to you that it would be as well to go to the fountain-head, in order to see what the value of the evidence was?

A. I had no more doubt of the accuracy of the report I had received than I have of any thing I have stated myself; and what I had heard was entirely confirmed by the pocket-book and all its contents.

Q. Then it did not occur to you to go to the fountain-head?

A. I did not do it.

Q. Nor did it occur to you to do it?

A. I daresay not.

Q. If it had occurred to you, you would have done it?

A. Perhaps so.

Lord Chief-Justice Cockburn: There was no evidence of what we should call overt act?

A. I have given evidence as to a list of the aristocracy of Oscott that was afloat in the college.

Mr. Coleridge: Did you see the list?

A. I think I saw the list.

Q. Where did you see it?

A. The Prefect found it.

Q. Where?

A. He came on a number of boys, to the number of eight or ten, in a place where they had no right to be; and at the moment of his appearance he saw that they shuffled away some paper, which he called for: that paper was given to him. The next day he was called upon by one of the clerical students on some other business, and this student told him that he had heard that he had seized, the day before, a list of the aristocracy of Oscott; and he made further inquiries from this clerical student as to what was going on in the bounds, and whether they suffered any persecution.

Q. Did you see the list?

A. I have said that I think I did.

Q. Have you got it?

A. Certainly not.

Lord Chief-Justice Cockburn: You say the inquiry was made as to whether they suffered any persecution?

A. Yes.

Q. Who made this inquiry?

A. Mr. Stone.

Mr. Coleridge: Who produced the list of the aristocracy?

A. It would be the Prefect, who had seen the list the day before.

Q. By the Prefect I understand you usually to mean Mr. Stone?

A. Mr. Stone.

Q. Has he got the list, do you know?

A. I do not know.

Q. What was the length of this list?

A. I really do not know.

Q. You saw it?

A. From my recollection of it, I should think it was ten or twelve names, perhaps.

Q. Ten or twelve names of the aristocracy of Oscott. Was it headed, "Aristocracy of Oscott"? "Nobbs"? or "Swells"? or what?

A. I do not think it had any heading at all.

Q. A list of names?

A. A list of names.

Lord Chief-Justice Cockburn: Was it a list of names as distinct from clerical students, or a list of the aristocracy?

A. I really do not at this moment remember a single name in the list, because I treated the matter lightly, until further acts came before me.

Mr. Coleridge: This was a formidable act; do you really say that you felt your throne tottering under you?

A. No, certainly not; but I felt that the peace of my subjects was very seriously endangered.

Q. When the list was produced to you, was any copy of the pocket-book also produced?

A. I think not.

Q. Did Mr. Stone merely tell you his recollection of it?

A. I think so.

Q. And it struck you as a formidable thing, with ramifications?

A. Certainly.

Q. You saw the pocket-book afterwards?

A. Yes.

Q. And it confirmed your worst suspicions, did it?

A. Yes.

Q. There seems to be a good deal which, I am sorry to say, is unintelligible to me: there is a good deal about "cosines" and "segments of circles," and so on; do you think that those segments of circles have any underhand meaning?

A. I think not.

Q. Then there is something about Governor Moody being elected by acclamation for his "magnanimous sentiments;" did not that strike you as an absurd thing?

A. Yes; I thought it perfectly absurd when I heard what it was.

Q. And did not that, in your mind, cast a shadow of ridicule over the whole of it?

A. Not of ridicule.

Q. Of absurdity?

A. Merely with reference to that entry,—not with reference to the other entries, which were substantial facts.

Q. It seems to be mixed up with a great deal of other matter; he seems to have kept the documents of this confederation very loosely?

A. I think that the entries follow on, page after page.

Q. Excuse me.

A. I do not know that there are any other facts that intervene.

Q. Here is one, at the beginning, I think. No; that is about the key of the bakehouse opening the paint-shop; was that told you at the same time?

A. No.

Q. That you discovered on inspection?

A. Yes.

Q. And "* * *" and "* * *." Do you attribute any thing to that?

A. That is a page which he told me had no reference to the society, and I asked him no further questions about it.

Q. And it seems to have no reference to the society, does it?

A. I do not know; I could not have understood the rest without his explanation.

Q. I observe that in the list here a good many are struck out?

A. I struck them out on David Fitzgerald's representation that those boys had nothing to do with the society.

Q. You say that the book confirmed your worst suspicions; had you told Mr. Stone before any thing about Mr. Fitzgerald's position in the house? had you told him that it was fickle and frail?

A. I certainly did not say it was fickle. When he has brought me complaints about David Fitzgerald, I have said, "I have given him his warning; his position in the house is extremely precarious; and if he commits any further offence, I must send him away."

Q. Did you tell him that he was in the house for his own purposes, and not for yours?

A. No; that is a misrepresentation. I think what I said was, that he was here for his own particular studies; and that if he did not conform to the discipline of the house, I must send him away.

Q. The Prefects could not overrule you in any way?

A. No.

Q. However much you might consult them, you would be the authority who did it?

A. Yes.

Q. As I understand you, before you proceeded to see him and the book, you had made up your mind that he should go?

A. Certainly, if the book contained that which I was told it did.

Q. Then he came, and you say that the book was brought with him?

A. Yes.

Q. Did Mr. Stone tell you how he had obtained the information that was in the book?

A. Yes; he had told me on the Monday morning.

Q. How long did he say he had got it?

A. He said that as soon as he received information of the existence of this association, and that each of the members of it had a list of the other members, he went to David Fitzgerald's room, to see if he could find the list; that he found his pocket-book on the table, and that in that pocket-book he found the list.

Q. And the rest of the documents?

A. And the rest of the documents.

Q. Had he gone there by your desire at all?

A. No; I was absent from the college.

Q. Are you quite sure that no letters of his were read at all?

A. Certainly—perfectly sure of it. I never even asked such a question, because such a thing is never done. I feel quite sure that it was not done:—I never asked the question, for I should have considered it an insult.

Q. Had you told Mr. Stone to keep an eye upon him, and to watch him?

A. When he complained to me of him for breaches of discipline, I said, "If he goes on so badly, I shall be obliged to send him away." But it is not likely that I told Mr. Stone to keep an eye upon him, it being part of his duty to do so.

Q. When you sent for him, you had got the information and the book, and you had made up your mind to act upon that?

A. If I found that the book contained what I was told it did contain.

Q. You say that the boy offered to show you a letter from his father. I ask you whether the passage in Mr. Justice Fitzgerald's letter was not, "What on earth is the A. B. C.? Pray enrol me as a member, and let me know what the subscription is"?

A. I never saw such words. The words, to the best of my recollection, were, "What is the subscription to the A. B. C.?"

Q. You told young David Fitzgerald that you would like to have seen what the Judge thought about it?

A. Yes.

Q. But you did not think it right to give him any opportunity of letting you know what he did think about it?

A. I could not.

Q. When you had made up your mind to expel him, you say you summoned the house by bell to see the expulsion?

A. Yes.

Q. I am sure I do not desire to see those notes; but you did, in fact, make notes of your speech, did you not?

A. You are perfectly welcome to see any notes I made.

Q. You must have written down, for instance, the passage which you read from Dr. Newman?

A. No; I took the books with me.

Q. I suppose the point of your speech was that he was not a gentleman?

A. That he had behaved in a very ungentlemanly way.

Q. You say that you have had occasion to send boys away before? Were there two boys sent away in the month of January or February, early in that same half-year?

A. I think not.

Q. Were there two boys who ran away?

A. Yes.

Q. I do not want to know their names,—very far from it; but had they been accused of some gross indecency?

A. They had been accused of holding immodest conversation.

Q. And they ran away?

A. Yes, while the matter was under investigation, which they knew very well; and I supposed therefore that they were guilty.

Q. Did you then assemble the house?

A. Certainly not; the matter was not one on which I should wish to speak to 120 boys.

Q. You did not speak to the boys at all?

A. It was a very delicate subject to speak about to boys under twelve years of age, of whom I had perhaps fifty or sixty; and I said as few words as possible to them. I said I found that it was known to some of the boys that these two boys had intended to run away; and I pointed out to them the extreme folly of allowing them to do such a fatal thing without reporting it to the authorities.

Q. Did you say that their case was not a case in which they would have been expelled?

A. I said that, as far as the matter had been investigated by the Prefect and myself, we had not been able to find them guilty, and that therefore if they had remained, I should probably have thought them innocent; but that from the fact of their having run away, I could not help thinking they were guilty, and that I should now refuse to take them back.

Q. Was that in this half-year?

A. I thought myself that it was between September and Christmas; but I cannot say at all.

Q. Then he was expelled?

A. Who was?

Q. Mr. Fitzgerald was publicly expelled?

A. Yes.

Q. And are you sure that you said nothing about the Oscotian Society?

A. I think it most likely that I did.

Q. That he was also to be expelled from that?

A. That he must be removed from that.

Q. Did you tell them also that he was a liar?

A. No; certainly not.

Q. Perhaps I do not use the right expression, but did you convey to them the same idea?

A. I should say certainly not. I do not know whether I told them any of the circumstances of the pistol-case; if I did, I may have said that he had been guilty of gross equivocation to a superior.

Q. Was it that he had been guilty of equivocation amounting to a lie?

A. Very likely.

Q. You say he went away from you expelled, and then you ordered him to be locked up. Did you give any order for him to be locked up?

A. I do not think I did; but I am responsible for it.

Q. Do you know the fact that he was locked up from that time until he left the house?

A. Yes; I have heard a great deal of it since.

Q. Does the Anti-Bunker Confederation now present itself to your mind in the same formidable light that it did in March 1865?

A. I have never heard a word to alter my opinion of it.

Q. The evidence that Mr. Fitzgerald gave yesterday does not alter your opinion?

A. Not the least.

Q. You still consider it a very formidable thing?

A. I think it was a most mischievous thing for the rest of the house, and for the happiness of the weakest part of the inhabitants.

Q. I should be sorry to misrepresent you by and by. Is that which you have stated really the whole of the evidence upon which you acted?

A. The whole, so far as I know.

Q. And upon that evidence you felt compelled, as I understand you, to expel David Fitzgerald?

A. Yes; this being the last step in a series of offences.

Q. As I understand you, you had made up your mind to expel him upon that evidence, supposing the book should turn out to be what Mr. Stone had represented it to be, before you had heard him?

A. No; I heard him, but he was unable to say any thing in his defence.

Q. You thought there was nothing in his defence when he said it was nonsense?

A. No, certainly not; his mere assertion proved nothing. I saw myself one entry on the 6th of March.

Q. About Governor Moody?

A. Yes.

Q. No doubt you considered that that was absurd?

A. Quite so.

Q. And that is the last entry?

A. No, it is not the last.

Q. However, there is nothing to show that any thing was entered after that date?

A. I speak from memory; but I think you will see that there was an entry after that date.

Q. When the other boys (the two other sons of Mr. Justice Fitzgerald, and their cousins) were removed, did you make another address to the house?

A. I made another address in consequence of telegrams that

I received. The boy was expelled on the Monday, and on the Tuesday I received telegrams to recall the two other sons of Mr. Justice Fitzgerald. The order was that they were to leave by the first train on Wednesday morning to meet the Irish mail. I arranged for them to leave at seven o'clock, which was necessary in order to catch the Irish mail; and I went to the boys in the refectory at a quarter-past eight o'clock, to explain the circumstances under which four boys disappeared so suddenly from the college. I thought that their leaving must necessarily cause a talk, and I therefore considered it right that the other boys should know under what circumstances they had gone. I said that, with reference to John, the eldest son, there was the distinct testimony of his brother that he had had nothing to do with the association, and that, so far as I was concerned, he might have remained happily in the house; that as to Gerald, his name was down, and his brother had not excused him, and I knew nothing about him; as to the eldest son of Mr. Justice Fitzgerald's brother, he was a boy who had been so long with us, and who was so universally respected, that I was sure that the mere fact of his name having been put down as a member of the association would not be enough to condemn him in their eyes,—that he had probably been seduced into it out of respect for the superior talents of his cousin, who was so much older than himself; as to the youngest Fitzgerald, the cousin of David, I forget what I said about him entirely, because he was so young. I then went on to tell them that I thought it my duty to repeat that when once a person was received into the college as a student, he should be received upon terms of perfect equality with the rest, and that I considered myself *in loco parentis;* that I was bound to look after and protect those who were least able to protect themselves; and that if I found any boy sowing the seeds of discord among different classes of the house, I must visit it with great severity, and that in proportion to the age of the offender, and his position in the college, must be the increased severity of his punishment. I believe that that is what I said.

Q. The result of what you said was, that you considered Mr. David Fitzgerald was the prime mover in the whole matter, and that he was responsible?

A. Certainly.

Q. Did you say that something had come to your knowledge with regard to him which was so bad that you could not mention it?

A. I think not. I think I know to what you allude; it has been rumoured, I am aware, that I made such a statement, but I believe the origin of the rumour was this: I did not choose to mention in the presence of 120 boys the offence of bringing spirits into the house on an occasion when one of the boys certainly drank to excess; but no imputation was made against the moral character of the plaintiff.

Q. Did you say any thing about that or not?

A. Certainly not; there was no offence to be laid to his charge in that respect.

Q. I mean as to the spirits?

A. I suppose that the sentence in my speech, which has been misrepresented in a way which has reached my ears, is a sentence in which I said there was another offence about which I did not choose to speak to them. I should not have liked to tell those boys that there were some among them who had been parties to the commission of such an offence as that of having spirits in the house and getting drunk.

Q. I suppose that Horace is studied at Oscott College?

A. Yes.

Q. And the Saturnalia you do not consider to be excusable?

A. No, not at all.

Re-examined by Mr. Karslake.

Q. You would consider it most detrimental to the discipline of the school that boys should have spirits either at breaking-up times or at any other time?

A. Certainly.

Q. Especially if the effect is to produce drunkenness?

A. Yes.

Q. Had you understood that on the occasion to which reference has been made they had drunk to excess?

A. I have no doubt that one boy had.

Q. You say that you never made, or intended to make, any

charge of immorality against young Mr. Fitzgerald either directly or indirectly?

A. Certainly never.

Q. I see here this, which I had not seen before: there are the names of John and James Fitzgerald in pencil, and * * * and * * * are struck through in this list of the A. B. C.?

A. Yes.

Q. Are the words "John and James" in your handwriting?

A. Yes.

Q. And were the names that are struck out in pencil struck out by you?

A. They were.

Q. Did you make those notes, "John and James," in the presence of David Fitzgerald?

A. I did.

Q. And did you strike them out in the presence of David Fitzgerald?

A. Yes, I did.

Q. How came you to put the names of John and James against "Fitzgerald, 5"?

A. Because David told me that he had asked his brother John to join the association, and he had refused; and I see now that James the younger Fitzgerald was also not a member, and therefore I struck out their names.

Q. Was it on the same occasion that you struck through those other two names in pencil?

A. I did.

Q. What led you to do that?

A. He told me that in one case only one of the brothers had to do with it, and in another case that his name was put down without the boy's leave; and I therefore struck them out.

Q. Were the other two boys you have spoken of who ran away foreigners?

A. They were.

Lord Chief-Justice: What is the good of asking this question, Mr. Karslake?

A. I don't know, my Lord; but questions were asked about this matter on the other side.

Lord Chief-Justice: I know; but when answers were given

from which it was impossible to elicit any thing on the plaintiff's side, there is no use in pursuing the matter any further.

A Juror: Did you say that upon investigating the case as to those two boys, you found there was nothing against them?

A. I do not think I said I found there was nothing against them, but that there was nothing to prove them guilty.

Q. And yet you expelled them?

A. No; they ran away.

Q. You would not receive them back?

A. No; because I looked upon their running away as a confession of guilt. I thought that if they were innocent, they would not have run away. I thought they were afraid of the result of the investigation; they did not know that we had not proved any thing against them, and they were afraid, and therefore ran away.

Mr. Karslake: There had been a charge made against them of using indecent language, which charge was under consideration; the proof had not been complete, and they ran away; and you told the assembled boys that as they had run away, though the charge was not proved, you would not receive them back?

A. I do not think I said any thing about receiving them back; I never dreamt of their applying to be received back, though one of them afterwards did apply and was refused.

Q. On the 12th you were absent from the college, I think you say?

A. In the afternoon I was.

Q. You told my friend that you made inquiries of young Fitzgerald about Governor Moody, and that he explained to you that it was not young Moody, but the elder one?

A. Yes.

Q. And upon his representation you believed that to be the truth?

A. I believed that to be the truth.

Q. Mr. Stone had told you previously that there was, as he understood, persecution in the bounds?

A. Yes.

Q. Did he tell you that on the Monday morning?

A. No; that was the week before.

Q. Mr. Stone had informed you of that?

A. Yes.

Q. Was that also mentioned when the superiors met on that morning?

A. We met once a-week always; therefore at what particular meeting that was mentioned publicly to us I cannot say.

Q. You told my friend just now that still, according to the rules, there is this distinction made with reference to the Church students, that they do not go home at Christmas?

A. Yes.

Q. Are there besides the Church students who have patrons other Church students who come to the college?

A. Not among the boys; there are a great number among the Divines.

Q. But among the boys are there students who are reading for the Church?

A. If they are, they do not make it public.

Q. They do not come distinctly as Church students?

A. No.

Q. Then are all these boys whom you call Church students, and who are not allowed to go home at Christmas under the present state of things, persons who come from patrons?

A. Yes.

Q. Upon funds supplied by Bishops?

A. Yes.

Q. The place is very large, and it would never do to keep it merely for the ecclesiastical students?

A. Certainly not.

Q. My friend has asked you some questions about young Fitzgerald measuring strength with Mr. Stone; Mr. Stone, you say, was a priest in orders?

A. Yes.

Q. Had he been educated at the college?

A. He had been at the college, I believe, eight or ten or twelve years; long before my time.

Q. My friend asked you whether it occurred to you that Mr. Stone might be measuring strength with Mr. David Fitzgerald; was Mr. David Fitzgerald under the control of Mr. Stone as Prefect of Discipline?

A. Certainly.

Q. You say that you do not include Divines in the Church students; I believe that among what you call Divines there are lay professors, are there not?

A. No; not lay professors among the Divines.

A Juror: About the public-house: you say the senior students in parties of not less than three are allowed to go out beyond the boundaries, and they may go for miles and not return for two or three hours?

A. Yes.

Q. Suppose they walk a long way on a very hot day, and go into a house where they sell ginger-beer or soda-water, are those boys, if they go there, to be visited with expulsion?

A. No, not necessarily with expulsion certainly.

A Juror: My Lord, I can only say that I believe every word that young Mr. Fitzgerald has said is gospel truth, and I think it was a most disgraceful thing to dismiss him from the college. That is quite clear to my mind.

Lord Chief-Justice Cockburn: Really, gentlemen, I cannot permit that.

Mr. Karslake: It is a very unusual course for a juryman to make such a statement before he has heard the case half through.

Lord Chief-Justice Cockburn: I have to attend the House of Lords now; and therefore the case must be adjourned to to-morrow.

(*Adjourned to to-morrow at ten o'clock.*)

THIRD DAY.

The Rev. William Stone sworn. *Examined by* Mr. Vernon Harcourt.

Q. You are a priest, I believe?

A. I am.

Q. And what is called the Prefect of Discipline at Oscott College?

A. Yes.

Q. What age are you?

A. I am now in my twenty-sixth year.

Q. How long had you been at Oscott College before you were appointed Prefect of Discipline?

A. I had been at Oscott ten years and a half.

Q. When were you appointed Prefect of Discipline?

A. In January 1865.

Q. I believe there are no written rules which prescribe your authority over the students, are there?

A. There are not.

Q. But of course there are certain traditions and habits which are known to limit the authority of the Prefect of Discipline for the preservation of discipline in the school?

A. Certainly.

Q. There are certain rules, are there not, for the government and conduct of the students?

A. There are.

Q. Are those rules read out every half-year?

A. They are read out every half-year.

Mr. Harcourt (to Mr. Coleridge): Have you the rules there?

Mr. Coleridge: We had them yesterday. If you want to refer to any thing, perhaps you will just call our attention to it.

Mr. V. Harcourt: The rules will be considered in, then.

Q. In all matters of discipline and breaches of discipline in the school, you have, in the first instance, authority to prescribe punishment, have you not?

A. I have.

Q. To the younger pupils, I suppose, corporal punishment?

A. Yes.

Q. And to the elder students other punishment?

A. Yes.

Q. From you, and from your sentence, the students can appeal to the President?

A. Yes.

Q. But, subject to such an appeal, you have the absolute control of the discipline of the school?

A. I have.

Q. Are all the students at Oscott, with the exception of those who are over seventeen years of age, governed by the same rules?

A. Those who are over seventeen years of age are exempt from corporal punishment.

Q. But in other respects are the students subject to the same rules?

A. Yes; they are subject to the same rules, except in the class of Philosophers, where there are certain extra privileges.

Lord Chief-Justice Cockburn: Being above seventeen places them beyond the reach of corporal punishment, independent of the class?

A. They are not subject to corporal punishment when they are in the poetry class. The *three* higher classes are exempt, and all those over seventeen years of age.

Mr. V. Harcourt: Except, of course, by the express orders of the President?

A. Yes.

Q. You say that the higher class—that is, the class of Philosophers—have certain privileges?

A. They have.

Q. Those are privileges which are well known and defined.

A. Yes.

Q. At the time you became Prefect of Discipline, the Plaintiff, young Mr. Fitzgerald, was in the class of Philosophers, and had those privileges, had he not?

A. He had.

Mr. Coleridge: We dispute that; you must not assume that.

Mr. V. Harcourt: Then I must ask you directly this question: Was Mr. Fitzgerald under you, and subject to that authority, in the same position as the Philosophers?

A. He was in the same position as the rest of the Philosophers.

Q. And subject to the same rules and discipline as the class of Philosophers?

A. With one exception; I do not know on whose authority it was, but he had permission to remain in bed an extra half hour in the morning.

Q. Do you happen to know whether he had had that permission for two years previously or not?

A. I do not know.

Q. That is not within your knowledge, is it?

A. No.

Q. I believe the matter about the drinking party occurred before you became Prefect?

A. Yes.

Q. And that did not come consequently under your cognisance?

A. No; it did not come under my cognisance.

Q. Was the first occasion on which you had to find fault with Mr. Fitzgerald on the subject of the matter which has been spoken of,—the pass-key?

A. Yes.

Q. Just tell us shortly, in your own words, what happened about the key.

A. David Fitzgerald returned home from the vacation, I think on the 31st of January,—I am not exactly certain as to the hour, but it was after ten o'clock.

Lord Chief-Justice Cockburn: After ten o'clock at night?

A. Yes; and I was undressing and going to bed. David Fitzgerald came to my room, and asked me to open his room, which had been locked during the time of vacation; and I lent him a pass-key.

Mr. V. Harcourt: Just state what that key was.

A. It was a key that opened all the students' rooms, all the masters' rooms, and all the class-rooms of the house, and several of the offices. I lent it him, with the express injunction that he should bring it back to me the first thing in the morning. About two o'clock on the following morning I met Fitzgerald in the cloisters.

Q. In the afternoon, I suppose you mean?

A. Yes, two o'clock in the afternoon. I met him in the cloisters, and reminded him that he had not given me the key. He produced it, and I remarked, "This is not the key, David." He said, "It is, sir." I then looked at it more closely, and saw that it was the key, but I noticed that it had been tampered with.

Lord Chief-Justice Cockburn: Tell us what you saw.

A. First of all, it was blackened, and wax was adhering to it; and I asked him what he had been doing with it. I said, "Have you been putting it to the fire?" He said, "No." I said, "What have you been doing with it?" He said, "Nothing at all;" and went upstairs. It then struck me that he had been taking an impression of the key in wax; and that same afternoon a wax impression of the key, and a rubbing of the key—a drawing of the key on paper—were put into my hands.

Mr. Coleridge: Which?

A. It was the wards of the key drawn with ink; these two were put into my hands by my assistant. I went to David Fitzgerald's room after night-prayers, and I showed him the impression in wax and the rubbing on paper, and I asked him if he recognised them. He said that it was a very faithful impression; he said it in a joking manner, passing it off as a joke; he said that it was a very faithful copy of the key. I then asked him if he considered it an honourable thing to do. To which he replied, that he saw no harm in it. I then said, "If you see no harm in it, perhaps your superiors will not think so lightly of it, and I shall inform them of it." I informed the Vice-President.

Q. That evening?

A. That same evening. I do not know whether I went to the Vice-President for the express purpose of informing him; but I know that I informed him the same evening.

Lord Chief-Justice Cockburn: You did inform him?

A. I did inform him.

Mr. V. Harcourt: Well, go on.

A. Some time after,—about a quarter of an hour, I should say,—David Fitzgerald met me again, and said to me, "I have come to you to ask you not to mention my taking an impression of the key to Dr. Northcote." He said he acknowledged that it was a dishonourable thing to do, and that he would not do so again.

Q. I must ask you this: did you say on that occasion, or on any occasion, with reference to this pass-key, that you thought there was nothing in it, and that it did not signify?

A. I never did.

Q. Well?

A. I then told him that I would not mention it to Dr. Northcote; and I went straight to the Vice-President, and told him that David Fitzgerald had been to me, confessing that it was a dishonourable thing to do; and I begged him not to mention the matter to Dr. Northcote; which he never did.

Q. I must ask you this question: had you at that time any desire to get David Fitzgerald into trouble?

A. Not the least; we had always been on very good terms, —on the very best of terms, I might say.

Q. Let me ask you about that key. Was that a key that David Fitzgerald, or any boy in the Philosophers' class, could be entitled to have at all?

A. No.

Lord Chief-Justice Cockburn: You may assume that.

The Witness: All the boys' rooms are opened with the same key; and it was against the tradition, and it was never allowed for any boy to have the key of his private room.

Q. Fitzgerald said that he had got the wax from which the impression was taken from the wax sacristy. Was that a room that was locked?

A. That was locked.

Q. With what key could that be opened?

A. It could be opened by this pass-key.

Q. You say that this matter, after young Mr. Fitzgerald had been with you, was not mentioned to Dr. Northcote till subsequently, at the last moment?

A. At the last moment.

Q. Was that when Mr. Fitzgerald's conduct was being investigated?

A. It was; and he released me from my promise of secrecy.

Q. It was not until he released you from your promise of secrecy that you mentioned it?

A. It was not.

Lord Chief-Justice Cockburn: Would not that have come better when the circumstances had been investigated? However, we may take it for the present, that it was not mentioned till that time.

A. There was no actual promise made.

Mr. V. Harcourt: That was the first occasion, as I understand you, on which you had to complain, seriously at least, of young Mr. Fitzgerald?

A. That was the first occasion.

Q. After you were made Prefect of Discipline?

A. Yes.

Q. Was your next subject of complaint about the 20th or 21st of February?

A. It was about the 20th or 21st of February.

Q. What did that relate to?

A. I am not sure whether it was the 20th or the 21st; but I found him up one night at half-past eleven o'clock, when he ought to have been in bed by ten o'clock.

Q. That was according to the rules?

A. Yes.

Q. And was he subject to those rules?

A. He was subject to the same rules as the others.

Q. There had been no exemption made in his case?

A. Not that I ever heard of.

Q. What did you do upon that?

A. I took away his privileges for three days.

Q. Was that the first time that he had done it; or had you reason to believe that he had done so on former occasions?

A. The first week I was in office I was told by a superior—

Mr. Coleridge: I do not know how far we can go into that.

Lord Chief-Justice Cockburn: It may account for what otherwise may appear to have been a severe enforcement of the rules.

Mr. V. Harcourt: Did you say any thing to young Mr. Fitzgerald about it having been done before?

A. I am not sure whether I did; I am pretty sure, but I will not swear to it.

Q. When you inflicted this punishment upon him, did you believe that it was a thing that had been done before?

A. I did; in fact, I knew it for certain.

Q. What did the punishment amount to?

A. His privileges were suspended for three days; he was confined to bounds, and he would not be entitled to go into the plantations.

Q. He was confined to bounds for three days?

A. Yes.

Lord Chief-Justice Cockburn: The plantations are beyond the ordinary bounds?

A. Yes.

Mr. V. Harcourt: While he was so confined to bounds by you, did you afterwards find him having broken those bounds?

A. It happened the very next day, or the day after. I will not be sure whether it was the 21st or the 22d that he went out with a party of Philosophers.

Q. Just tell us what you saw about that.

A. I took no notice of it at the time. It so happened that at that time I was busily engaged in getting up plays for the Shrovetide vacation; and although I remarked it, I had not time to speak to him upon the subject.

Q. Was that the occasion on which you saw him at the Swan Inn?

A. No; that was the day following.

Q. Then you saw him out of bounds before the occasion at the Swan Inn?

A. I did not actually see him; but he put a party in my rooms, with his name at the head of the list.

Q. Let us go on to the next day: what happened the next day?

A. The next day one of the superiors informed me (the Vice-President) that he had seen two boys on the road,—or two who looked very much like our boys,—and he told me that I had better see into the matter. I was going to Birmingham that afternoon, and I thought that they might very possibly be at this inn; and I turned out of my ordinary way about a quarter of a mile, and went into the inn, and found them.

Q. Whom?

A. I found those two, of whom David Fitzgerald was one, together with two others—three others altogether: himself, the boy who was with him, and two others.

Lord Chief-Justice Cockburn: Four altogether?

A. Yes.

Mr. Harcourt: What was David Fitzgerald doing when you went there?

A. He was hiding himself.

Q. What did you do thereupon?

A. I knew, or at least I guessed, that David Fitzgerald was there: the other three I saw; but I could not see Fitzgerald. I called his name out, and I discovered him covered up in the fire-place. I said nothing to them at the time, but sent them home.

Q. What did you do then?—did you report that?

A. I went to Birmingham that same evening; the President was out on the following day; but I reported it on Saturday morning the 25th.

Q. We have heard from Dr. Northcote what he did upon that. Did Dr. Northcote, or did young Mr. Fitzgerald, tell you what punishment Dr. Northcote had inflicted on them?

A. Dr. Northcote told me himself.

Q. That punishment, as we have heard, was that young Fitzgerald was to be confined to the bounds until Easter?

A. Until Easter.

Q. That was on Saturday?

A. That was on Saturday the 25th of February.

Q. On the Monday following—which would be the 27th—did you again find young Fitzgerald out of bounds?

A. I found him about five o'clock in the housekeeper's room.

Q. Was that contrary to the bounds which Dr. Northcote had inflicted on him?

A. Yes.

Q. That was out of bounds?

A. Yes; and I told him so at the time.

Lord Chief-Justice Cockburn: The housekeeper's room, I suppose, is in the college?

A. Yes.

Mr. Karslake: If the rules are read, it will be seen that there are certain parts of the college in which they are not to be.

Lord Chief-Justice Cockburn: That would hardly be within the bounds; it is more a general prohibition to be in that part of the house: whether they have their privileges or not, they are not allowed to go there?

A. It is especially down in the rules that they are not allowed to go there.

Mr. Harcourt: You told him, at all events, that he ought not to be there?

A. Yes.

Q. Did you tell him to return to his bounds?

A. I did.

Q. Did you soon after that find him again out of bounds?

A. A quarter of an hour after that I found him in the plantations with another student.

Q. Were the plantations out of bounds?

A. Certainly.

Q. Who was he with?

A. He was with another student, of the name of * * *.

Q. Was * * * a boy who was entitled to be out of bounds?

A. Certainly not.

Lord Chief-Justice Cockburn: What class was he in?

A. He was in one of the lower classes.

Mr. Harcourt: Therefore he had no right to be in the plantations at all?

A. No right whatever.

Q. What were young Fitzgerald and * * * doing?

A. They were shooting in the plantations.

Q. Shooting with a pistol?

A. Yes, shooting with a pistol.

Q. Just tell us what passed between you and young Fitzgerald on that occasion.

A. As soon as they saw me they took to their heels; I followed them, and called them back. I then said to them, "Who owns that pistol that you are shooting with?" David Fitzgerald answered, "I do." I then said, "Give it to me." He said, "I have not got it." I then said, "Go and find it;" to which he answered, "I do not know where it is." I then said, "That's a lie;" to which he answered, "It is not." I then repeated the affirmation that it was a lie; and I told him that if he did not mind, I should box his ears.

Q. What happened about the pistol? where was it?

A. It was a few yards from where he was standing.

Lord Chief-Justice Cockburn: How was it found?

A. I forget whether it was actually found by himself or the other student, but I believe it was found by himself.

Mr. Harcourt: It was on the ground?

A. It was lying close by the hedge.

Mr. Coleridge: Flung into the hedge?

Lord Chief-Justice: How near to where he was standing?

A. I cannot exactly say the distance, but I should say that it was not more than four or five yards at the very outside. Previously to this, I had said to him, "If you do not instantly give me up that pistol, you shall leave the house to-night." I think that was the expression I made use of; it was more as a threat—

Mr. Coleridge: Never mind that.

Mr. Harcourt: He found the pistol, and you took it?

A. I took it.

Q. What then happened?

A. I told them to return to their bounds.

Q. And they went?

A. I told Fitzgerald, at the same time, to go to his room, and bring me every thing connected with his pistol—the cartridges and powder.

Q. Did you tell him that you should report him to Dr. Northcote?

A. I do not believe I made use of that expression then.

Q. Did you?

A. I did report it to Dr. Northcote.

Q. What passed further between you and Dr. Northcote?

A. Dr. Northcote sent for me.

Q. When you went to Dr. Northcote, did you find that young Fitzgerald had been to see Dr. Northcote upon the subject?

A. I found so.

Q. And did you give your explanation of the matter to Dr. Northcote?

A. I gave my explanation of it.

Q. After that, as we have heard, Dr. Northcote again saw young Fitzgerald.

A. He did.

Q. And after he had seen Dr. Northcote the second time, did you see young Fitzgerald again?

A. David Fitzgerald came to me on the night of Tuesday the 28th.

Lord Chief-Justice Cockburn: Was that the day on which this had happened?

A. The following day he came to my room about ten o'clock, and he said he wished to have a conversation with me.

Mr. V. Harcourt: Did you ask him what punishment Dr. Northcote had awarded him?

A. That was almost the close of the conversation. He began by saying that he wished to speak to me on three points. First of all he prefaced it by saying that he had been conducting himself so badly, and that his character was so lowered in the estimation of his superiors, that it would little avail him to try to extenuate his faults; or some words to that effect.

Mr. Coleridge: This is what you told him?

A. This is what he said to me; and then he said, the first point he wished to speak to me on was with regard to the expression I had used to him in the plantations, "It is a lie," and threatening to box his ears; and he excused himself by saying that he did not mean to tell a lie; that it was not a lie, for that he did not actually know where the pistol was. I then pointed out to him that if it was not a lie, it was certainly an equivocation, and almost amounted to a lie; and with regard to the other expression, threatening to box his ears, I said, "Of course, David, I should not think of carrying such a threat into execution. It is not generally customary for a superior to apologise to a boy, but I am not ashamed to confess my fault when I have committed one." I think I also explained it by saying that I was out of temper at the moment, and that I meant it as nothing more than a threat. He then came to the second point.

He denied, or at least he said it was his impression, that the Prefect had not the power to take away the privileges of the Philosophers. I knew perfectly well what had been done in my own time; and I told him that the Prefect always had that right, and frequently exercised it; and he moreover added that he had gone out in order to see if I should press the right.

Q. At the time when he was in the plantations, I understand from you that he had been confined to bounds by Dr. Northcote?

A. He had.

Q. That was not a taking away of the privileges by you, but by the President?

A. That was by the President.

Q. Was that all that passed on that occasion?

A. I think there was another point; I forget at the present moment what it was. It was then that I asked him what punishment Dr. Northcote had inflicted upon him.

Q. And he told you?

A. He told me, and the next morning—

Q. Just tell us the punishment that had been inflicted upon him.

A. He told me that Dr. Northcote had degraded him to the ranks, and told him to study in the common study-place.

Q. Did you proceed to put that order of Dr. Northcote's into execution?

A. I went to Dr. Northcote the next morning; and he then told me himself of the punishment that he had inflicted upon Fitzgerald, and I then proceeded to put it into execution.

Q. Did you after that, on a subsequent occasion, again find him up after hours?

A. I found him up, I should say it was about four or five days after. I am not sure as to the number of days; it may be four or five, or seven or eight, that I found him up again at night.

Q. What did you do then?

A. I told him that I did not wish to bring him to any further trouble, and that I would overlook it; but I think I also reminded him that I should not overlook any further offences. I think it was on that occasion that I made use of the word "fickle," which is attributed to me. I told him that his position in the house was rather fickle.

Q. And I understand you to say that you said you would overlook it at the time?

A. I said I would overlook it.

Q. Had Dr. Northcote told you the substance of what had passed between him and Fitzgerald as to his future position in the school?

A. He told me all about it.

Q. Before this occasion, when you said you would overlook it on account of his fickle position, did you know that Dr. Northcote had told young Fitzgerald that for the next offence he would have to leave?

A. I did.

Q. Was it with reference to that that you made that observation, and used that word "fickle"?

A. It was.

Q. Was it subsequent to that that it first came to your knowledge of there being a party in the school against the clerical students?

A. The first tangible trace of the existence of the evil spirit that came within my knowledge happened on the 4th of March, on the occasion of my seeing this list.

Q. It was just about that time that you say the first tangible knowledge came before you?

A. I had previously heard from others that there was a very ill-feeling in the bounds.

Q. What do you mean exactly by the bounds?

A. It means the students in the bounds.

Lord Chief-Justice: You mean amongst the students?

A. Yes, amongst the students.

Mr. V. Harcourt: Was that a feeling which in former days had existed in your time?

A. A most violent feeling existed in my own time.

Q. Had that died out before that?

A. I was under the impression that it had altogether died out, or pretty nearly died out.

Lord Chief-Justice Cockburn: A bad feeling about what? You say there was an ill-feeling amongst the students?

A. Amongst the lay students against the Church students.

Mr. V. Harcourt: And I understand you to say that your impression was, before this came to your knowledge at this period, that that ill-feeling had died out?

A. Certainly.

Q. Just explain to us (you can do it best) what was the character of this ill-feeling of which you have spoken; how did it manifest itself?

A. It manifested itself in the frequent use of this word "Bunker."

Lord Chief-Justice Cockburn: That is when it existed, to your knowledge.

A. Yes; and in petty annoyances.

Mr. V. Harcourt: Had it been the cause of great annoyance to the persons who were the objects of it?

A. It had been the cause of very great annoyance, and it led to very serious quarrels amongst the two bodies.

Lord Chief-Justice Cockburn: It manifested itself in the use of the term "Bunker," and what else?

A. Petty annoyances; serious annoyances sometimes.

Mr. V. Harcourt: And you say these petty annoyances had resulted previously in serious quarrels?

A. In my own time there was scarcely a week in which there was not some open manifestation of this feeling.

Q. Had there been great pains taken by the authorities to remove this?

A. I do not believe that the authorities were aware of it up to a certain point. It came to an open issue on one occasion; I forget exactly now what date it was, but it was about 1857.

Q. I think we need not go into the details about that; but what I want to ask you is this: Had it been Dr. Northcote's object, and the object of the authorities, as much as possible to remove all distinction and feeling of jealousy between the two classes of students?

A. It had.

Q. As far as you can judge, had they succeeded in removing the feeling between the two classes of students at the period we are speaking of?

A. So much so, that I had frequently denied to other people that there was an ill-feeling in the bounds; I felt almost certain that it had died out.

Q. In your position of Prefect of Discipline, that was a matter that would come very much under your observation?

A. Certainly.

Q. Now, if you please, tell us what were the circumstances which led you for the first time at this period to believe that the old feeling was breaking out again?

A. I had heard observations from other priests in the house that the ill-feeling was springing up, and had manifested itself; but I refused to believe it until on the evening of the 4th of March I went into the study-place, and there I found several students, to the number of about a dozen, amongst whom was the plaintiff, laughing, and perusing some paper that they had before them. As soon as I appeared, the paper instantly disappeared. I demanded it from one of the boys—he gave it to me rather reluctantly—and I found it was a list of all the students in the house, marked, some with a cipher, and others with a cross.

Mr. Coleridge: What became of that?

A. I took it to my room.

Q. What has become of it?

A. I am not sure whether I have it in my possession now, but I almost imagine that I burnt it shortly after young Fitzgerald was sent away. I will not be sure whether I have it now or not;* I almost imagine that I burnt it, because I thought—

Q. Never mind what you thought; have you looked for it?

A. I know I had it in the vacation-time, but I was burning a lot of papers.

Q. Have you looked for it for the purposes of this examination?

A. I have not.

Mr. Coleridge: Then you cannot go into the contents of it.

Mr. V. Harcourt: Then we will not go into that. I mentioned it as the thing that led to the investigation. That was the first thing—seeing this paper?

A. Yes.

Lord Chief-Justice Cockburn: How many ciphers were

* It has since been found, and is in Mr. Stone's possession.

there, and how many crosses? Can you tell me the proportion of one to the other?

A. I should say about ten to one. The crosses, I think, were intended for the Church students.

Mr. V. Harcourt: Did the finding of this paper put you upon further inquiries as to what was going on?

A. The whole of that night and the next day I could not come to any satisfactory conclusion as to what the paper meant, although a thought did strike me that it might be intended for this.

Mr. Coleridge: We need not go into that.

The Witness: The next night one of the Church students met me and said to me: "So I hear you have a list of the nobility of Oscott." And then for the first time positively I was assured of the existence of this ill-feeling in the house—that it had begun to manifest itself again.

Mr. V. Harcourt: I understand you to say that you had not heard any thing of this for some time before?

A. I had not heard any thing.

Q. This put you upon further inquiries?

A. It did not put me upon further inquiries then. He told me of this ill-feeling that was springing up in the bounds.

Q. Who told you this?

A. This student. He also gave me two names of boys who he felt sure were at the bottom of it.

Q. Did you hear from other quarters also of the existence of this spirit?

A. On the very next Sunday, March the 12th, one of the Divines came to my room and informed me that he had just heard that a conspiracy had been got up in the bounds—that a confederation or society had been got up in the bounds against the Church students. I asked him where he got his information from. After some time he told me that he had got it from a lay student who had been asked to join the society. He also gave me David Fitzgerald's name as the head and originator of it.

Q. In consequence of what you heard in the way you have told us, what did you do?

A. I went to David Fitzgerald's room.

Q. Before you go to that, tell me this: beyond what you

have told us, had you heard any thing else before you went to his room?—had you heard any thing about lists?

A. I am not sure whether he told me that there were lists afloat—I am almost sure he did; I think he told me that David Fitzgerald had a list, but I do not think he told me that the others had.

Q. He told you that David Fitzgerald had a list?

A. I think so; I will not be positive.

Q. Tell us what you did upon the information that you then received?

A. I went to David Fitzgerald's room, and I found an open pocket-book lying on the table; I opened it at random at one page—a certain page—and turned the leaves over very quickly. The first letters that caught my eye were the letters "A. B. C," written on the top of one of the pages.

Q. Did you know what that meant?

A. I had heard from this Divine that the society went by the name of "The A. B. C.," and he interpreted it for me "Anti-Bunker Club" or "Confederation"—I do not know exactly which. It was known generally by that name.

Mr. Coleridge: He did not say so?

A. It was only known to the members.

Mr. V. Harcourt: What did * * * tell you?—tell us what further you did.

A. I found under this "A. B. C." a list of the members.

Q. That is the list we have already seen?

A. Yes.

Q. I think that Dr. Northcote explained most of these initials; but I see opposite "* * *" there is "C. M." Can you tell us what young * * * at Oscott was, or what his father was by trade?

A. I do not know whether I am at liberty to say what a person told me no later than yesterday as to what he thought the letters meant.

Q. Do you know what his father was?

A. I did not know at that time.

Q. Do you know now?

A. He did not tell me positively what it was, but he inferred—

Mr. Coleridge: Do not tell us if you do not know yourself; if you do not know, do not say.

Mr. V. Harcourt: What did you do further upon that?

A. I found certain notes.

Lord Chief-Justice Cockburn: In this pocket-book?

A. Yes.

Lord Chief-Justice: We have seen all those, you know.

Mr. V. Harcourt: I must ask you this question, which has been put in the Plaintiff's case: did you open, or did you read any letters of young Mr. Fitzgerald's on that occasion?

A. Not one.

Q. After you had found these entries in the pocket-book with reference to this society, or whatever it is called, what did you do?

A. After night-prayers I accidentally met the Vice-President, and I told him what I had then discovered; but he went away at once. He had not time to go into it, and nothing further passed between us then.

Q. Did you tell Dr. Northcote the next morning?

A. I told him the next morning; he was absent that night.

Q. Was that the first information, as far as you know, from you that Dr. Northcote had upon the subject?

A. I do not know whether the Vice-President told him the night before.

Q. I mean from you?

A. From me that was the first time.

Q. What happened next after you told Dr. Northcote?

A. I think it was somewhere about nine o'clock—

Q. Nine in the morning, you told Dr. Northcote?

A. Yes, I told him before that time; I told him, I think, about eight o'clock; and at nine o'clock we met in his room—the Vice-President and myself met in Dr. Northcote's room.

Q. And you gave him further information, I suppose, upon the subject then?

A. He asked me to relate the information then.

Q. After you and the Vice-President and Dr. Northcote had been together, did Dr. Northcote tell you to do any thing?

A. I think it was at eleven o'clock that he gave me distinct orders to go and get the pocket-book.

Mr. Coleridge: Dr. Northcote said there were two meetings.

Mr. V. Harcourt: There was another meeting at eleven?

A. I think there was.

Q. After the meeting at eleven, what did Dr. Northcote tell you to do?

A. He told me to go and get the pocket-book from David Fitzgerald—that he wished to judge for himself.

Q. Did you go to his room?

A. I went to the study-place first of all, because he ought to have been in the study-place; but I believe I met the Prefect of Studies on the way, who told me then that David Fitzgerald had been studying in his room contrary to orders; and having that information, I went to his room and found him there again.

Q. Now tell us as accurately as you can remember what passed between you and him.

A. I told him I wished to speak to him, and I told him to come to my room. As soon as I got inside, I bolted the door to prevent intrusion.

Q. That was in your room?

A. In my own private room.

Q. Let me ask this, as to bolting the door to prevent intrusion: was that a habit usual with you?

A. Always, whenever I had any one in to punish, because I did not know who might be coming up; and I always did so whenever I was punishing a boy or speaking to him,—I always had the practice of bolting the door inside.

Q. Was that the usual practice at Oscott?

A. Yes; and as soon as I had bolted the door, I said to him, "David, I am afraid you have done for yourself at last;" or "David, I am afraid you have done for yourself now." He said, "I do not understand you."

Q. I see that Mr. Fitzgerald says you said it with a triumphant smile.

A. My back was turned towards him at the time. I am not aware of any triumphant smile. I then said to him, "You have a pocket-book." He said, "I have;" and he put his hand upon his pocket. I then said, "I want you to give it to me;" he said, "I do not see what right you have to demand it." I said, "If you do not give it to me, I shall take it." He again said, "I do not see what right you have to demand it." I then said, "Are you going to give it to me?" to which he answered, "No." I then said, "Very well, I must take it;" and I took the book without any opposition on his part.

Q. Is it true that there was any struggle between him and you about this pocket-book?

A. Not the shadow of a struggle.

Q. You took it out of his pocket, I understand?

A. Yes.

Q. And did he resist at all?

A. He did not resist at all.

Q. What passed after that?

A. I opened the book.

Lord Chief-Justice Cockburn: Did he draw his hand from his pocket?

A. He had his hand upon the pocket, but not to prevent me at all; I think he had hold of the corner of his coat: it was a motion something like *this* (describing it).

Q. It was his coat-pocket?

A. Yes; it was a loose coat.

Mr. V. Harcourt: An outside pocket?

A. Yes.

Q. The pocket in the flap of the coat?

A. At the side.

Q. It was a shooting-jacket?

A. I think it was.

Q. Then you took the book, and what passed after that?

A. I opened the book to see if the information was there—if the notes were still there; and when I had seen that they were, I closed the book. I think I said, "It is all right." He then said, "Are you satisfied?" I said, "You may pretty well guess" (or some words to that effect) "what the consequence of this will be." He said, "What do you mean?"

Q. This, as I understand, was subsequent to the two meetings of the superiors in the morning?

A. It was subsequent to the two meetings.

Q. He said, "What do you mean?"

A. He said, "What do you mean?" I then taxed him with getting up this conspiracy—this society—in the bounds.

Q. Which term did you use?

A. This "society." I will not be certain.

Mr. Coleridge: What did you say when you taxed him?

Mr. V. Harcourt: Put it in your own words.

A. I said, "You have been getting up a society in bounds against the Church students." He put it all off as "humbug" and "nonsense"—he said it was humbug and nonsense.

Q. After that you took him to Dr. Northcote?

A. I made some further remark, to the effect that it was, I was afraid, too late for him to help himself, but that it was not too late to help others—I alluded to some of the other names down on the list—and he then asked me if he might see Dr. Northcote; and I said, "Certainly."

Q. And you went with him to Dr. Northcote?

A. Yes; Dr. Northcote had previously told me to get the pocket-book from him and bring it to him.

Q. You were not present at the whole of the interview between Dr. Northcote and Mr. David Fitzgerald?

A. Not at the whole of the interview.

Q. After young Fitzgerald left Dr. Northcote on that occasion, when did you see him next?

A. The next time I saw him, I think, was about a quarter after one.

Q. Do you know what led to your seeing him?

A. I was under the impression that he had taken himself away, in order to save himself the disgrace of public expulsion.

Q. Had Dr. Northcote given you any directions, after this last interview with young Fitzgerald, as to what you were to do?

A. He told me that he was going to expel him publicly; and I went to his room to find him, but I could not find him; and I therefore concluded that he had taken himself away. I looked about the house for some time, and could not find him, and therefore I concluded that it was very likely he had taken himself away.

Q. Then afterwards you saw him?

A. I found him waiting at the President's room.

Q. That was after the very last meeting of the Superiors?

A. Yes.

Q. That was after the very meeting of the house at which Fitzgerald was expelled?

A. Yes.

Q. Now, tell us what you did then.

A. He went into Dr. Northcote's room; I did not. Dr. Northcote told me to go down to see about his dinner. I went down and ordered his dinner into the parlour, and then I went to get money from the Procurator, which the President had told me to do.

Lord Chief-Justice Cockburn: You ordered the dinner into the dining-room?

A. Yes; not the public refectory. There are two or three dining-rooms.

Q. He was to dine alone, was he?

A. He was to dine alone.

Q. It was a dining-room?

A. Yes.

Mr. Harcourt: After that, what did you do?

A. After that the President ordered me to take Fitzgerald and to get him his dinner. I went up to David Fitzgerald's room with him, and locked the door,—this being somewhere about between half-past one and a quarter to two. He came from the President's room; and then I went down again to see if his dinner was ready; but he previously called me as soon as I locked his room. He kicked at the door, and he asked me as a special favour to allow him to have his dinner in his own private room.

Lord Chief-Justice Cockburn: What did you lock him in for?

A. Because it has always been the custom.

Q. Did you intend that he should dine downstairs?

A. Yes.

Q. Then why lock him in to prevent him from dining downstairs?

A. It was merely while I went out to see if his dinner was getting ready.

Mr. V. Harcourt: The room you spoke of was the visitors' dining-room?

A. Yes.

Q. Was it your intention that he should have dined down there?

A. I had given orders to the servant to put his dinner in that room.

Q. In that room he would have had no communication with the other boys?

A. He would not; I should not have allowed it. There would have been nothing to prevent it. I do not believe that I should have locked that door.

Q. You say he asked you as a special favour to allow him to have his dinner in his own private room?

A. Yes; and I consented without any demur.

Lord Chief-Justice Cockburn: Did he give any reason?

A. He gave no reason whatever.

Mr. V. Harcourt: You say when he first went into his room you locked the door?

A. Yes.

Q. Why did you lock the door?

A. It has always been the custom, as long as I can remember, when a person is expelled, that all communication between him and the rest of the students should be forbidden.

Lord Chief-Justice Cockburn: Have you so many cases of expulsion, then?

A. In every case that I recollect in which a person has been sent away that has been the case.

Q. How many cases of expulsion have you had?

A. I can recollect one only for certain; but I am sure it was the universal custom.

Q. Universal custom depends upon the number of instances in which the particular thing has happened.

A. I can give an instance of it.

Q. How many have you known in your time?—within a dozen?

A. I should say it was within a dozen.

Q. Have there been a dozen expulsions?

A. I really do not know; I should say perhaps there have been,—I do not know.

Q. As far as your recollection goes, what do you put it at in your time,—the outside number? Surely you can say?

A. It is a long time to go over.

Mr. V. Harcourt: You say there have been several expulsions at Oscott. In your recollection, on those occasions have the boys, from the time of their expulsion to the period of their leaving the school, been always locked up?

A. Yes, if they are not sent away directly.

Lord Chief-Justice Cockburn: What do you mean by "directly"?—within what time?

A. Immediately—as soon as the President had seen them.

Q. They have always had time, I suppose, to pack their things up, and so on?

A. I have heard of a case occurring in which the boy has been sent away, and his luggage has been sent after him. I know a case of several of the senior students being confined to their rooms during the whole of the evening; and it was an extra punishment to lock the students in their rooms.

Q. When you have expelled a boy, there is an end of it, you know?

A. He was not actually out of the house.

Mr. V. Harcourt: At all events, rightly or wrongly, that had been the custom at Oscott?

A. It had been always.

Q. After you became Prefect of Discipline in Oscott, in your opinion would it have been injurious to the school if access had been allowed to young Fitzgerald and the other boys?

A. It did not strike me at the time; I simply acted on the custom.

Q. You simply acted because it had been the custom to do it?

A. Yes.

Q. If the door had been opened, of course the other boys during play could have entered the room?

A. They could have done so—several of them—not all of them.

Lord Chief-Justice Cockburn: It would depend on what orders you gave them?

A. If it were wet, for instance, they were at liberty to go to their rooms at two o'clock.

Mr. V. Harcourt: I understand you to say that what you acted upon was the custom of the school?

A. Yes.

Lord Chief-Justice Cockburn: You must show a reasonable ground under the circumstances of the case—you must show it to be a reasonable thing.

Mr. V. Harcourt: Young Fitzgerald's dinner was brought to him in his room?

A. It was brought to him in his room at his request.

Q. Did he ask to see any other boys there?

A. He asked me, about ten minutes after that—as soon as his dinner was brought up—if he might be allowed to see his brothers and his cousins. I consented, and went down to bring them up. I locked the door on him again. He then said, "Why do you lock me up? I have done nothing disgraceful." I said, "I must do so." I locked the door, and then went down to bring up his brothers and cousins. They came up—I should say it was about twenty minutes after two or a quarter-past two—they came into the room, and I came in with them; and after that the door was not locked.

Lord Chief-Justice Cockburn: Not after they went up.

A. No; I was there with them.

Q. You remained with them?

A. Yes.

Mr. V. Harcourt: That was the end of the locking-up, was it?

A. Yes, that was the end of the locking-up.

Q. How long was he locked up?

A. Not more than thirty-five minutes.

Lord Chief-Justice Cockburn: There is not much difference between locking the door and the gaoler being present. You would not have allowed him to go out?

A. Certainly, if it was a matter of necessity.

Q. But, supposing he had proposed to go out?

A. I should not have allowed it, certainly.

Mr. V. Harcourt: Did you see him about his packing-up his things?

A. I was with him while he was packing-up his things?

Q. Something has been said about your pushing him?

A. Only on one occasion I put my hands on his shoulders; I did not push him at all.

Q. What led to that?

A. He was taking his time, and was rather tedious over packing-up his things. I think he had been a long time over it, and I told him that if he did not be quick and pack-up his things, his things would be sent after him.

Lord Chief-Justice Cockburn: You put your hand on his shoulder, did you?

A. I did.

Mr. V. Harcourt: Did you use any roughness or violence towards him on that occasion?

A. None whatever.

Q. Mr. Fitzgerald has said that you pushed him, so that he nearly fell; is that so?

A. I have no recollection of having done any thing of the kind.

Q. Before he left he asked to see Dr. Northcote again?

A. He did.

Q. Did you take him to Dr. Northcote's room?

A. I did.

Q. You did not go with him, I think?

A. No.

Q. When he left Dr. Northcote, what did you do?

A. I took him downstairs, and he got into the cab.

Q. And he went away?

A. He went away.

Cross-examined by Mr. Coleridge.

Q. I observe in these rules there are a good many alterations,—some are scratched out, and some are put in in another handwriting: are they altered from time to time?

A. There are certain rules that I think have been altered according to circumstances. There have been alterations in the building.

Q. Just take almost any page; take *that* page which opens quite at a chance. You will see there are a couple of the rules there struck out and altered in pencil (*handing the rules to the Witness*).

A. Yes.

Q. First of all I will ask you, is it your duty, as Prefect of Discipline, to keep the rule-book, or what?

A. It is.

Q. It belongs to you?

A. It belongs to me.

Q. It belongs to the Prefect of Discipline at the college?

A. Yes.

Q. Do you make the alterations in them yourself?

A. I think I have; but this is one that is made by my predecessor.

Q. I see throughout there seems to be a great number of alterations and scratchings out?

A. Yes; they have been necessitated—

Q. I do not find any fault with it; but that is so as a fact?

A. Yes.

Q. Are those done by your predecessor or by you?

A. I think I have made one or two alterations; but most of them were made by my predecessor.

Q. Is that the only copy that there is of them? Is there no fairer copy?

A. I do not know of any.

Q. However, that is the one you keep?

A. Yes. We have been compiling another for some time.

Q. You say they are read out. Who reads them?

A. I do. The Prefect reads them in the presence of all the superiors and all the boys.

Q. When is that done?

A. At the beginning of every half-year.

Q. Do you mean that it is always done,—that you have always done it recently?

A. I did not do it this half-year, because we had not the book.

Q. That is a very good reason for not doing it. But before that was it done?

A. I have done it for two half-years.

Q. Were you present when Mr. Martin read them over?

A. Yes; on every occasion.

Q. Did he always read them?

A. He always read them when he was Prefect.

Q. Did he not omit for some time to read them?

A. I do not remember.

Q. Will you undertake to say that you have a distinct impression that he did read them?

A. Sometimes he would not read them when there were very few new boys, and most of those in the house knew the rules.

Q. They did, as we do in court sometimes, take them as read, perhaps?

A. Very likely.

Q. You knew, I suppose, that David Fitzgerald was there in the house for a special and particular and limited purpose?

A. I heard so afterwards. I thought, when he came, that he was just the same as the others. In fact, I understood that he was the same as the others.

Q. You were not Prefect of Discipline at that time?

A. When he returned after the vacation?

Q. Yes; between September and Christmas?

A. No, I was not.

Q. Between September and Christmas 1864 Mr. Martin was Prefect?

A. Yes.

Q. That was when his course was over, and when he came back for the purpose of reading for matriculation.

A. I had nothing to do with his studies.

Q. When you found him in this position in January 1865, you assumed that he was there as he had been before?

A. That he was there exactly under the same circumstances.

Q. That you assumed from seeing him there?

A. Yes.

Q. And from nothing else?

A. Nothing else.

Lord Chief-Justice Cockburn: You assumed that he was subject to the ordinary rules?

A. Just so.

Mr. Coleridge: As to the exalted people who go by the name of Philosophers, have they a set of rules for themselves?

A. Yes.

Q. Are these read out?

A. Generally at the beginning of each academical year.

Q. When does the academical year begin?

A. After Midsummer.

Q. One reading does for the Philosophers for the year?

A. Yes; that does for the class of Philosophers.

Q. You say that Mr. Fitzgerald disputed with you as to whether you could take away his privileges, and whether that was not a matter reserved for the President?

A. He did.

Q. And, as I understand you, he had, after you had taken them away, put his name down at the head of a party which assumed that he had still a right to continue his privileges?

A. It was after he had done it that he noticed that.

Q. That was not my question. He put the party down as any other Philosopher would have done who was going out with a party, and who had a right to do so?

A. Yes; I suppose so.

Q. Can there be any other interpretation put upon it? because if there can, put it.

A. I do not think there can.

Q. That being the only interpretation possible, he had given you notice by that, as far as he could, that he meant to act in defiance of your taking away his privileges?

A. Yes.

Q. There was nothing underhand in it?

A. He put the party in my room.

Q. With his own name at the head of it?

A. Yes.

Q. You say you thought he might possibly be at the Swan?

A. Yes.

Q. Had they been playing bagatelle?

A. Some of them had.

Q. You found the bagatelle-table open, as if the balls had been knocked about?

A. One of them was playing at the time I went in.

Q. I suppose no more than one could play at once?

A. It requires two for a game.

Q. But only one person can knock the balls about at the same time?

A. I suppose so.

Q. You found some of them playing?

A. Yes.

Q. Pray, have you ever played bagatelle?

A. I have not played at that place; I have played in the college.

Q. Never in old days—the days of your youth?

A. Never.

Q. You have never dropped into the Swan?

A. I did not say so. I said I never played at bagatelle.

Q. O, I beg your pardon. Then you have dropped into the Swan?

A. When I was a Philosopher I sometimes did as Philosophers did.

Q. We know that Plato was very fond of a drop of the best he could get—we will not say beer—but still he got something which he drank; was that your case?

A. Circumstances were different in those days.

Q. You got the best you could?

A. I suppose so.

Q. And I suppose so too; and you would have been uncommonly surprised if you had been told that you had done something which was the worst possible offence you could be guilty of?

A. On the contrary.

Q. You hardly sinned against the light even at that time, I suppose?

A. I do not know: I did not go there frequently; it was not an ordinary thing.

Q. However, on the subject of this beer; pray, has it a good reputation—the Swan—for beer?

A. I am sure I do not know.

Q. Where was the cover of the bagatelle-board?

A. It was over David Fitzgerald.

Q. The cover of the bagatelle-board was against the place where the fire might have been, and instead of the fire there was David Fitzgerald?

A. Yes.

Q. And then you dragged him out; at least, I will not say that you dragged him out, but you evoked him, and he came?

A. Yes.

Q. Was he in company, on that occasion, with any of the (might I call them) Bunkers?

A. I think he was.

Q. All but himself?

A. Yes.

Q. At all events he did not mind going and taking a drop of beer with them at the Swan?

A. He was there with them.

Q. He was there with three Bunkers. My learned friend says I am wrong. Am I right or wrong?

A. He was there with them.

Q. I thought I was right. I suppose you, after this, looked after him to see how he got on, and attended to him?

A. Not particularly.

Q. Did you see who he associated with?

A. I did not.

Q. Did you never observe who his friends were?

A. He was confined to the bounds after this.

Q. But I suppose he might have friends in bounds?

A. Yes, I think he had.

Q. Do you know that three of his intimate friends were * * *, * * *, and * * *?

A. They were not his intimate friends.

Q. Were they friends?

A. They were not friends.

Q. Did he associate with them?

A. Very seldom.

Q. That you saw?

A. That I saw.

Q. But you did see him with them?

A. I do not remember; he generally went about by himself.

Q. Solitary?

A. On almost every occasion he was by himself.

Q. When he was not by himself, was he either with * * *, * * *, or * * *?

A. He was obliged to be, because they were the only Church students in the class. I do not remember whether there were any other lay students in the class.

Q. Do you mean to say that you do not know perfectly well that * * *, * * *, and * * *, were friends of David Fitzgerald's?

A. I can say that they were not friends of his.

Q. Did he not associate with them constantly?

A. He did not.

Lord Chief-Justice Cockburn: Were these the three at the public-house?

A. Yes; but he did not go out in company with three of them.

Q. He went out in company with one?

A. He went out with one, and joined the others.

Mr. Coleridge: Were the three students that he was with, * * *, * * *, and * * *?

A. No; one name was * * *.

Q. Put it right for me, if you please.

A. * * *, * * *, and * * *.

Q. I thought * * * was a Divine?

A. There were two * * *—one a Philosopher, and one a Divine.

Q. Then he was there with these three, was he?

A. He was.

Q. But you say he was not intimate with them?

A. He was far from intimate with them.

Q. Who was the one he had gone out with?

A. * * *.

Q. Was he a Church student?

A. He was.

Q. Was he intimate with him?

A. He was not.

Q. He merely chose him for this occasion.

A. I do not know what his motive was. I suppose he chose him for this occasion because he could find no other.

Q. That is what you really suppose, is it?

A. Yes.

Q. You mean that?

A. Yes.

Q. Now we understand you. Where do you suppose he found the other two?

A. I believe he found them at the Swan.

Q. Did they come home, and was it after that you took away his privileges?

A. I reported the matter to the President.

Q. We had not heard of this matter about the housekeeper's room before.

Lord Chief-Justice Cockburn: What was done with the other students?

A. They were subjected to the same punishment.

Mr. Coleridge: This is the first I heard about the housekeeper's room. You say he was found in the housekeeper's room; was that where the wine is given out?

A. It is.

Q. Had the Fitzgeralds wine to have?

A. I do not know whether they had or not.

Q. Boys have wine, some of them, do they not?

A. Yes.

Q. And if they have wine, it is in the housekeeper's room that they get it, is it not?

A. Yes.

Q. And they get it at what is called "beer-time"?

A. They do.

Q. Was he there at beer-time?

A. No; it was not beer-time.

Q. What was he doing there?

A. He was sitting in the chair; there was no one else in the room.

Q. Was the housekeeper not there?

A. No.

Q. What time in the day was it?

A. I am not sure whether it was immediately before beer-time, or shortly after.

Q. Then it was not beer-time, but it was very shortly before or shortly after?

A. I think it was after.

Q. If he was going there to get his wine, would that have been a mortal sin or not?

A. No sin at all.

Q. I mean against school discipline?

A. It would have been a very venial sin.

Q. But it is mentioned here as a thing you had to overlook. If he wanted his wine, where could he get it but in the housekeeper's room?

A. He must get permission.

Q. Who had to give permission to him?

A. I was to give permission to him.

Q. Had the other Fitzgeralds wine?

A. I suppose what one had the others had.

Q. Had they, or not?

A. I really do not know.

Q. Will you undertake to say they had not?

A. I will not.

Q. Will you undertake to say that he was not there, like any one else, getting his wine?

A. He was not getting his wine.

Q. Will you undertake to say that he was not there for the purpose of getting his wine?

A. I will not.

Q. Would that have been any offence?

A. He should have asked my permission first.

Lord Chief-Justice Cockburn: As I understand you, the place to get it is the housekeeper's room?

A. Yes.

Q. Had they to ask leave every time?

A. Yes, every day.

Mr. Coleridge: There is not a general permit?

A. No, there is not.

Q. I think you said you would overlook that?

A. I overlooked it.

Q. But you mentioned it now?

A. I mentioned it now.

Q. To do his general character a service?

Mr. Karslake: Do not make those observations, Mr. Coleridge.

Mr. Coleridge: Now as to the pistol. You heard the pistol go off, I suppose; is that it?

A. I did.

Q. Two or three times?

A. I did.

Q. And you came up when the pistol had just gone off?

A. Yes; it had gone off.

Q. Perhaps there was a blue smoke in the air?

A. I saw the smoke.

Q. It was not a very big pistol?

A. It has been produced.

Q. It was manifest to every body that there had been a pistol shot off?

A. Yes.

Q. And it was hopeless to disguise the fact?

A. Yes.

Q. And at that spot?

A. Yes; at that time.

Q. There was the smoke, as you tell me?

A. Yes.

Q. When you asked him for the pistol, he said it was his pistol?

A. He said it was his pistol.

Q. When he told you that he did not know where it was, were you misled by it; I mean when he denied that he had it?

A. I was not led to that at all;* he told me he did not know where it was.

Q. Now did you so understand him, for a moment, that he wished to deceive you?

A. I thought that he intended to deceive me most certainly.

Q. Did you see him throw it away?

A. I did not.

Q. Did he not tell you that he had thrown it somewhere in the hedge?

A. That was some time afterwards.

Q. After you called him a liar?

A. After I told him it was a lie.

Q. Had you ever heard him shoot a pistol before?

A. I do not remember to have heard it before.

Q. Would that be a thing permitted or not?

A. Certainly not.

Q. You say he came to you that night, and told you that he

* Mr. Stone did not hear this question correctly.

had been getting on so badly that it was useless to defend himself with his superiors?

A. That it was useless for him to say much in excuse of himself; or some words to that effect.

Q. And, as you say, you then said you were out of temper; and you said you were sorry for it, like a gentleman; and therefore I will say nothing more about it. You were angry with him, and you said that which afterwards you regretted?

A. I did.

Q. Did he say, at that time, that he had gone out of bounds, and had done this on purpose to see whether you had or had not the right?

A. He did.

Q. You say he was up at night. You knew he was then reading, and reading hard, for his matriculation, did you not?

A. He was not reading when I found him; he was writing a letter.

Q. You do not answer my question. You knew that he was reading, and reading hard, for his matriculation, did you not?

A. His matriculation was over.

Q. For his B.A. degree then?

A. Yes; I was aware of that.

Q. Is it, according to your notion, so very immoral a thing for a boy who is reading hard to sit up reading till twelve o'clock?

A. It is not immoral at all.

Q. Is it an offence for which he was to be visited with punishment, if you found him up at half-past eleven at night?

A. Yes; the rule is very strict.

Q. I suppose that your boys who are working hard—if they are like other boys—do, in fact, sit up late a good deal at night, when they have got separate rooms?

A. No; they do not sit up after ten.

Q. Well, there is some magic in your school, I suppose. Do you mean when the examinations were coming on at Oscott, when you were a boy there, you were not aware of the fact that the boys sat up late at night?

A. They may have sat up once or twice; but the Prefect has very soon been down on them.

Q. That is, if he found them out?

A. The Prefect goes round to the rooms every night at ten o'clock to see if they are in bed.

Q. But you can light a candle after that, I suppose. But, however, I daresay you do not do those things at Oscott. Now as to the great key case. As I understand, the key, it had got sticky things upon it; he made no disguise about it, that there had been a copy taken of it, did he?

A. He did not say any thing about it.

Q. He gave you back the key?

A. Yes; he gave me back the key.

Q. And when you asked him about it, he told you?

A. Yes; when I asked him about it, he told me.

Q. Have you got the "rubbing"?

A. I have not. I kept it for a few weeks afterwards; but, when looking over some things, I said, "This will never be needed again;" and I threw it into the fire.

Q. The wax impression?

A. Yes, and the paper.

Q. Well, that is gone, and we cannot have it. You say that the next thing that alarmed you—or which you found against him—was the list. When did you last see that list of the nobility?

A. I think, this last Christmas.

Q. It is a good while since this action was brought: the action nearly came on this last Christmas, you know?

A. Yes.

Q. You saw it then?

A. Yes; I saw it then.

Q. You did not yourself see the student; you trusted to the narration of the Divine?

A. I think I asked him the name before.

Q. You did not see him?

A. I think I saw him the next morning.

Q. Before you saw Dr. Northcote?

A. I forget whether it was before or after; I think it was before.

Q. The boy was not there himself—I mean Fitzgerald?

A. He was not there.

Q. What time did you go?

A. I think it was just as they were going in to night-prayers; I went straight from my room when the Divine left me.

Q. They were just going to night-prayers?

A. Yes.

Q. Did you go to night-prayers yourself, or what?

A. I went in afterwards.

Q. You did what you wanted, and then you went in afterwards?

A. I did.

Q. How long were you there?

A. Not more than three minutes.

Q. You saw enough to satisfy you in that time?

A. I saw the list of names; that is all.

Q. Did you see that about Governor Moody?

A. I will not be sure, but I think I did: I thought it had reference to the boy.

Q. And the "magnanimous sentiments"?

A. I did not understand for some time afterwards what that meant.

Q. But you thought that serious?

A. No; my first impression was—I could not understand it at all—I thought it was a boy who had been admitted into the society.

Q. The "magnanimous sentiments"?

A. When I heard it explained by the person himself, then I saw that it was a joke, and that there was nothing serious about it.

Q. It did not throw a shadow of doubt upon the seriousness of the whole thing, to your mind?

A. It did not, to my mind.

Q. You were sent to get the book from him by Dr. Northcote, I think.

A. Yes.

Q. Was it necessary to have all this long conversation with him before you got the book?

A. It was not a very long conversation; I think the whole thing did not take two minutes.

Q. I mean about his having "done for himself," and so on?

A. It did not take longer than two minutes.

Q. You positively aver that you did *not* use any force?

A. I used no force further than my taking it out of his pocket.

Q. Did he resist?

A. He did not.

Q. You were aware of the correspondence between Mr. Justice Fitzgerald and Dr. Northcote, were you not?

A. Yes.

Q. And you knew of the fact that the Judge had taken away his sons, and was waiting to make inquiries?

A. Yes.

Q. And I have no doubt you supplied Dr. Northcote with information upon the subject of his letter?

A. Dr. Northcote wrote the letter, and then asked me if it was correct.

Q. Did you see the Judge's letter?

A. Dr. Northcote read it to me.

Q. Then you heard this, I suppose: "In addition, I think I am not unreasonable in asking you whether it was with your sanction that Mr. Stone, the prefect, took from David's person, by superior force, a note-book, containing some papers;" and so forth. And then the answer of Dr. Northcote, which you say was submitted to you, is: "But, upon hearing of its contents, I desired the Prefect to ask David for it; and if he refused to give it up, to take it from him, and to bring it to me; and this was done in accordance with the practice of this, and, I suppose, every other society, in proceeding against those who conspire against its rights;" and so on. Were you aware at that time that David Fitzgerald represented it had been taken from him by main force, or superior force? you knew that that was what Mr. Fitzgerald said?

A. I do not know whether I did not tell him.

Q. Will you say you did tell him?

A. I will not say that I did; I only told him, "Here is the book." I do not think I made any observation about it.

Q. Here is the letter of the Judge, which was read to you for the purpose of being answered.

A. He authorised me to use superior force, if necessary.

Q. Did you?

A. I did not.

Q. But here you are accused of doing it; the Judge said that that had been done?

A. "Superior force" I might understand as moral force.

Q. Why did you not deny that there had been any superior force?

A. "Superior force" might include moral force.

Mr. V. Harcourt: Vis major.

Mr. Karslake: He means that he did not use any actual physical force.

Mr. Coleridge: Do you really suppose that he meant that by the moral energy of your looks you extracted it?

A. I will not say that I did, and I will not say that I did not.

Q. What time was it that young Mr. Fitzgerald left Dr. Northcote's presence to be locked up in his room; was it about a quarter-past one?

A. It was a quarter-past one when he first went into his room; I think that was when he first went into the President's room.

Q. How long was he there?

A. I should say a quarter of an hour, or a little more; he came out at half-past one.

Q. Did his brothers and cousins come to him at half-past one?

A. They came to him about ten minutes to two, I think.

Q. How long did they stay?

A. I should say they remained in his room about ten minutes or a quarter of an hour.

Q. And then he was got rid of about three?

A. About three o'clock.

Q. All that time he was locked up?

A. No.

Q. Or you were present?

A. He was only actually locked up a little over half an hour.

Q. And you were present, preventing him going out, the rest of the time?

A. Yes.

Q. He was locked up by superior force for half an hour, and by moral force for the rest. Now I see how it stands. I should really like just to pursue that matter about the expulsions and the custom. Is there a custom as to expulsion at Oscott?

A. If a boy is not fit to remain there, he is expelled.

Q. Is there a well-ascertained *cursus expulsionis* at Oscott?

A. I never heard of one.

Q. You never heard of any?

A. No.

Q. Tradition would do as well?

A. I never heard of any.

Q. You only yourself recollect one?

A. I only recollect one.

Q. And you are not sure about any more?

A. I am morally certain about that.

Q. Then I cannot follow that.

A. I am sure that it was done.

Re-examined by Mr. Karslake.

Q. You say by tradition you have known of it. Have there been cases where boys have been sent away immediately?

A. Yes.

Q. In this particular case a fly or a post-chaise had to be brought in order that Mr. Fitzgerald might go to Birmingham to catch the train, I believe?

A. Yes.

Q. And as soon as the fly did come, and he had prepared his portmanteau, did he go?

A. He went.

Q. I think he told us the fly had to be brought from Erdington?

A. Yes, from Erdington.

Q. You have been asked about Governor Moody. Did you know a boy in the school who had that nickname?

A. I thought that was his name; I never heard his nickname till that time.

Q. You knew that there was a boy called Moody, and that he had a father who was also a master?

A. Yes.

Q. I think you told us fairly that Fitzgerald, when you asked him for the book, did object to give it to you, and refused to let you have it, and that you did take it from him against his consent?

A. Yes.

Q. And, rightly or wrongly, you call that superior force?

A. Yes.

Q. I do not want to mention the name of the student who had told you things, but you say you know the name of the student who had stated this to the Divine, and I ask you this: Did you believe that statement to be true?

A. Yes, I did.

Q. Did you know the man who had made that statement?

A. Yes.

Q. And you knew his character?

A. Yes; he gave the Divine permission to use his name.

Q. Some fun has been made about sitting up late at night, and whether you did so or not?

Mr. Coleridge: I did not make any fun about it. It was a serious thing.

Mr. Karslake: Was it the duty of the Prefect to go round night after night to see that the boys were in bed?

A. Yes, it was.

Q. And, as far as you know, where the Prefect had forbidden the boys to do so, did they go on doing it in defiance of the rules?

A. I cannot say. They would have been punished if it had been found out.

Q. They were liable to punishment if they did so?

A. Every time.

Q. You have been asked about the pistol—I suppose there is no written rule against fire-arms in the college?

A. There is no written rule.

Q. I suppose that rests on tradition?

A. Yes.

Q. You do not know of any rule?

A. No; and there are no rules against a great many other things.

Q. Did you know of its being the practice?

Mr. Coleridge: I shall not say that shooting a pistol was within the rules of Oscott College.

Mr. Karslake: You have been asked about the public-house. At the time that he was in the public-house he was actually under orders to remain within bounds?

A. He was.

Q. Just let me ask you this with reference to a question which has been put to you as to his sending in his name to you. It is one of the rules, is it not, applicable to the Philosophers and to the higher classes only of the school—the members of the philosophy class are allowed to go out in parties of three?

A. Yes.

Lord Chief-Justice Cockburn: We have got this two or three times over. They can only go out in parties of three, and they must hand in a list before they can go.

Mr. Karslake: It has been suggested that he was contesting the rules on that occasion, and I was going to ask whether it was one of the rules.

Lord Chief-Justice Cockburn: He was treating himself as though he were not in the position of having had the Philosophers' privileges taken away.

Mr. Karslake: If it is admitted that he is a Philosopher, and that he is under the Philosophers' rules, well and good.

Q. Did he give you any notice at all that in going out in that way he was testing your authority?

A. No.

Q. Did he say any thing at all about it until after the pistol affair?

A. No.

Q. At that time, as we understand, he was under Dr. Northcote's punishment, and not yours?

A. Yes.

Q. At the time you found him in the housekeeper's room what did you say to him?

A. I told him to go to his bounds.

Q. Did he say at the time that he had come to get his wine?

A. He did not.

Q. He made no such excuse?

A. No.

Q. Just let me look at these rules. You talk about there having been alterations made from time to time. Are there many of these rules which apply to parts of the house to which boys may go and may not go?

A. Yes.

Q. And since these rules have been made are there parts of the house that have been altered?

A. Yes.

Q. And are many of the alterations in the rules made for the purpose of meeting that?

A. Yes.

Q. Now as to these Philosophers' rules, that I shall have occasion to have read, were they all in existence at the time he was there?

A. I think they were.

Q. Just look at them.

A. (*after looking at them*) Yes.

Q. I believe the Philosophers are bound by the rules and regulations that affect other students in the house except where the rules are stated not to apply?

A. Yes; all these rules were in existence with the exception of the last, about the academical cap and gown.

Q. What is that rule?

A. They used to be required to go out with their caps and gowns; but the academical dress was abolished, and the rule was altered.

Q. But the other rules remained in force?

A. Yes; there was one other rule that was not strictly enforced—it was against the rules, but it was not strictly enforced —and that is entering the Serpentine Walk.

Q. Were they allowed to do so, or not allowed to do so?

A. It was tolerated.

Mr. Coleridge: The written word was one way, and the tradition the other.

Mr. Karslake: You say you became Prefect in January. When Fitzgerald came back, had you any orders from the President to alter your course as regarded him, or to do any thing different with him than the rest of the Philosophers or students?

A. Not the least.

Lord Chief-Justice Cockburn: Throughout the time that you were Prefect when young David Fitzgerald was there, did he ever arrogate to himself the right to be exempt from any of the rules applicable to the philosophy class?

A. On no single occasion.

Q. He never questioned your authority?

A. No.

Q. The only time he questioned your authority was so far as it extended to taking away the privileges of the Philosophers?

A. Yes.

Q. On no other occasion did he assert that he was exempt from the obligation to submit to the ordinary rules?

A. He never asserted it.

Mr. V. Harcourt: Now, my Lord, I am going to read some of the rules: my friend Mr. Karslake wishes them to be read. They are the rules in reference to parties: "1. In all parties which leave the bounds each student is required to keep in advance, within sight and call of the master. 2. No student on a party is allowed to purchase or procure any article whatever. 3. No student or party is allowed to enter any town, village, or house, without the permission of the President. 4. No party is allowed to leave the bounds for any other object than that for which special leave is given. 5. Every student is required to go out with a party once a week unless excused by the Prefect."

Mr. Coleridge: There is a question which Mr. Justice Fitzgerald wishes me to ask him: it is as to the terms of his letter. Mr. David Fitzgerald only mentioned that he had offered to show the letter to Dr. Northcote, which he would not read. The terms of that letter the Judge is very anxious that I should ask him about. The learned Judge says that he had not the least idea that there was any thing serious, or he should have answered it. It is that passage in the letter about the A. B. C. Club.

Mr. Karslake: O no, certainly not.

Mr. Coleridge: He did not know in the least what it was that was meant.

Mr. Karslake: I do not in the least degree impute that he did.

Mr. Coleridge: Then my learned friend has put in the letter.

Mr. Karslake: No; you put it in.

Mr. Coleridge: I have put in a letter of Dr. Northcote's to the Judge of the 12th of December; and I desire to put in a letter to which that was an answer, of the 11th of December:

"DEAR DR. NORTHCOTE,—I have to thank you for yours of the 7th. My intention at present is to meet David in London, on the 7th prox. I can remain with him until the evening of the 12th, and I'll have no fear of leaving him alone at Ford's Hotel for the remainder of the time. A week's vacation then, another at Easter, would be, I think, sufficient. As to the other two boys, I leave it to themselves to determine whether they will travel on the night of the 22d, or by day on the 23d; and I have no doubt what their decision will be. My reason for suggesting that David should remain at St. Mary's during the Christmas vacation was, that he might have the benefit of that period for the active preparation for the entrance examination, as I infer from his letters that he has yet much to do to afford him a fair chance of honours; he would do nothing if at home. In relation to the future. You commanded me in September last to suspend my determination about David's future, *i. e.* as to his entering University College immediately after his matriculation at the University. I obeyed. I now transmit you a copy of the Calendar of University College; I am informed that the Professors are generally very superior teachers, and that the Professor of Mathematics stands A 1. The distinction in favour of University College is, that the Professors not only afford the students an opportunity of learning, but teach them; and their teaching is of the first character. The question seems to be whether the advantages of St. Mary's will enable D. to compete on equal terms with his competitors from University College.—Praying you to excuse me, I remain yours faithfully, J. D. FITZGERALD."

And it is in answer to that letter that the letter of the 12th was written, which is before the Court.

Lord Chief-Justice Cockburn: I should like to see that letter of the 12th.—(*It is handed to his Lordship.*)

Mr. Karslake: Gentlemen of the Jury,—There are cases, very exceptional cases, in which an advocate may be justified, after strong expressions by the jury, formed upon consideration of all the facts of the case upon both sides, in declining to exercise the privilege to which he is entitled of withdrawing from a case. There are other cases, gentlemen, and this is one of them, in which a barrister would betray his client and disgrace himself in his profession if he took such a course. And, gentlemen, notwithstanding the expressions of opinion, somewhat unusual, by some of those gentlemen whom I address, I have to discharge my duty, and I shall do so to the best of my poor ability; and then you, under the direction of my Lord, will have to discharge your duty in the way in which you think it ought to be discharged.

Gentlemen, forgive me if I say, that although you may have formed, or some of you may have formed, opinions which have been pretty loudly expressed, you have done so before the whole case has been heard, and before probably you really knew the exact issues which you had to try. This case is put forward as if Dr. Northcote was answerable to a jury for the exercise of the discretion, the large discretion, which Mr. Justice Fitzgerald, in common with all the parents of the children who were at the college, had invested him with. This case has been put forward as if some cruel act of expulsion had been committed causelessly and unjustly, and that Dr. Northcote is to have his judgment reviewed by a jury as to the justice of his acts; acting, mind, upon the belief and the information which he had at the time he did the acts which are complained of. Gentlemen, I am quite sure of this, that if I can succeed in putting before you the real issue which you have to try, I have no fear that, if you will keep your minds open, you will do that which any man has a right to do, and which as a gentleman he may do properly, justly, and fairly, namely, to review the decision to which he has come, and to ask himself whether his first impressions are not incorrect; and that is what I ask some of the gentlemen of the jury who have expressed an opinion here to do.

Gentlemen, Mr. Justice Fitzgerald—because I do not view this as the boy's action—has asserted his right to bring this case before a jury, in order to have their decision and their verdict between himself and the defendants in this case. He appeals not merely to you to decide the simple issues raised upon this record between himself and Dr. Northcote and his co-defendant, but he appeals to society and to the public; and to them I also appeal for a justification of Dr. Northcote in what he has done. Gentlemen, some of you may in your youth have been at a large public school, or at all events a school in which it was necessary to keep up a considerable amount of discipline. To Oscott College young David Fitzgerald went, knowing that the rules were unusually strict; and when I read the letter to you which I shall read, you will see that his own father sent him back there in December 1864, at the suggestion of Dr. Northcote himself, in order that he might be under the strict rules of that college; and by being under the strict rules of that college he might, to some extent, get rid of a little of the pride and haughtiness which had been his failing up to the time when he had passed through his early degree and left the college in July 1864. Gentlemen, whoever went to that college knew perfectly well, or ought to have known, that he was liable to every rule that was made for the discipline of the students there. And when I hear my learned friend suggest, or indirectly suggest, that each of these different rules which were infringed by Mr. Fitzgerald at the time he was there was a trivial rule, and that the matter might have been looked over as one of no importance at all, I say this, gentlemen: He was never charged with having gone to a public-house for the purpose merely of getting a glass of beer; a thing which sounds ridiculous when placed in that way before a jury. He was never charged with simply going into the plantations for the purpose of shooting off a pistol. He was never charged with merely abstracting the key, and then omitting to return that key as speedily as he ought to have done. Nor was he charged with having sat up late at night, when he knew he had no right to do so; and the Prefect, in exercising his authority over him, only did that which, by Dr. Northcote's commands and orders, he was bound to do. The things upon which he was arraigned and charged were these: that, knowing those rules which were applicable to his case, he wilfully measured his strength against that of Dr. Northcote and the Prefect; and at last, after the most solemn warning, when he had pledged his word of honour that he would not again infringe the rules of the college, he advisedly did so, and for that fault he was detained until he could be sent away; and he was sent away at the earliest moment at which he could be sent away, and to return to his father, disgraced to the extent of this—and only to the extent of this—that, having so much pride and so much conceit in his composition, he would not obey the rules of the college in which he was; and that he chose wilfully to infringe those rules, after the most ample warning from Dr. Northcote as to what would be the consequence. He infringed them once too often, and received the punishment which Dr. Northcote had told him would be the necessary consequence of his next offence. Therefore, gentlemen, let me get rid of the sort of playful cross-examination which my learned friend administered. Is it really a mortal or a venial sin to go to a public-house? Venial. Is it a mortal or a venial sin to shoot off a pistol in a plantation? Venial again. But is it in Mr. David Fitzgerald's case, when you see the whole of the facts, a case in which Dr. Northcote, in justice to himself and to those who appointed him to Oscott, and to those who have boys there, could have overlooked that which he believed to exist, and which he still believes to have existed,—a combination or association, of which David Fitzgerald was the head, which was formed for the express purpose—and the ungenerous purpose—of annoying boys not in the same position of life as young Mr. David Fitzgerald, and rendering their lives at the college miserable so long as that association was continued? Now, gentlemen, that is why Mr. David Fitzgerald suffered as he did; and that is the act which is justified, on behalf of Dr. Northcote, in the face of you, and in the face of the world, who shall judge of his acts. Gentlemen, in July 1864 young Mr. David Fitzgerald left college, he having passed through the classes. The first matter which was suggested by my learned friend was this: that young Fitzgerald came back again upon exceptional terms, and that young Fitzgerald when he came back was entitled to an immense amount of respect, to which the other students in the college were not entitled. Gentlemen, I deny that. I show you his own acts. I submit he virtually remained in the same class as that in which he had been before,—namely, the highest class, that of the Philosophers. The boys in that class were those who had passed through the different classes, and had attained to the highest degree in the college, and were, more than any other boys, of course bound, so far as they could, to maintain discipline, and bound also to take care that they did not infringe the rules, when they knew there was no adequate punishment except that of being sent away.

Now, gentlemen, let me call your attention to what I think may be material for your consideration. Under what terms did David Fitzgerald come back? He came back upon the representation made by Dr. Northcote that there would be but a very small portion of the subject-matter for the honours which would be discussed or lectured upon in the class, and that for many reasons it would be expedient that he should have a private tutor. "In other words," says Dr. Northcote, "having a class of three candidates for honours, we shall do our best to prepare that class directly for the examination. I do not profess to be A 1 in every thing; but I think this direct preparation under Professors *B* will be more likely to attain the end than indirect preparation under Professors *A*,—to say nothing of what I should also set a high value on, the continuance for six months longer *in statu pupillari*, and under quiet Catholic discipline. In London University the discipline depends wholly on the individual. I am told a student may run into all kinds of excess." Gentlemen, therefore, in 1864, after young Fitzgerald had been back for one quarter, or term, or whatever they call it, from July down to September, when he was going up for the London University matriculation, he was going to return to Oscott for the purpose of resuming his studies, and continuing *in statu pupillari;* because his father believed that the discipline of that college would be beneficial to him, and that, having regard to all things, it would be better that he should go back to that college and be subject to its discipline, rather than go to a private tutor, or be at once launched in London at the London University. Those were the terms on which he came back again.

Gentlemen, I daresay that a great deal of that which young Fitzgerald did he did from exuberance of spirits, or even from that pride which is in his composition. But, gentlemen, Mr. Fitzgerald might have remembered that, having been taken back by Dr. Northcote on the terms that he was taken back, rather as a matter of favour than otherwise, it was all-important for him to do nothing which could loosen the discipline of the college, and do nothing which could either directly or indirectly be deemed to be an infringement of the rules. Let me call your attention to this. Supposing young David Fitzgerald, when he chose to go out into the plantation, where he had no right to go,—when he chose to go to Erdington, when he was under penance, or not allowed to go out of bounds,—had not had serious notice taken of those acts of insubordination by Dr. Northcote and those who were in the college, what right would Dr. Northcote have to punish another boy in an inferior position? He would be at once told by that boy, "There is a system of favouritism going on here. Fitzgerald comes back here, and his peccadilloes are overlooked; I come here, and find myself punished for precisely the same fault which in young Fitzgerald passes unnoticed." It was impossible that Dr. Northcote could do that; for if he did, his whole authority as head master of the school, I venture to say—after having been at a public school for nine years—would, under such circumstances, be gone. He could not in any one single instance allow a boy, however eminent for talent, or however high in position, to infringe the rules, and then overlook that infringement; and then the next day punish a boy for an infringement of the same rules, because that boy happens not to be in so high a position, or in a lower grade than the boy who is passed by unpunished.

Now, just let me look at the evidence which is now before you, as the history of what David Fitzgerald did. He returned in January 1865. You will have to judge of these matters; but there is one thing which I have to remind you of,—that Dr. Northcote and Mr. Stone, in acting as they do, have not the power of submitting the whole of their scholars to examination, or cross-examination, for the purpose of sifting the truth. They must act on the best of their judgment and to the best of their belief, exercising that judgment and belief on what they believe to be the facts brought before them. Now, just look at the first instance in which Fitzgerald did that which unquestionably he ought not to have done, because nobody can doubt that. Mr. Fitzgerald is in the position, as I say, of one of the Philosophers, having a right therefore to occupy a room by himself. He has no right to have a key of that room, or so to lock-up that room as that the Prefect of Discipline may not have an opportunity of seeing what is going on there. He has got a room, to which other boys may have access; but he chooses to infringe a rule of the college, to which I will call your attention. There is a master-key—not only of that room, but of other rooms, and some of the offices and the masters' rooms: it was lent by Mr. Stone for a special purpose to young Fitzgerald, and was given back to Mr. Stone, bearing an impression of wax upon it, or something which gave rise to some suspicion. He is taxed with it, and admits that something has been done to that key. I ask you, how can you have the least doubt in the world that it had been arranged by David Fitzgerald and his companions that it would be useful—as he himself says—or desirable, that there should be a duplicate of that made; by which any boy, at any time, may have access to the room of another boy, and to the masters' rooms, or if necessary, the offices, which by means of that key could be opened? That is what Mr. Stone tells you, when he taxed David Fitzgerald afterwards with it; and David Fitzgerald himself says it was done by way of a lark. Of course, that is the explanation which a boy always gives when he is found out doing something which is wrong. But when he is afterwards taxed with it, and it is pointed out to him that that key having been lent to him for a particular purpose, it was an improper act, to say the least of it, for him to have an impression of that key made, for the purpose of getting a duplicate constructed in Erdington, or elsewhere, he admitted to Mr. Stone that he had done an act which was not an honourable act; and he begged him to overlook that act, and not to mention it to the President. He knew perfectly well that if that act had been brought before Dr. Northcote, it was a matter which Dr. Northcote could not have failed to take serious notice of. And supposing, as I say, gentlemen, another boy a week afterwards had done the same thing, and had been brought before Dr. Northcote for the offence of having attempted to get a key made which should open different students' rooms, and some of the offices and masters' rooms in that establishment; and he had come before Dr. Northcote, and Dr. Northcote had degraded him for the remainder of the term, and inflicted some severe punishment upon him,—what would that boy have done? He would have turned round and said: "Why, Dr. Northcote, this is the grossest injustice that could possibly be. Young David Fitzgerald did the same thing only last week. It is reported to the Prefect of Discipline; he knows it; he passes it by, and David Fitzgerald goes unpunished; and now, because I do the same thing, you turn round upon me and give me the punishment which David Fitzgerald was subject to at the time he committed a like offence, but which you did not inflict upon him, either from his position, or because he was a favourite of yours." Gentlemen, I take leave to say, that in one of the public schools in this country there is nothing so dangerous as not taking every case which is brought before the head-master, and noticing the case at once; because, if you do not, you at once establish the precedent that one boy may go unpunished, and the next boy who is brought before the master for the same offence is to have a different punishment dealt out to him, or the offence is to be punished in some way in which the other boy has not been, and from which he has been allowed to escape altogether. Gentlemen, it was never mentioned to Dr. Northcote. It is said that Mr. Stone was a person who had been conspiring from first to last against David Fitzgerald. It was a little ungenerous, to say the least of it, to make that statement until the statement was proved. My learned friend knew that he would have another opportunity of making it. I ask, on what grounds was that statement made? Is there a suggestion that Mr. Stone has, from first to last, attempted to impose duties or burdens on this young man to which he was not properly subject? I say there is not the slightest foundation for it. I will take the first instance, in which Mr. Stone was perfectly justified and authorised, if he thought fit, in going to the President, and mentioning to him that which was beyond all doubt an infringement of the rules of the college. He did not then make that known to the President, on account of the promise which young David Fitzgerald made, that the thing should never again occur. That was passed by without any notice, upon an implied promise, perhaps, that it should not be noticed; and it never was noticed until Mr. Stone was released from that implied promise which had been given by him to David Fitzgerald, just before the occasion when this dismissal from the college took place.

Now, gentlemen, let us come to the next matter. The next matter that I have to refer to, and about which a laugh has been raised frequently in the course of this cause, because it suits my learned friend to take that view of it, is the occasion when young David Fitzgerald goes to Erdington and is found there contrary to the rules and regulations of the college. It is said it is not a very mortal offence to go to Erdington. Granted that it is not; but it is a perfectly well-known offence. Now supposing on that occasion young David Fitzgerald, who is said to have committed only a venial offence, were allowed to escape without any punishment being inflicted on him, could the other three boys who were with him have had any punishment inflicted on them? and if on a future occasion the boys had been found at Erdington, when punishment was about to have been inflicted upon them, they would have quoted this, and said they were only following the precedent which they would have said was established in the case of Fitzgerald. How could Dr. Northcote turn round and say, "I look upon the circumstances of your case as different, and I intend to punish you, although I did not punish David Fitzgerald and those who were found with him in the Erdington public-house"? Remember, that which was done to David Fitzgerald upon that occasion was not a punishment only for being in the public-house; it was a punishment for having acted contrary to the rules and discipline of the house, and in a spirit of insubordination, because at the time he did infringe a positive rule which he knew of as being among the rules of Oscott College; and that when he was under another rule which forbade him to go out of the bounds at all. Therefore he was doubly offending against the rules of the college. At the time he did so, the other boys who were with him might have done that, which I daresay many other Philosophers may have done. But in Fitzgerald's case it was a determination on his part, to use the expression of Dr. Northcote, "to measure his strength with the Prefect." He was at that time under the orders of the Prefect that he should not go beyond the bounds. He committed the double offence of going beyond the bounds and going into the Erdington public-house. That he knew he was doing wrong is proved beyond a question by my friend's cross-examination, which established beyond all doubt that he was hiding himself at the time he was in the public-house, and attempting to screen himself from the vigilance of the Prefect of Discipline, who was looking after him at the time. If he was merely testing the authority of the Prefect, which is the sort of suggestion which has been put forward, why did he not come forward boldly and say, "Here I am, although confined to bounds; I am here for the purpose of testing your authority: I will go back with you to the President and contest your authority"? He never suggested that the Prefect of Discipline had not authority over him, until it suited his purpose to do so by making a complaint against the Prefect of Discipline when the next instance of insubordination manifested itself. Before that time he had been told that it was against the rules, as he perfectly well knew it to be, remaining up until between eleven and twelve o'clock at night. He says, "Stone came in and blew me up because I was sitting up between eleven and twelve o'clock at night." Now, gentlemen, that sounds very harsh indeed: but it is not merely for his being up late at night; it is because he, being placed in a position of considerable importance—at all events very nearly, if not quite, the head boy at the college—had chosen to give a great deal of trouble to the Prefect of Discipline, who is empowered and authorised by the President of the college, who cannot himself control and look after all these boys,—it is because of his refusing to obey the Prefect, or because he is infringing the discipline of the college, that the offence is looked at as an offence of weight, and treated as an offence of weight.

Now I will go to the next occasion. In consequence of what was done at Erdington, David Fitzgerald was then under punishment; and therefore his offence being not merely going into the Erdington public-house, but having, at the time he went there, done so in defiance of a sentence which had been passed on him before confining him to bounds, he is brought before the President of the college, Dr. Northcote; and Dr. Northcote at that time, in lecturing him upon the impropriety of his conduct, confined him to bounds until Easter. Therefore, beyond all question, he had no right to be in the plantation at all. What do you find, only a day or two after this? Dr. Northcote's account is this: "I talked to him about the difficulty there was in treating with him, placed in the position in which he was." Why, he not only goes himself, but he induces another boy of the name of * * *, who beyond all doubt had no right to be, under any circumstances, in the plantation at all, for the purpose of doing that which every boy, even at private schools, knows is against the rules, namely, firing off a pistol, and amusing himself in that manner; he knows perfectly well that that is against every rule and regulation of the college to which he belongs. But, gentlemen, it does not stop there. Young David Fitzgerald gives his own account of the story; and according to his own account the insolence with which he treated the Prefect was almost unparalleled. He treated the Prefect as if he was his inferior in every respect. He told him he would not go; and because the Prefect told him to go faster, he replied that he would go his own pace. He threw away the pistol. He gave him, according to his own statement, a very haughty and insolent answer indeed, when the Prefect was only discharging his duty, and when he asked him where the pistol was. You have heard the statement which is made on the other side. Such was his conduct on that occasion that Mr. Stone said he would do that which, according to the rules of the college, he had no right to do, and which probably he never intended to do, although he threatened it. It was very easy for my learned friend to say that young David Fitzgerald stated that he had thrown away the pistol. The way in which those things are said makes all the difference. What Mr. Stone observed about him was this, not that he mentioned that he had possession of the pistol, but when he was asked where the pistol was, he said he did not know where it was. He might not literally have known where the pistol was at that moment, because he had thrown it into the hedge about four yards from where they were standing; and that is what Mr. Stone said he considered was a lie, or, at all events, an equivocation equal to a lie; and it was beyond all doubt deserving of that appellation, when you come to look at the circumstances under which that statement was made by David Fitzgerald. What does he do upon that? He sets at defiance Mr. Stone's authority. He goes to the college, and he goes to make a complaint against the Prefect to Dr. Northcote. Dr. Northcote hears both sides. He did not refuse to hear David Fitzgerald, as David Fitzgerald chooses to say. He pointed out to him at that time that it was his intolerable conceit, and his refusal to be bound by the rules and discipline of the college, which were bringing him into disgrace, and when he was there for a special purpose he ought to be taking particular care of what he did; that he was infringing the rules at the time when he was under punishment; and that his position in the college, if he went on in that way, was extremely precarious. Dr. Northcote pointed out to him, "You are now in this position, David: I have almost exhausted punishment upon you; and the next time you do infringe the rules of the college, I shall have nothing to do but to send you away from it." He had taken from him his right to read except at certain hours in his private room; he was degraded to the ranks; he could not undergo corporal punishment, because that was against the rules of the house; he had had every punishment inflicted upon him that it was in Dr. Northcote's power to inflict, and he was told at the time by Dr. Northcote of what would be the necessary consequence if he infringed the rules of the college again.

Now let me call your attention again, when the charge of hardship is made against Dr. Northcote, to that which is Dr. Northcote's excuse for not having given warning before he sent this boy away. On that occasion Dr. Northcote, when he sent for young David Fitzgerald, told him, "You have now committed so many breaches of discipline and offences against the rules, that it will be my duty to do that which I regret to do. I have never yet written, David, to your father except in terms of the highest approbation; I must now write to him and tell him how you are going on, because, unless I do so on this occasion, after having told you that the next breach of discipline will subject you to dismissal from the school, the consequence will be that your father will turn round on me, and say that, never having given him notice, or never having given him any warning, your dismissal will be a harsh act on my part." Now, gentlemen, how came Dr. Northcote to give up his intention on that occasion of writing to Mr. Justice Fitzgerald, and telling him what was going on in the college? Young David Fitzgerald said he was going to write to his father himself, or, at all events, he intimated that he should do so. He came back after prayers and begged and prayed Dr. Northcote not to write to the Judge to tell him of what his conduct had been, and what the consequences of future breaches of discipline or of the rules would be.

He promised him, on his honour as a gentleman, that he should never have occasion to find fault with him again. It was after that promise that Dr. Northcote said to him, "Now mind, David, you are placing me in a dangerous position, because I am trusting to your word of honour as a gentleman that you will not infringe the rules again; if you do infringe them again, I have already told you the punishment which it will be my duty to award to you. I am placing myself in this position: if that punishment is awarded to you, your father may think it cruel and harsh in my not having given him notice of your former faults which you have committed, and in allowing the world to think that this was the first offence which you ever committed against the rules of the college." Dr. Northcote, perhaps weakly at the time, but trusting to the honour and promise of young Fitzgerald, gave up his intention of writing to the Judge, and allowed the young man to stay there without any complaint being made of his conduct, on the solemn promise which he gave, that he should never be found infringing the discipline of the college again. You will remember, not only on that but on other occasions Mr. Stone had passed over faults as well as Dr. Northcote; and it was, as they believed, after punishment had been exhausted, that his honour as a gentleman might be trusted, that Dr. Northcote allowed him to stay, degraded as he was, until the end of the term, on the promise that he should never be found infringing the rules of the college again.

Now let me come to that which was done afterwards. You have heard from Dr. Northcote and Mr. Stone what the constitution of this college is: there are boys there who, like David Fitzgerald, probably consider themselves the aristocracy of Oscott. There are boys there who come for the purpose of pursuing their studies aided by the funds which are found by the Bishops, and who are sent there, as a matter of course, for the purpose of being educated as priests. Many of those boys, if not most of them, come from a preparatory school called Sedgely Park; and, as you hear, years ago the term "Bunkers" had been applied to those boys, and there had been petty annoyances to which they were subjected, and there was a feeling exhibited against them which made their position in that establishment any thing but an enviable one. I do not stop to discuss the question as to whether the college could or could not have been maintained with clerical students only, or whether it was necessary to have lay students there also. This I do say, that if young Fitzgerald could so far swallow the pride of the Fitzgeralds, as I think my learned friend called it,—"although he was a Fitzgerald," said my learned friend,—if he could so far swallow his pride that he could, with his father's consent, come and sojourn at that college for the purpose of pursuing his studies, he ought at least to have taken the rough with the smooth there, and to have allowed those who came to it supported with charitable funds to pursue their studies there without molestation or annoyance. He had been there for years; he knew what the character of these students was. He may have had friends among some of them; but one thing is manifest, that years ago this feeling against the so-called Bunkers was so manifest, that almost every person who had the interests of Oscott at heart had done his best for the purpose of crushing out the feeling which existed against the class of boys who were subjected to this annoyance, which, as a matter of course, made their lives miserable as long as it was allowed to be practised upon them. Now, gentlemen, was Dr. Northcote wrong in applying his best energies for the purpose of preventing that feeling getting into existence again? How could Dr. Northcote justify to the parents of those boys, or the patrons as they are called, granting permission to any other boys to treat them with slight or indignity, or practise annoyances, however petty, upon them? How could Dr. Northcote justify class being set against class in that establishment, and boys who were meeting daily in the playground, and in the study-rooms, to be setting themselves up against another class of boys whom they found in the same playground and study-rooms as themselves? It was one of those duties which Dr. Northcote had to discharge in the most conscientious manner; and he most carefully looked to see that there was no outbreak of that sort again, because if there was, it was his duty to put it down with a strong hand the first time he saw that spirit manifested. Now what happened? Several days before this pocket-book was found, Dr. Northcote and Mr. Stone—Mr. Stone being the person who is more particularly brought into communication with the boys and the masters of the college—he had found, on what he believed to be reliable information, that there was in existence an association which had for its object the revival of this spirit against the Church students in the college. He found that it had been so far organised that boys were actually suffering annoyance from it. He knew at Midsummer 1864 that the spirit had so completely died out, that Church students, old Oscotians, and others, who could meet in the playground or the cricket-ground, met there without the least disaffection or feeling one against another. He finds all of a sudden, after David Fitzgerald had returned in 1865, that it had manifested itself again, and that there were students who were complaining of the existence of this spirit, and who pointed out young David Fitzgerald as being the ringleader and originator of that association which it was suggested was being formed for the purpose of annoying these Church students. Further, Mr. Stone was informed, on perfectly reliable authority as he believes, that there had been this association formed, or at all events in the course of getting up, and that active measures had been taken, and that those measures had already borne some pernicious fruit; and he finds also that there is a belief in existence that David Fitzgerald has in a pocket-book various papers in his possession, and among them a list of those whom it was proposed should join this association, and a list of those against whom the association was going to take active operations—that is, whom they had made up their minds to annoy and insult. On Sunday the 12th of March this matter was unknown comparatively to Dr. Northcote; but the history of it had been given to Mr. Stone. Mr. Stone ascertained that there was this feeling in existence, and, according to the best of his belief, upon the information he had, that association was in existence and in active operation at the time. Now let me call your attention to that which he did. On his own behalf and on Dr. Northcote's behalf, although Dr. Northcote had no act or part in it at the time, I say I do fully justify in Dr. Northcote and Mr. Stone the taking of that pocket-book for the purpose of ascertaining whether it was true that there was any society in existence. Now let me call your attention to what the pocket-book discloses. The only answer which is given to the entries or information which this book contains seems to be that which young Fitzgerald himself has given. It seems curious that a young man, who was at that time about seventeen years of age, who was pursuing his studies at Oscott, who had his time so fully occupied that it is suggested that he might sit up till midnight, although he had to rise at half-past six in the morning, for the purpose of pursuing his studies, should have been occupying his time on any thing so trivial as merely jotting down on several pages of a pocket-book the history of an association which had no existence. I ask you to place yourselves, if you can, in the position of Dr. Northcote and Mr. Stone; and, having placed yourselves in the position in which they were, knowing what the effect would be which would be produced in this college by such an association carrying on its operations, ask yourselves whether you would not have come to the same conclusion that in the result Dr. Northcote did, when he was informed what was in this pocket-book, and had examined young David Fitzgerald, as he did, with reference to the entries which he found there. You have not seen this book yourselves, but it is necessary you should see it. I will just call your attention to some of the entries. You will find, "* * *, S. P.," Sedgely Park; "* * *, S. P.," Sedgely Park; "* * *, N. S. M." N. S. M. means National schoolmaster. This young David Fitzgerald said was all humbug, or merely for a lark. But he had taken care to ascertain the calling of the father or relative of this boy against whose name this N. S. M. is placed. Against the next name is again put "S. P." I will not mention the name. You will find that so the names go down until we come to "J." Somebody, "S. P." Then there is this mark against him, which has been explained "London Irish;" the lowest class of pariah apparently, according to Mr. Fitzgerald's view. Then come the names of two others, one described as "The Bell Inn, Stourbridge;" both of those having left in January 1865. Now those are the names. On the next page we find that young David Fitzgerald has taken the trouble of investigating this matter still further; because one of these gentlemen appears to have an uncle or brother who keeps a small grocery establishment on Wednesfield Heath, and another whose father is a general inspector of canal locks. Authority, "Honorary Secretary A. B. C." It is a fact beyond all dispute that there is a boy there who has an uncle or brother who keeps a grocery establishment at that place; and it is admitted that there is another boy whose father is an inspector of canal locks. What on earth was David Fitzgerald doing when he was at college, in taking the trouble to investigate the history of these boys and the occupation of their parents, if it was not for the purpose of carrying out those objects which it was believed at the time, beyond all question, he was carrying out? Then we go on; and we find in the next page that which I shall call your attention very closely to. What is it that appears upon the next page? "A. B. C." We then find, "Fitzgerald, 5." There were five Fitzgeralds in the house; that is beyond all dispute. "* * *, 1; * * *, 2; * * *, 2; * * *, 1; * * *, 1; * * *, 1; * * *, 1." That is the entry as originally made; but underneath that, and apparently written at a different time, and it is written in pencil, there is this, "Governor Moody elected for his magnanimous sentiments about Sedgely Park." Some remark was made against Sedgely Park by a master, which seems to have struck them as being quite in consonance with their views; and therefore this memorandum is made. Then there is the name of another person, and this entry: "N. B. Consult the Honorary Secretary about this 'gentleman'"—"gentleman" being in inverted commas. We all know what that means. Then after that there is a list of names with crosses against them, and there are other marks against others, which it is said by young David Fitzgerald have nothing at all to do with the A. B. C. Society. The next page is prepared to contain a list of the members of the A. B. C. Society, but that list of members did not find its way into the book. Then, in a further page, we have this, "We want all particulars about any of the undermentioned as to birth, parentage, qualification, and patrons." Now nobody could entertain a doubt on reading that book; which book, you will remember, was first seen by Mr. Stone, who conveyed the information, and who looked at it in consequence of what he had heard; he brought the information which he had acquired to the knowledge of the Vice-President on Sunday evening; the Vice-President mentioned it that evening non-officially to Dr. Northcote; and on the following morning Dr. Northcote called all the Superiors of the College together, and the information which was in existence with reference to this movement was brought before them; and it was not until they had determined upon a particular course of action that young David Fitzgerald was summoned, and told to bring his book with him. Now, gentlemen, you have the history. I am sure I do not think it signifies what occurred; but I fully admit that when David Fitzgerald was sent for by Mr. Stone, and told to bring his book with him, as he did, he positively refused to give up the book to Mr. Stone. Mr. Stone took it from him, and I venture to justify his taking it from him by what is called in one of the letters "superior force." Mr. Stone says, "he did not actually resist, but I took it from him after he had told me in so many words that I should not have it." I have not the least doubt in the world that I should have ventured to justify that act if it had been asserted that superior force, in the sense in which it was used by my learned friend, had been expended upon young David Fitzgerald. I say, as a master of that school, as Prefect of Discipline, that Mr. Stone was perfectly justified in taking it from him by force if he should have found it necessary so to do. But, however, it was taken from him. He is then summoned before Dr. Northcote. When he is summoned before Dr. Northcote, he tells him that the whole of this is humbug. Gentlemen, do not suppose that I for a moment think that Mr. Justice Fitzgerald, when he gave implicit confidence to his son, and put implicit faith in the statements which he made to him, knew of the existence of the Anti-Bunker Society as a dangerous society to some of the classes in that college. But when young David Fitzgerald comes down before Dr. Northcote, and tries to represent at first that which he has represented here—namely, that it was all humbug, and only done for a lark—there was a very important statement which he made afterwards. He admits that a portion of this book was written at a time when he was in a splenetic humour, or something of that sort; and Dr. Northcote tells you that on inquiring more closely into it, he had said it was all humbug, or only done for a lark; and after he had gone away to his room for the purpose of fetching a letter from his father, which he would not allow him to read, I think, from the position in which Dr. Northcote was towards him, he need not be trying to exculpate himself if Dr. Northcote had read the whole of the letter from beginning to end. Whatever secrets it might have contained were perfectly safe with him; but he points to one particular passage, and says, "This is my exculpation." This is the passage, "Pray, what is the subscription to the A. B. C.?" Is that sufficient to satisfy Dr. Northcote that the whole thing was humbug from beginning to end? He says, "That is what I vouch;" and when he is first called upon to give an answer to this, he admits afterwards that he has done it in a fit of spleen; he goes into the history of the different boys whose names you will find in his own book—that his brothers John and James have nothing to do with it; and you will find Dr. Northcote's own pencil-marks against John and James, showing that that explanation was given at the time. You will find further that as regards * * * 2 is put down. He explained to him that there was only one of them who was a member of the A. B. C. Club, and that the other had nothing to do with it; and with regard to * * *, who is mentioned afterwards, and against whom the figure 1 is put, he says he refused to give in his adhesion or alliance, and therefore he too had nothing to do with it. That is the statement that is made to Dr. Northcote. After young David Fitzgerald had tried to explain the thing by saying, "This is all nonsense and humbug," he had been told, "You may do this in a fit of spleen, and think nothing of it, but remember that what may be a very good joke to you is death to the frogs;" meaning thereby that if this sort of association was to exist, if this sort of feeling was again to be fomented in the college, and manifested throughout the college, they might as well shut up the gates of the college as far as the clerical students were concerned, because it was impossible that the clerical students could live there under that system of annoyance which Dr. Northcote believed was again about to be revived against them. I do say, then, that if Dr. Northcote had not taken the strongest measures at once to crush out that spirit that was again rising up in the college, he would have failed most grossly in his duty towards those who appointed him to the supervision and the presidency of that college, and to the fathers and every one of those boys whose names are set down as being boys who were to be the objects of insult and annoyance at the hands of those who claim a superior position,

—namely, the Anti-Bunker Society, which Mr. Fitzgerald admits himself to be the originator of. The whole thing is investigated. Dr. Northcote takes every means that he thinks right, and which are at hand, for the purpose of ascertaining the extent of this. He examines young Fitzgerald most carefully upon the matter; he forms his opinion upon such materials as he has before him. But that with which he is charged is proved against him. He reminds him at that time of the promise that he had made before; he is told, "You know what must necessarily be the consequence." Young Fitzgerald had freely exculpated many of those boys whose names were mentioned from any complicity in this association. After the whole interview had taken place, Dr. Northcote had told him, "You will now go to your own room; you know what the consequences, as I called to your attention only a week or two ago, would be of again infringing the rules and the discipline of this house: I find you engaged now in doing that which is subversive of all discipline, and dangerous to the inmates of the house, and the consequence is that you must go at once, because you are no longer to be trusted among your former companions here."

Now I will just call your attention to what David Fitzgerald does. It is said that he was dismissed from that time; and I hear a sort of suggestion that at that time, having been dismissed, Dr. Northcote had no more power over him. Had he not, gentlemen? Was Dr. Northcote to let that young man do any thing he liked until he left the roof under which he had been? I say he was not removed from Dr. Northcote's care and supervision until he was actually sent from that roof to his father. So long as he was there, it was the duty of Dr. Northcote not only to protect him from the violence of the other boys in the house, but also to protect the other boys from him, and prevent his having any communication with them before he left. He is told to go to his room, and he again evinces that spirit of insubordination which he had evinced on so many other occasions; he leaves his room, after Dr. Northcote had expressly told him to remain there. The bell is rung for the purpose of summoning the boys in the house to hear the sentence, and the reasons for the sentence, which was about to be inflicted upon David Fitzgerald. He does not appear, and is not to be found in his room, although Mr. Stone goes for him. He is found standing at the door of Dr. Northcote's room, having come there for the purpose of meeting him; and it is upon that occasion, after all that had passed between them, that he is again told to go. "You must pack up your things, and be in readiness to leave this afternoon." It is next suggested that he should dine in the private room, or in the visitors' room; but at his own request, instead of dining there, he occupied his own room, and Mr. Stone saw his dinner taken up there. Then it is said that he was locked in, which is a gross indignity. How on earth, carrying out that which Dr. Northcote believed to be necessary—namely, the exclusion of young David Fitzgerald from the other boys—that was to be effected without some such plan as that being adopted, I do not know. What had he done before when he was told to keep to his room? He had refused to do so; he had left his room. What warrant was there that he would not do exactly the same thing again? No one could doubt that he would have done so, if he had been allowed. Therefore I say that Mr. Stone, in locking him up in his own room when he goes down for the purpose of giving orders, was merely locking him in for the purpose of preventing him leaving his room and having communication with the other boys, and also preventing the other boys from having communication with him. The earliest time at which he can go is about three o'clock, and a carriage is sent for for the purpose of taking him to the station. He is requested to pack up his things; but he packs up his things very slowly indeed, intimating to Mr. Stone that he will not obey his authority, and will not obey his orders, although Mr. Stone is only carrying out Dr. Northcote's instructions. At last, having been told that if he does not choose to pack up more quickly and to go, his things will be sent after him, the carriage waiting there to take him to the station at Birmingham, in order that he might get on the railway on his return to Ireland, he does pack up his things; and he has one further interview with Dr. Northcote after that time, and he leaves the house.

Now, gentlemen, that which is charged here is an assault on Sunday the 12th of March by Mr. Stone; two upon the 13th, when Mr. Stone saw him and took the pocket-book from him; and one other on the 13th, when Dr. Northcote ordered him to his room, and had him kept there. There are other matters, and I do not know that it may not be right to refer to them; but certainly it did strike me, having read the letter from Mr. Justice Fitzgerald, that this charge of assault was placed on the record, not for the purpose of determining the main question, if that be a question for the jury at all, but for the purpose of suggesting that in carrying out the object of Dr. Northcote the book was kept a little too long, or that something was done in excess of what was authorised; and therefore the verdict may be hung on that peg, if it cannot be hung on the main question which is to be decided on this occasion.

Gentlemen, it is said that there should have been a telegram sent. "Why did you not telegraph to me, Dr. Northcote?" I know of no charge in this case which was made before to-day about not telegraphing. We have been very far a-field in the charges which have been made. Charges have been made of having imprisoned him during the time that he was in the college, and taking the book from him during the time he was in the college. Dr. Northcote did not then send any telegram; but having sent off this young man by the evening train from Birmingham, by that same night's post Dr. Northcote wrote the letter which my learned friend would not read in his opening, and which would have given you a very different impression indeed at the outset of Dr. Northcote's conduct, if my learned friend had thought fit to read it, instead of allowing the whole of the examination of young Fitzgerald to be gone through before you were apprised of the contents of that letter. Now, gentlemen, I do not know whether, in addition to the charge which Mr. Coleridge made against him, that he was utterly unfit to deal with gentlemen in a school of this description, it is going to be said that Dr. Northcote advisedly abstained from sending any letter in order further to harrow up the Judge's feelings on finding that his son was sent away from this place. I do not trouble you with that. I appeal to every letter which my learned friend has read, and I ask you whether Dr. Northcote did not do that which he thought it necessary to do with the utmost pain and reluctance, and only because he had found that by his previous conduct he had rather encouraged young Fitzgerald to go on in that spirit of insubordination which he manifested, and to prevent his committing other acts of insubordination, and that it was because he had found that there was no hope of any amendment; and it was with the deepest regret that he sent him away from the college, without the slightest imputation, as was at one time suggested, that it was on account of any breaches of the rules of morality, or on account of any thing immoral in his conduct, but simply because young Fitzgerald, having attained high honours, had got so proud or so full of conceit, as Dr. Northcote himself says, that he measured his strength against the constituted authorities of the college. At last, having been warned of what would be the consequence of again infringing those rules which it was Dr. Northcote's duty to support, having infringed one of those regulations made for the discipline of the college,—one of those rules which although it was a traditional one, he knew to exist; one which, above all others, it was the duty of Dr. Northcote to take care was not infringed, namely, that rule which had been known perfectly well among all the boys, that, so far as the President and the Master of that college could do it, the position of those boys who had been admitted as accredited students should be considered equal to those who considered themselves richer and stronger than their humbler brethren, and who chose, because they were in that position, to treat them with indignity and scorn—now, gentlemen, that was the reason why Dr. Northcote took this course. Having said that, let me read you the letter which my learned friend would not read, and which was on the table of Mr. Justice Fitzgerald, I should think, a very short time after he found his son under his roof in Merrion Square. It is suggested, gentlemen, that a telegram ought to have been sent. Supposing a telegram had been sent, saying, "David Fitzgerald is expelled," do you think that would have been a kind course to have taken? It was impossible within the limits of a telegram to have explained fairly and justly to the Judge, or towards the heads and authorities of the college, what the reason was for David's going home. Gentlemen, let me call your attention to the letter. I think it was unnecessary, and I venture to say so in his presence, that Mr. Justice Fitzgerald should have taken the course which he has taken in bringing forward this case to exculpate his son. So far as we know now, he has passed through the

London University, and is reading for the profession of which I have the honour to be a member. I hope the youth will follow in the footsteps of his father, and that his talent will enable him to command a position such as his father holds in that profession. It is said there may be some imputation against his morality; and it is necessary, therefore, to bring this action on his behalf. Was there ever a suggestion in this letter, or elsewhere, that there had been any such accusation made against young David Fitzgerald? None whatever. The whole course of his being sent away is explained at length to his father. He might have been sent home without any explanation at all; but here is this letter. Therefore, to say that it may be suggested that there was something which had happened which was not explained, seems to me to be entirely in contradiction to that which was the real state of the case. Let me just read it, and you will then see how Mr. Justice Fitzgerald acts upon it. I can perfectly understand that he hears the boy's own account of what occurred. Every schoolmaster in the world well knows that there is nothing more dangerous than to place implicit confidence in a boy's account of what has happened when he is subject to punishment, because he would not be a human being if he did not make out as far as he could that he was not to blame, and that the master was unnecessarily harsh. Mr. Justice Fitzgerald acts at once on his son's statement, although he has this letter from Dr. Northcote before him. Now let me call your attention to what is explained here. I read it before, but I will read it to you again, because it is a justification, which I submit to you, of Dr. Northcote's conduct on this occasion.*

What was done upon that? Mr. Justice Fitzgerald immediately telegraphed to Oscott, and had all his sons and nephews taken away. Some suggestion was made, as I understand, that when Dr. Northcote, as he found it his duty to do, informed the boys assembled on the 13th of what had been David's offence, that he made use of expressions which were unnecessarily harsh. You have heard what the observations were. I need not repeat them. He pointed out that a gentleman does not consist merely of a man who may be of gentle birth; but a gentleman consists

* See the letter, p. 5.

mainly in this, that you shall never give offence, by word or act, to others who happen to be your inferiors in station. After that lecture had been given it was, that David Fitzgerald, who was not present at it, was dismissed from Oscott. The Judge takes away his other sons and relatives; and upon that occasion also it was suggested that Dr. Northcote had done something harsh or unkind. I will tell you exactly what he did. He explained most fully that, as regards many of these young Fitzgeralds, they had been exculpated by young David Fitzgerald himself; and as regards the others, he thought they would not have joined this association or this combination, if it had not been that they had been led into it by the older boy. I think the learned Judge must have been a little out of temper when he received the letter dated March 17th from Dr. Northcote, in which Dr. Northcote said:

"I confess I was somewhat surprised at the request for information to enable you to form a correct judgment of the course pursued towards David. Two days before, I had received a telegram ordering the immediate removal of the whole family from the college; a course of proceeding which seemed to me to indicate in no doubtful manner a judgment already formed."

He naturally thought it a little strange then to request information to enable him to form a correct judgment on the course pursued against David. I think Dr. Northcote not incorrectly argued: "If you have taken your other sons away, I cannot hope to alter the impression which you have already formed upon it." What was the answer which was given by the Judge? I cannot help saying that I think it is an answer which Mr. Justice Fitzgerald ought hardly to have given to a man in Dr. Northcote's position:

"Rev. Sir,—I have received your letter of the 17th in answer to mine of the 15th inst. There was nothing in my letter, nor in the subject to which it related, to call for or warrant a sneering or offensive reply. You complain that my judgment stands committed on one side by the removal of my second and third sons. I ordered their return because, on consideration of your letter of the 13th, I felt convinced they were no longer safe at Oscott."

I should like to know the passage in that letter of the 13th (written *bonâ fide*, and in the belief that every thing there stated was correct, and Mr. Justice Fitzgerald having no means whatever of knowing that that statement was not strictly accurate) which rendered it justifiable that Dr. Northcote should have been written to in that way by the Judge, and his letter written in answer to one that the Judge had sent him stigmatised as "a sneering and offensive reply." Gentlemen, that was the course which Dr. Northcote took in answer to Mr. Justice Fitzgerald's letter. Then Mr. Justice Fitzgerald talks about "poisonous slander," as to which there is not the least foundation. Then he says:

> "I cannot permit my son to enter life, to join a high and honourable profession, with the stain that you have thus fixed on his name; and I will, therefore, endeavour to procure for him an early opportunity for public investigation. In doing so I will be actuated solely by a desire to perform my duty to the public and to him, in seeing that truth and justice shall prevail."

And for the purpose of making truth and justice prevail, I suppose these long pleadings containing these technical pleas are raised, in order that, if they can prove that the book was kept one hour too long or one day too long, the verdict may be given on that technical ground, although on the main points of the case Dr. Northcote is entitled to succeed.

Gentlemen, you will hear again, I have no doubt, from my learned friend, a very able speech on behalf—I will not say of David Fitzgerald, but—of Mr. Justice Fitzgerald. I daresay you will again hear Mr. Stone called a gaoler, and possibly you will hear Dr. Northcote called an executioner, for aught I know; because it seems to me just as proper to call Dr. Northcote, who orders a boy to be flogged, an executioner, as to call Mr. Stone, who is ordered to confine a boy for breach of discipline to his room, a gaoler.

Lord Chief-Justice Cockburn: I think, Mr. Karslake, that was my phrase. Do not blame Mr. Coleridge for that.

Mr. Karslake: I thought it was my learned friend's, my Lord.

Lord Chief-Justice Cockburn: Not at all; it was mine.

Mr. Karslake: I beg your Lordship's pardon. I was merely endeavouring to point out that the imprisonment, as it is called, under lock and key made no difference. I say, if it was necessary to send him away from the college, as it was thought under the circumstances absolutely necessary, that then Dr. Northcote, in the exercise of the wide discretion which was vested in him, was bound to take care that that young man should not have any communication with the other students of the college, so long as it was necessary to keep him within the walls of the college, until his carriage could be sent for to take him away to Birmingham.

Then, gentlemen, what does it result in? Dr. Northcote, upon the grounds which he has stated to you, believing that there was this association and combination existing at the time that he took these measures towards young David Fitzgerald, there was no other course for him to adopt than the course which he did adopt. Gentlemen, my learned friend has asked the question of Dr. Northcote, after having heard what young David Fitzgerald has said here, "Do you still believe that you were justified in what you did, even supposing this combination existed?" Dr. Northcote knew what his previous conduct toward the Church students had been. He had not only the opportunity of making up his mind from the information which had been furnished to him, but from the very manner of young Fitzgerald himself, when he came before him, as to whether this association existed or not. That he believed it to exist, there can be no question; and that he acted on that belief, there can be no question. He is a person who has a right, in a case of this sort, to award such punishment as he thinks fit for such an offence; and if he thinks it right that he should be detained—as young Fitzgerald was detained—either with some person on guard over him, or some person who had authority to lock the door, until he left the college, I contend that he was justified in so doing, and that his discretion in such a matter as that must be absolute; and there can be no appeal from his discretion, and no review of his discretion, by a jury, as to whether he was right or wrong in so doing.

Lord Chief-Justice Cockburn: There I should differ from you, Mr. Karslake; and I should lay it down that the jury have a right to see whether he had reasonable grounds for the course which he pursued. I hold that there is an implied contract between the parent and the preceptor, when a parent sends his child to be educated at that establishment, that the preceptor will continue to educate him, so long as the conduct of that child does not warrant him in expelling him from the institution. He may cease to do that under reasonable circumstances; but if he expels him, he does break his contract with the father, so long as the conduct of the child has not rendered his expulsion reasonably necessary. Then, when we consider what the consequences are to the young man who is expelled from an institution of this kind, it becomes the more essential that that implied contract should not be broken. Therefore it will be a question for the jury, whether they think that, under all the circumstances, making due allowance for the discretion which undoubtedly is vested in the master, and which certainly ought not to be overruled upon light grounds, that the Defendant has or has not broken his contract; and if they think he has, it is a question for them whether they think the circumstances of the case reasonably warranted him in exercising that discretion.

Mr. Karslake: Of course, gentlemen, I bow to my Lord, when he states what he shall lay down to you; and taking what his Lordship says he shall lay down to you as my guide, I contend that there are fair and reasonable grounds to warrant Dr. Northcote in acting as he did. I submit to you, gentlemen, there can be no doubt whatever, that if he did act in the belief that there was an association in existence,—that belief being supported on grounds which would have made any person in Dr. Northcote's position act as he did, knowing, as Dr. Northcote knows better than any other man, what would be the consequence if such an association or combination was not crushed out at once; having regard to the fact that young David Fitzgerald had already been warned that any future infringement of the rules of that college would necessarily result in his dismissal, —that that is a complete justification of Dr. Northcote in acting as he has done.

Now, gentlemen, I have made these remarks to you, because it was my duty to place the case before you as it seemed to me the facts warranted. I lay it before you with the confident hope that when you have heard that which is much more important than any address which I can make to you, or any address which my friend can make to you, because we are acting here merely as advocates on one side and on the other,—when you have heard what my Lord shall leave to you as being the real issue for your determination in this case, that you will pause before any one of you adopts an opinion—which some of you have already expressed—without having had the most ample means of knowing what the real issue before you to try is. Although you may sympathise with a young man like David Fitzgerald—as you naturally do—who comes and tells you that although his position in society is injured in no way by what has been done—for no suggestion has ever been made that any thing has been ever done in consequence of this expulsion, as it is called, or dismissal from the school—I submit to you, that whatever sympathy you may feel for a young man so situated, you will look at all the difficulties under which Dr. Northcote was placed, and all the circumstances under which he deemed it right to do that which he did with pain and with sorrow; and I trust, gentlemen, that your verdict in this case will be one of acquittal of Dr. Northcote, and those who acted with him; and I venture to hope also that the opinion which you express, justifying Dr. Northcote, will be an opinion which will be endorsed and confirmed by that society to which the learned Judge has appealed.

(*His Lordship and the Jury then retired for a short time.*)

Mr. Coleridge: May it please your Lordship, Gentlemen of the Jury,—Dr. Northcote in this case has had his will. He has had this case tried out to the very dregs; and it is now for you, having heard his case presented to you by one of the ablest men in England, to say what verdict you will pass upon him.

Most of you, I should think, must have hoped that at the end of Mr. Fitzgerald's examination, at all events at the end of the plaintiff's case, Dr. Northcote would have said, and have gracefully said, "Whatever was my opinion at the time I expelled Mr. Fitzgerald, I have heard his account of the matter; he is a young gentleman who has manifestly told the truth; he has told this story under the sanction of an oath; I now see what he has told is the truth, that this conspiracy was a pack of stuff, and that I acted too precipitately and harshly; I am sorry for what I have done; I acted for the best under the belief that it was as represented to me; I now find I have made a mistake, and am sorry;" and there, gentlemen, as far as Mr. Fitzgerald is concerned, would have been an end to the case. That has not suited Dr. Northcote; it has not suited Mr. Stone; it has not suited, I suppose, the interests which Dr. Northcote and Mr. Stone represent; and one of the ablest men in England has been put up to make a laboured attack on the character of Mr. Fitzgerald, and, although not in words, yet in fact to suggest that the account which Mr. Fitzgerald has given of the transactions was not a correct one: that not only was Dr. Northcote not mistaken in point of judgment, which any man might be, but that he was not mistaken in point of fact, although Mr. Fitzgerald has sworn that he was. I should think that any one who has heard this case, and any one who has had any thing to do with it, from the beginning to the end, must exceedingly regret that it did not suit Dr. Northcote, that it did not suit his character, that it did not suit his position to do that which any gentleman might have done with dignity and grace, and with advantage to his character and to all the best interests he represents.

But, gentlemen, it is my duty, as counsel for Mr. Fitzgerald, to address you now in reply upon this case; and I shall be as brief as I can, because, divesting the case of all irrelevant matter, the points for your consideration are very few, and singularly simple. First of all, was there on Dr. Northcote's mind a reasonable belief, not a mere vain imagination, not a foolish delusion, but was there a reasonable belief,—such a belief as a reasonable man in any other important affair of life would act upon,—that there was the existence of this conspiracy which he has represented to you; and did he do what was done in the pursuit of that reasonable belief? Next, if there was that reasonable belief, did Dr. Northcote in what he did transcend or not transcend those limits of reasonable necessity which you are to be the judges of and which must be the limits under which all persons in Dr. Northcote's position are to act?

I said to you before, and I say to you again, that I admit, as any man of common sense must admit, that a large discretion is of necessity to be intrusted to a person who is at the head of an educational establishment,—no man of sound judgment will attempt to interfere with even a strong exercise of that discretion if it is *bonâ fide*,—but at the same time there are reasonable limits, of which juries are to be the judges; and it is for you, gentlemen, to say, not for the purpose of catching a miserable verdict, as my learned friend has a little unkindly imputed to me—not for the purpose of catching a verdict on a peg too small to hang it upon—but because it is the real question in the cause. Admitting that Dr. Northcote must have a reasonable discretion, as the head of an establishment of this nature, has he or has he not transcended the reasonable limits which must be reasonably imposed upon every such discretion? My Lord has pointed out the first question to you in language far better than any I can use. There is on the part of every parent who sends a child to an establishment of this sort a contract entered into that he shall be there left until his expulsion from the school shall become a reasonable necessity on the part of the head. In the circumstances of that expulsion there must be a limit of reasonable necessity to justify it; and if a man acts with unwarrantable harshness and cruelty, he is answerable to a jury for so acting.

Gentlemen, the questions I have pointed out will be the two main questions for your consideration. Then there is a third question—but one entirely unimportant compared with the others, as far as Mr. Justice Fitzgerald or his son is concerned—namely, what amount of damages ought Dr. Northcote to pay for the conduct of which he has been guilty in this case?

Now, gentlemen, I have said to you that I thought Dr. Northcote might gracefully have withdrawn from the case after hearing Mr. Fitzgerald's evidence; and I think I may repeat that, on the authority of Dr. Northcote and Mr. Stone themselves, for you have had yesterday occupied, and the greatest part of to-day occupied, with the contradiction of Dr. Northcote and Mr. Stone; and I appeal to you if in any material particular they have contradicted or qualified the story which Mr. Fitzgerald has told you. Does not the case remain, as far as the facts of it are concerned, substantially where it was when young Mr. Fitzgerald left the box? I am therefore relieved of a part of the difficulty—an onerous and a very disagreeable part very often of an advocate's duty in reply—the duty of sifting certain statements against others, and pointing out why one set of statements is to be believed, and another set of statements is to be discredited. In the present case, substantially speaking, the statements are the same. About the main general features of the transaction there is no dispute; and I will not waste your time about whether this particular form of expression was used, or that particular form of expression was employed, because you will all agree that substantially Mr. Fitzgerald has told the truth. I do not ask you to believe that, although you might reasonably do so, from the frankness of manner and the general conduct of the young man himself; but because Dr. Northcote and Mr. Stone do not contradict him: they do not substantially contradict one single important fact which Mr. Fitzgerald has stated.

Now what appears from this? Why, I say, first of all appears from it the entirely trumpery rubbish of the whole of these miserable subjects into which we have been inquiring at the instance of Dr. Northcote, and upon which he founds his cruel and unjustifiable expulsion of this young man. Not a thing has been proved against Mr. Fitzgerald which can be said to be an act that is not done in every school in the kingdom by hundreds of boys; and when Dr. Northcote is asked the question, he is obliged to say that, with the exception of the spirits, there is not a single offence of which Mr. Fitzgerald was guilty that he did not class under the head of venial sins. Then nothing can be more trumpery or unworthy of consideration than the fact upon which Dr. Northcote has based his extremely strong and cruel proceedings in this case; nay, as I before stated with reference to an important part of this case, I assert this not upon Mr. Fitzgerald's authority, but upon Dr. Northcote's own authority; for if you refer to the letter of the 13th of March, which he writes to Mr. Justice Fitzgerald after he has expelled his son, he treats these matters as not being worthy of consideration,* and does not go into them, and puts the whole of it upon this miserable "A. B. C." confederacy. He says: "I pass over the breaches of discipline and offensive conduct to his Superiors, which by degrees led to my having a serious conversation with him, and inflicting a severe punishment on Shrove Tuesday,"—and so on; therefore he does not pretend to say that upon those breaches of discipline he would have undertaken, or

* The reader is requested to read the letter itself, p. 5.

have justified to any body, the extreme measure to which he had recourse; but now, when an action is brought against him, and when he has to justify himself for having expelled Mr. Fitzgerald, and having affixed a stigma for life upon that young man, he goes back for years, and seeks to rake up these miserable peccadilloes, and bring them as make-weights to justify the course he adopted.

Mr. Harcourt: I think my learned friend has forgotten that all these matters are referred to in the letter of March the 17th.

Mr. Coleridge: If I am misstating any thing that I am dealing with, I am exceedingly glad to be corrected. I have not yet arrived at the position of my learned friend Mr. Harcourt; but I must tell my learned friend that no one in my position can deal with more than one thing at a time. I have been quoting from a letter of March the 13th; when I come to the letter of March the 17th, I shall deal with that: I cannot deal with the two at one time, even to please my learned friend Mr. Harcourt: I have not the power.

I am now on the letter of the 13th of March, and there the passage occurs which I have already read to you. In that letter, which he writes to explain on what grounds he expels Mr. Fitzgerald, he says he passes over, and will not rely on, the previous breaches of discipline of which the young man had been guilty. Mr. Justice Fitzgerald, in answer to that letter, says: "In order to judge of your conduct, I want to know of these previous breaches of discipline;" and when he asks for an account of the previous breaches of discipline, in the letter of March the 17th, it is true, upon the requisition of Mr. Justice Fitzgerald, those answers are given; but they were not given, and would not have been given, if the Judge had acquiesced in the course adopted, and had not inquired into its justice. I say more: not only are these miserable matters raked up for the purpose of attacking and casting a stigma upon the character of Mr. Fitzgerald, but Dr. Northcote goes back into a matter which he does not refer to in his letter of the 17th of March, and which, as far as I am concerned, I never heard of, nor any body else, I presume, until he came into court to support his case. He actually goes back to the Midsummer of 1862, at the time of the International Exhibition, when it seems that Mr. Fitzgerald and two or three other persons were all guilty of the unpardonable offence of singing in the dormitory, "We *will* go home in the morning." That is a thing he marked with the severity of keeping him back for the best part of a day from his schoolfellows; and that is raked up as a proof of what my learned friend calls this young man's ungovernable conceit and indomitable pride, because he sings "We *will* go home in the morning!" No doubt such conduct may have disturbed the gentlemen in the dormitory, and doubtless it was annoying to those who were not going home in the morning; but as it affects Dr. Northcote in a case like this, where he makes no charge of a moral kind against Mr. Fitzgerald, that he should rake up these miserable peccadilloes to the discredit of the plaintiff, I leave you to deal with it, and to say whether that is to his credit or his discredit.

With regard to this conspiracy or society, one cannot help remarking that a great deal of the feeling displayed arises from the mistake which Dr. Northcote is not answerable for, but which must be considered to be a grave mistake, of endeavouring to mix up in the same educational institution the strict and ascetic training of priests, which may be extremely necessary for their education, with that more free and liberal education which we, as laymen, are entitled to have, and do most of us have. No doubt, speaking without prejudice, there may be some positive advantages and disadvantages in each of the two systems; and I am far from saying that there may not be good reasons why the eminent men who conduct the Roman Catholic system in this country should not be trained in separate establishments. We think it right that our clergy should be educated amongst us, and should be educated with no distinction with laymen until they come to take the oaths of the Church. That is our system, and that may or may not have advantages; but this is an attempt to mix up and commingle the two systems in one public school for clergy and laymen; and I think that the endeavour to conduct in the same institution a seminary for priests, having regard to the strict discipline to which they are subjected, with a public school for laymen, can only result in mischief to both, and certainly to the lay element in the institution, as has been abundantly shown in the present case.

Now, what would have been the treatment dealt out to proceedings of this kind at the hands of any sensible English clergyman at the head of a public school? Instead of making a solemn matter of it and reducing the young fellow to the ranks, and speaking about humiliation and Ash Wednesday and Lent and so forth, I should think any sensible head-master would have administered perhaps a little corporal punishment, or would have sent for the boy and given him an imposition, or told the young fellow in a few kind and generous words that it must not happen again. He would have treated it with lightness, but at the same time with temper, which most English public scholars would appreciate; and which is the system that results in moulding the scholars into high-minded English gentlemen. Now that Dr. Northcote does not so treat his scholars, although he appears to have done so, is evident from his own account; for he says, if he had known of the breaking-up supper, he would not have allowed them to come back; and it was only the interest which he felt in young Mr. Fitzgerald and his position there which induced him to overlook it; and after all, he does not pretend to say that except on account of this miserable matter of the Anti-Bunker Confederation would Mr. Fitzgerald have been sent away from Oscott College.

Gentlemen, allow me in passing, with regard to this matter about conceit and grumbling, and the various complaints which we now hear of for the first time, to say that the only letter which my learned friend called for, and which was put in, was a letter in which it appears that all the young fellows complained of their fare and want of cold water; and Dr. Northcote made a reply on that, that he seemed to be a little too delicate, and that nothing was good enough for him. Why, gentlemen, we all know that it is not at all unknown to boy-nature to grumble about such matters, and that there are boys who think that nothing is good enough for them; but after all, Dr. Northcote hardly ventures to say that, except for this miserable matter about the club, any thing serious would have been done to Mr. Fitzgerald.

Then let us consider the question of the Anti-Bunker Association; and this Anti-Bunker Association is founded chiefly upon the evidence supplied by this pocket-book which I have before me. I should have thought that the proper way to have met this matter would have been to treat it with supreme contempt; or, if the matter really required notice, to have noticed it in a way which I ventured to suggest when I opened the case to you: it might have been noticed, namely, to have sent for the boy and endeavoured to find out whether there was any thing serious in the matter at all; and if there was any thing serious in the matter, to have pointed out to him that it was unkind, ungenerous, nay, ill-bred and ungentlemanly, to set himself up, or to set any one class against another class of students, especially in regard to worldly means. Gentlemen, I freely admit, and I agree with my learned friend, that there is nothing so unworthy of a gentleman as to make any distinction founded on birth and parentage. It is a mark of a low mind, an ill-bred mind, and for which I have not a shadow of sympathy. But at the same time it would have been fair to the young man to have pointed out to him, if it was found that he was serious and in earnest, that he was open to great blame upon the score of his own feelings, and to great blame upon the score of the feelings of those with whom he might come in contact, and upon whom he might produce exceedingly painful and irritating impressions. Surely it was the duty of Dr. Northcote to have dealt frankly with the young man, and to have endeavoured to discover what really was the foundation of the imputation which had been made against him, and to have resisted it, if he found out that it really was a piece of nonsense, that there was no confederation, that there were no meetings, no objects, and no society at all: that it was simply an effusion upon the leaves of this unhappy pocket-book, which was poured forth in a moment of spleen, but which, the moment his better nature was appealed to, he would have repudiated as strongly as my learned friend Mr. Karslake or I could do. That would have been the way to treat a thing of this kind. This, at all events, is clear, that so far from having his feelings or his conduct seriously affected by the entries in the pocket-book, Mr. Fitzgerald has stated to you upon his oath in the witness-box that amongst these very Church students were some of his friends; and Mr. Stone, whose mode of answering the questions on that matter I leave to your recollection, has not ventured to deny that at all times he did associate with clerical students, and was out walking with them, and that the three persons he was with when he was found in the public-house drinking and playing at bagatelle, and when Mr. Fitzgerald concealed himself under the bagatelle-table, were three Church students; therefore, when he is accused of having conspired against all the Church students in the house, that must be taken as evidence of the unfounded nature of that charge; and I think Mr. Stone need not have put upon me that he went with the three Church students because he could get no one else. At all events he goes out and drinks at the public-house in company with three Bunkers; therefore, whatever he chose to write down in the pocket-book, and whatever he talked of to the Secretary, he had no objection to the society of the Bunkers, for he went out with them, and drank with them the best ale he could get. It is known to Mr. Stone at the very time, and on these very occasions, that three of the men whom he was supposed to be conspiring against the peace and welfare of, were his companions in a cross-country expedition; and he is actually found in the Swan public-house drinking ale with them. If Mr. Stone had chosen to look at the circumstances before his very eyes, it would have been apparent to him that what the young man said was the truth,—that it was a piece of pure foolish nonsense.

But more than that, it was found that there was a Governor Moody, and that Governor Moody, on account of his magnanimous sentiments, had been unanimously elected. Now, gentlemen, it really does seem that the clerical mind is not appreciative of a joke; they deal with serious things in a serious way: they have grave responsible duties to discharge, and they are quite right to discharge them gravely; but I do think that any layman reading this entry about Governor Moody, for his magnanimous sentiments being unanimously elected, would have seen that it was a joke: the very words themselves would have suggested a joke. I once belonged to a society, a rule of which was, that any one who did any thing offensive or contrary to the government was to be had forth and publicly pitied! No one would seriously imagine that a member was to be actually had out and publicly pitied! Any one reading it, or hearing it read, must perceive that it was mere nonsense. Here, in the midst of entries,—here, in the midst of various other entries of the most suspicious nature, we find this—"Governor Moody elected March 6, for his magnanimous sentiments about Sedgely Park." Gentlemen, I ought to tell you that this is a memorandum-book, in which these things seem to have been jotted down with a singular disregard to dates. Here is this matter about the key of the bakehouse opening the paint-shop, and so forth, and the only date is October the 6th; and then there are some other entries about a chaffinch; and then there is a note concerning a bottle of rosemary which was to be obtained, which I suppose was to make his hair greasy; and then there is a lot about mathematics, and things which I do not understand, although I daresay Mr. Fitzgerald does. Gentlemen, if you take that book in your hands, you will find it is as innocent a book as any jury need have to deal with, and you may touch it without fear of finding any thing in it which can militate against your peace of mind: it is as safe as it looks, and you need not be afraid to handle it. But Dr. Northcote and Mr. Stone put on their terrible magnifying-glasses, and look at all these things through the haze of a strong clerical imagination. They say they believe there was a conspiracy against the house, and to invade the laws of the house; and the whole thing was treated as if we were living in the Dark Ages, and as if the conspiracy was as dangerous as the conspiracy of Guy Faux. But even Dr. Northcote could not help appreciating my question when I asked him, "Did you think your throne was tottering?" "No," he said, in reply to the pleasantry; "but I thought the peace of my subjects was seriously endangered." Gentlemen, how could he think that the peace of his subjects could be endangered by these entries in the pocket-book amidst entries of bottles of rosemary and chaffinches? If Dr. Northcote had not been a clergyman, and could have gone back to what he was many years ago, and have looked at the matter in the light in which he would have regarded it in earlier days; if he could have remembered what he was when he was in King Edward VI.'s Grammar School; if he could have allowed himself for a moment to look at the matter as if he were—what no doubt he was once—a schoolboy, he would have seen that Mr. Fitzgerald's account was true,—that really it was a mere piece of pleasantry, and that really all this conspiracy and A. B. C. was pure nonsense.

On the one hand you have had placed before you Mr. Fitzgerald's account, and on the other hand you have had placed before you every thing which ingenuity could suggest by one of the most able Counsel I know of, for the purpose of discrediting Mr. Fitzgerald. His books were taken away from him when he was not in his room; and his pocket-book lying open upon the table was read by Mr. Stone. He was taken at a disadvantage: I will pass by whether that was right or not; some people would not do such a thing, others would; but at all events, we find that every thing that could be raked up against Mr. Fitzgerald has been raked up from the time he went to Oscott to the present hour, and that really nothing has been made of it. And remember this, gentlemen, that if what the young man said was not true, there was a class of evidence at the command of Dr. Northcote to prove that what he said was not true. There are at least nine or ten members of the A. B. C.; there are some of the clerical students and the Divines, the persons who gave the information upon which Dr. Northcote acted; and there are boys still remaining in the school, who could, if Mr. Fitzgerald was not correct, have come forward and told you that he was utterly incorrect in what he has stated,—for that there was a conspiracy going forward. The names are before you: there is the honorary secretary, whose name has been mentioned, and of whom Mr. Fitzgerald says, "I appointed him;" in fact he said, "I am the Confederation, I make you the secretary;" and he is the person who is referred to for these various sources of information. Mr. Fitzgerald said it was all nonsense. If that is not true, where is this young gentleman whose name has been mentioned? If there was a syllable of actual foundation for this supposed conspiracy, why do they not bring the conspirators before you? Why do they not bring the secretary and the other young gentlemen who are at the school before you, and let them say, "It is all a mistake of Mr. Fitzgerald's; it *was* a serious thing, and he is mistaken in saying that there was nothing in it." Gentlemen, they have not chosen to adopt that course; and I am therefore entitled to say that he is uncontradicted in the most important parts of his evidence; for when it lay in the easy power of Dr. Northcote and Mr. Stone to contradict him by the means I have suggested, all they have done has been to bring forward every sort of accusation except what might have been substantial evidence—namely, the evidence of his schoolfellows—to say that the colour he has put upon the matter is not the true colour.

Now, gentlemen, consider again the spirit in which this matter has been conducted. I pass by my learned friend's repeated observations about the young man's conceit, pride and conceit and so forth, which, considering his youth and all things, might have been spared. Why did not Dr. Northcote, if he really meant fairly by Mr. Fitzgerald, if he really meant fairly by his father,—why did he not write to the Judge, or telegraph to the Judge, not an entire account of Mr. Fitzgerald's expulsion—I never suggested any thing so absurd—but why not telegraph to the Judge and say, "Things are going on badly; come and take away David"? Can you doubt that the Judge in the course of a few hours would have been at Oscott, and would have brought his practised intellect to bear upon the matter, and that he would have been able to show to Dr. Northcote that he was making a mountain out of a molehill, and that the whole matter had crumbled into the dust of which it was made? But Dr. Northcote says in his letter—and here I convict him out of his own mouth: "I have never written to your father any thing but good of you. If I were to dismiss you from the college without warning, he would have a right to complain: he would think I had lost my temper, and been unreasonably harsh with you for the first offence. To protect myself, therefore, I must make him informed of all that has happened." The boy was pressing him not to write to his father; and he says to the boy, "What will the Judge say, if some morning you appear at the breakfast-table without any explanation?" That is his own account; but when the matter comes to be acted on, and when this A. B. C. Club turns up, he does the very thing which in the letter he said would justly excite the suspicions of Mr. Justice Fitzgerald. It is perfectly true, he says, that he did not write at that time owing to the entreaty of the boy; but it shows what he knew Mr. Justice Fitzgerald would think of that conduct which he afterwards did pursue. When my learned friend says gravely that the safety of Oscott House and the security of Dr. Northcote's dominions could not be secured for five or six hours—that it could not be maintained with the presence of young Mr. Fitzgerald there—he talks of course as an advocate, who is obliged to say so in aid of a very difficult and hopeless case. That is Dr. Northcote's own view of what the Judge would say. Why on earth, that being his own view, the letters showing that there had been intimate, I may say affectionate terms of friendship between Dr. Northcote and Mr. Fitzgerald, the Judge being an eminent Roman Catholic,—why, I ask, did he not telegraph to him, if there was not time to write, and say, "Pray come, for things are not going on well, and your son must be removed; pray come and satisfy yourself of the necessity for his removal"? Gentlemen, I do say that the cruel harshness of expelling this boy without any warning, sending him to his father—his father being utterly unprepared for any such proceeding, but being surprised and deeply grieved and wounded at it—was a want of consideration which, if Dr. Northcote had been well advised, he might have said he regretted, but for which he has not expressed any regret, insisting, as of course he is entitled to insist, upon his rights in this or any other Court.

Then, gentlemen, there is a matter which I approach with regret, because it does show a spirit which I cannot help thinking is not creditable to Dr. Northcote, and a spirit which I think he ought not to have exhibited. You recollect the day before yesterday, when Mr. Fitzgerald was in the box, he came to a part of his narrative, when my learned friend was cross-examining him as to what had become of him when Dr. Northcote sent him to his room, and when Mr. Stone went to his room and did not find him. Young Mr. Fitzgerald said he had gone into the chapel, for reasons which any body could appreciate. He was overwhelmed with the calamity which had come upon him, and he had gone into the chapel to pour out his overcharged heart before the God and Father of us all. He knew, I suppose, that "God will hear, if man will call to the blue sky that bends over all;" and my learned friend, like a manly and generous person, as he always is, declined to ask him why he went into the chapel, knowing why he went there, and appreciating — and I may say, reverencing — the feeling. But two days elapse, and my learned friend replies, as Dr. Northcote's advocate; and then my learned friend charges as an act of disobedience that Mr. Fitzgerald went to pray to God for the calamity that had befallen him. Although he would not put a question in a marked way upon the subject, he afterwards makes the charge; and I think therefore I am justified in saying, that Dr. Northcote has not shown that feeling which a clergyman—the head-master of a school and a priest—might be expected to have shown in dealing with a former pupil.

But more than that, the boy is subjected to every imaginable ignominy before he is locked-up: he is handed in by Mr. Stone. Mr. Stone, as he says, did exercise superior force, although he will not admit that he had a struggle with him. That is the only point upon which Mr. Fitzgerald, Dr. Northcote, and Mr. Stone, are at direct issue. Now, you recollect Mr. Fitzgerald says there was a struggle, and the book was taken from him by force; and on the 13th of March, when he went home to Dublin, he told his father so; because Mr. Justice Fitzgerald writes to Dr. Northcote in answer to his letter, and asks: "Was the book taken from David with superior force with your sanction?" So that it is plain, at that time, that that was the story the boy had told. Now, Mr. Stone admits that the letter was read to him: Mr. Stone admits further, that Dr. Northcote's letter was read to him, or he saw it, and supplied the materials for it. What is Dr. Northcote's answer at the time? Not that it was not taken by force, but that he told Mr. Stone to go for the book; and said, if Mr. Fitzgerald would not give it, he was to take it from him. That is an answer from Mr. Stone, because Dr. Northcote was not present; that lies between Mr. Stone and Mr. Fitzgerald, for they only were present. It is clear—and Mr. Stone does not deny it—that he used force; and Mr. Stone must excuse me when I say that he quibbles about moral and physical force, when he said that by "superior force" he thought was meant moral force. Mr. Stone is a clergyman, and speaks under the solemnity of an oath, and so does Mr. Fitzgerald; but I see by the letter what Mr. Stone said then, and that is contradicted by what Mr. Stone says now, and is confirmed by what Mr. Fitzgerald says now.

Then I have a right to assume, in that state of facts, that you will believe Mr. Fitzgerald, confirmed as he is by the contemporary Mr. Stone, and the letters of Mr. Justice Fitzgerald and Dr. Northcote. Then, why is the boy to have this book taken away from him after a struggle? If it is wanted, let the boy be taken to Dr. Northcote, and let him say, "I want to see the book. If you do not produce it, you know the inference I must draw"? Do you suppose that if that had been said to a boy of sense, as Mr. Fitzgerald is not denied to be, that the book would not have been produced? But it is taken from him, and he is lectured; and Dr. Northcote gives you the account of the lecture. Upon what evidence did Dr. Northcote act? I have his own words for that, and we will see. He says he heard of it from an official communication by Mr. Stone, to the effect that a lay student had reported to a Divine the existence of a conspiracy against the Church students, known as the A. B. C., or Anti-Bunker Confederacy; and that there were afloat in the institution lists of the aristocracy, as they were called. One of these lists has been traced to the possession of Mr. Stone. Now, I pass by the great key case, and will not revert to the key and the wax; but it seems that the documents were in Mr. Stone's possession at Christmas.

Now this case stood for trial at Christmas, but was put off because Mr. Justice Fitzgerald was engaged in Ireland, and could not attend. Where are the documents and the lists of the aristocracy now, which were in Mr. Stone's possession at Christmas? Why were they not treasured up in the archives of Oscott College, and produced on the trial at Westminster Hall? They knew the importance of it. Mr. Stone had them at the time the trial was to come off at Christmas. Where are they now? Then it appears that the superiors met and went over the evidence, and at the second meeting the evidence was gone over again. Now what was the evidence? The evidence was that a lay student of the house had reported to a Divine the existence of a conspiracy against the Church students, known by its members as the A. B. C.; that each member had a list of the other members, and that David was the prime mover in it. Now Dr. Northcote had this evidence. Mr. Stone said that a Divine said that a lay student said that there was a conspiracy against the Church students of the house: name unknown, objects unknown, acts unknown, character undescribed. But it was too important to treat it as gossip, and must be laid before the authorities. It is laid before the authorities, and they are going to proceed to the last extremity of expelling Mr. Fitzgerald and fixing a stigma upon him for life. A poor lawyer would say, you know, "You had better just look at your evidence before you proceed." That is a poor vulgar way we have of proceeding; but of course you would expect that evidence that did satisfy a lawyer would not satisfy a Divine; that a schoolmaster, and a man standing *in loco parentis*, if he had evidence, would be glad to escape from the conclusion that was unwillingly forced on his mind. I should have thought so; but not so Dr. Northcote, Mr. Stone, and the superiors at Oscott House. No; a lay student tells a Divine, who tells Mr. Stone, who tells Dr. Northcote, and that is sufficient. I do not know whether you know the "Game of Russian News," where a party of people being seated at a table, one man tells a story to his neighbour in an undertone, and the neighbour tells it to his neighbour, and so it travels on until it reaches the other end of the table in a condition in which no one would recognise it who had heard it at the beginning. Gentlemen, that is what hearsay evidence comes to; and, gentlemen, hard, dry, and technical as no doubt Dr. Northcote thinks all these proceedings must be, let me tell him it is sometimes an exceedingly important thing, when you are going to act, to be quite sure of the evidence upon which you are acting; and when you are going to convict a man of something that is excessively disagreeable, and when you are going to punish him in a way from which you cannot retract, it is very important to be sure of your facts. Here A. tells B. something about C., upon which D. is to expel C. The very least, surely, that could be expected would be that before Dr. Northcote acted upon the evidence which had so reached him, an inquiry should be made, and all the students should be seen upon the subject. The first thing to do would be that. But I asked Dr. Northcote, "Did you send for the lay student?" "No." "Did you send for the Divine?" "No." "Did you hear what they said?" "No." "Then all you trusted was the narration which Mr. Stone had given of that which somebody else had said that somebody else had said of somebody else?" Is that satisfactory? "Well," he says, "that was not all: there was a pocket-book, and I sent for the pocket-book, because if I had seen that the pocket-book did not confirm what the lay student had told the Divine, who told Mr. Stone, who told me, I might then have altered my opinion; but things looked very black." "You did send for the pocket-book?" "Yes." "And what did the pocket-book disclose?" "It confirmed my worst fears." Gentlemen, the pocket-book is before us; and although the list of the aristocracy, and although the key and the wax do not appear, here it is, a natural history of chaffinches and so forth; and you will say how far that does or does not confirm the story which, entirely without sifting, Dr. Northcote chose to act upon.

Well, gentlemen, Mr. Fitzgerald is expelled; and what happens thereupon? Why, that happens thereupon as to which it is for you to consider the effect you will give to it when you come to make up your minds in this case. The boy is expelled; the boy is sent to his room by Mr. Stone; he is locked up by Mr. Stone; he is kept, in fact, in confinement by Mr. Stone from half-past one until something like three o'clock, and during the whole of that time is not allowed to leave the room. He is hurried in his packing, as Mr. Stone admits he did hurry him; pushing him, and telling him he must make haste, for he wants to get rid of him as soon as possible, and treating him with about as much kindness and as little consideration for his feelings as any human being could show a gentleman. He is sent off to Mr. Justice Fitzgerald. He arrives at Mr. Justice Fitzgerald's house next morning without the smallest warning; and Mr. Justice Fitzgerald finds his eldest son—the son in whom his hopes were centred, upon whom he had fixed his best expectations in life—expelled from a religious institution to which he had been sent to be educated, as not fit for the society of its members, and as a young man who was likely to contaminate them if he had remained in the establishment any longer. Gentlemen, I do not know whether any of you have children or a child at school; but I do think that if any of you are men of feeling, it would almost break your hearts to have one of your children sent home in that kind of way, without any explanation,—a child of the highest promise, of whom you have heard nothing but good, of whom the man who has himself expelled him had written in the most flattering terms; to find that that child had been suddenly expelled from a school of this kind as being utterly unfit to remain an inmate—expelled under circumstances of peculiar hardship, for he was sent there, and his pension paid in advance, I believe—

Lord Chief-Justice Cockburn: That is not the gravamen of the present charge, which is the assault and the imprisonment, not the expulsion.

Mr. Coleridge: No doubt, my Lord, that is so; he was there with his pension paid in advance; and no doubt, if it was necessary for the discipline of the institution,—if it was essential to the maintenance of order in the institution,—that he should subscribe to the rules, he was bound to do so.

Lord Chief-Justice Cockburn: But it is not the complaint here.

Mr. Coleridge: To be sure, my Lord, that is true.

But still it is for you, gentlemen, to say, under all the circumstances of the case, whether it was necessary for the discipline of the institution that he should be so expelled, and whether the circumstances of his expulsion were such that you can say the reasonable necessity of it was not exceeded.

Lord Chief-Justice Cockburn: The declaration does not complain of his expulsion; and therefore the only way the question of expulsion arises is quite incidentally, as a stepping-stone to the real complaint.

Mr. Coleridge: That, no doubt, my Lord, is true.

But, gentlemen, it must be a matter for you to consider what has been the injury committed, in coming to a conclusion upon the question of imprisonment and assault. That is a matter upon which you will take my Lord's direction. They expelled him; and it will form a subject for your consideration in estimating the damages which he has sustained from the legal cause of action. They expelled him, as far as I can make out, for something perfectly childish,—for something that it was not at all reasonably necessary should be treated in so serious and harsh a manner. He was expelled from the walls of Oscott College; and in expelling him, they read to him a noble passage from the works of a great writer, who turns every thing he touches into gold, which intimated to him and to those he left behind that he was not a gentleman; that he had not the attributes of a gentleman; that he was unfit to remain at Oscott College, because he had not the attributes which that great writer has laid down as necessary qualifications for the character of a gentleman. But there is a much greater writer, who, in a very much nobler passage, written 1800 years ago,—whose just authority, I hope, has not been impaired in Dr. Northcote's estimation by any change of religious opinion through which he has passed,—and that greater writer describes, not the character of a gentleman, but the grace of Christian charity; and he says: "Charity suffereth long, and is kind: charity thinketh no evil, is not puffed up, is not easily provoked, believeth all things, hopeth all things, endureth all things." How far you will think the spirit of priestly authority has or has not impaired the just authority of that passage in Mr. Stone's mind is beyond our province to inquire; but it is not beyond my province to ask you for, and it is not beyond your province to give, such damages as, under all the circumstances of this case, you think have been sustained by the injury inflicted upon young Mr. Fitzgerald, under what I venture to call singularly slight provocation. Do you think there was any justification for the assault and the imprisonment? I am sure you will be of opinion that beyond all doubt there was none, and that you will say so by your verdict.

SUMMING UP.

Lord Chief-Justice Cockburn: Gentlemen of the Jury,—You must consider what are the causes of action which the plaintiff brings forward to justify his claim to your verdict for damages against the defendant.

You have heard many observations made upon the expulsion of the plaintiff, young Mr. Fitzgerald, from this scholastic institution; and they have been made to you with all the feeling and eloquence of which no one is more capable than the very learned counsel who has just addressed you. But I am bound to tell you that, except as incidentally connected with the question of the imprisonment, the expulsion of Mr. Fitzgerald from that institution is not what is complained of in this action. I suppose there were some reasons, best known to those who brought the action, or who advised it, for omitting that which appears to me to be, after all, the essential part of the complaint, —if there was any complaint well founded: there was some reason for omitting that from the declaration. But it is omitted; and therefore I am bound to tell you, that if you should be of opinion that that expulsion was not justifiable under the circumstances, you cannot, in the conscientious exercise of your duty, and you are not entitled to, give damages in respect of it.

What the plaintiff complains of in the present action is that he was assaulted and that he was imprisoned, and that his property, namely, his pocket-book, was taken from him and detained from his possession. Those are the matters which are for your consideration. The first question for you to consider is, whether he was assaulted as he represents, and whether he was imprisoned as he states; and then you will consider whether his pocket-book was taken from him, and whether the circumstances under which these different matters took place were such as to justify the conduct which the defendants adopted towards the plaintiff.

Now that the plaintiff was assaulted, so far as assault in the eye of the law is concerned, I think there cannot be the slightest doubt in the world. Whether the pocket-book was taken from him by superior force, notwithstanding his resistance, as he alleges; or whether he having the pocket-book in his pocket, it was taken from his person by the hand of Mr. Stone, he objecting;—that in the eye of the law would be an assault.

Again, with regard to the imprisonment, it is alleged in the declaration that he was twice imprisoned; once, I presume it is intended to say, when the door was locked by Mr. Stone in order to get the pocket-book from him, and when he was taken down to the President. I suppose that is intended to be one of the imprisonments; and the other is after he was expelled, or when he had received notice that he was to be expelled, and he was confined to his own room; first, for half-an-hour under lock and key, and afterwards by the corporeal presence of a stronger man than himself, who tells you that if he had attempted to go out of the room, he should not have allowed him to do so. Therefore, as to the fact of the imprisonment you cannot entertain much doubt; and that his pocket-book was taken away is equally beyond all question. That is admitted on all hands. But the main question which you have to consider is, whether the circumstances were such as to justify on the part of the defendants what was done. The more active proceedings appear to have been carried on by Mr. Stone; but if Mr. Stone assaulted and imprisoned Mr. Fitzgerald, and did so by the authority of Dr. Northcote, both Mr. Stone and Dr. Northcote would be responsible, unless they can justify their proceedings.

Now then we come to the great question, which is, whether or not the acts complained of were justifiable under the circumstances? And the first branch that presents itself is, what was the position in which Mr. Fitzgerald stood on his return to Oscott College with reference to the authorities there? You remember he had gone through the usual course at Oscott College, and that it was then intended that he should go to some University. For some reason or other, which is not explained, it did not coincide with the views of his father that he should go to any English University, nor did it coincide with his views that the youth should go to Trinity College at Dublin; and it was determined that he should become a member of the London University, and take his degrees there. Now the London University is unlike the other Universities to which I have referred. It has two colleges connected with it in the neighbourhood of the metropolis; but it has other scholastic establishments affiliated to it, in which the students may reside during the interval of time that elapses between their education at college and taking the degree of bachelor of arts, which is the first degree conferred by the University. It was recommended on the part of Dr. Northcote, and I have no doubt with the most honest desire to promote the welfare of the young man, that under these circumstances he should come back to Oscott College, and continue his studies there during the interval that was to elapse; and consequently we find that he does so come back. He goes up to London and matriculates there; and having gone through his matriculation, he goes back to Oscott College, and continues his studies until the time should arrive for his going up to take his first degree of bachelor of arts.

Now one can quite understand that a young man going back under such circumstances, instead of being subjected to the ordinary discipline in the school, and to the authority of the head-master and the subordinate masters—that is to say, his masters relatively to a boy at school—might be placed in a different position; although his father paid a certain amount for him, he might have gone back as a sort of pupil at large, or guest, and not subject to the general discipline of the establishment. The question is, whether it can be said that young Fitzgerald stood in that position; for that would make a material difference. Any body can at once understand the difference in their relative positions, both as regards the authority of the tutor or the master, and the obligations of the young man so circumstanced. It would be a very different position to that which each would hold towards the other if they stood in the relation of schoolmaster and school-boy, call it what you will.

Now I must say that it seems to me the evidence on this point was all one way. I do not find, in any of the different letters that passed between Mr. Justice Fitzgerald and Dr. Northcote, that any claim is put forward, or any desire intimated, that the son should be exempt from the ordinary discipline of the school, or from the authority of the master. On the contrary, I find, in a letter in which Dr. Northcote recommends Mr. Justice Fitzgerald to send his son to the establishment, for him to continue his studies there with a view to his progress at the London University, that Dr. Northcote especially refers to the advantage it would be to the young man still to continue in the relation of a pupil and in the position of a pupil, subject to the authority of the institution. And I find that, from the moment young Fitzgerald went back until the hour he left, he never asserted the slightest shadow of a claim to be considered as in a different position from any of the other pupils in the establishment; that he took his place willingly, and without the slightest murmur of dissatisfaction, in the class to which he had previously belonged; with this distinction only, that he did not pursue there the studies appropriate to that class, because it would not have suited the position in which he was with regard to the object he had in view. But throughout, step after step and time after time, we find the authority on the part of Dr. Northcote and on the part of Mr. Stone exercised towards him, and invariably submitted to on his side, with as much recognition that he was subject to that authority as any of the young men who were members of the institution were subject to it.

Now, supposing that to be the state of things, then we approach the question as to whether the treatment to which he was afterwards subjected was justifiable. I cannot help thinking that his position was an anomalous and a somewhat unfortunate one. He had gone through the whole course of that school; he had gone to the London University and matriculated there, and had been admitted into that University. He went back, therefore, in a different position from that in which he stood at the time he was a schoolboy going through the school course. It seems that in January a new Prefect had taken the place of the former one; and without saying any thing to the disparagement of Mr. Stone, who does not seem to show any semblance of ill-nature or ill-temper, as far as we could judge, we do know that sometimes, when a man comes first into authority he does exercise it rather more harshly than a man who is well fixed in his seat, and who has been accustomed to rule and govern others; and it may be that, seeing this young man in an anomalous position, and who, if we may judge from his antecedents, whatever merits he may have, seems to be a young man who was not as submissive to authority as young men generally are; who seems to have been to a certain extent of a somewhat mutinous disposition; who had complained, as Dr. Northcote tells us, of his former Superior in the establishment, although he was more mild and more moderate in the exercise of his authority than Mr. Stone,—young Fitzgerald and Mr. Stone soon got into circumstances not perfectly pleasant to each other; and one cannot be altogether surprised at that. But I must say that I think there is a good deal as to which Mr. Fitzgerald is open to blame. He had at this time passed from the mere position of schoolboy; he was a young man who had become a member of a University, and he was bound to show a good example to others in this institution,—at all events, he was bound not to lead them into mischief. But he does certainly appear, between the month of January, when Mr.

Stone entered into the office of Prefect of Discipline, and the month of March, to have got into as many scrapes as a young gentleman could well do, although possibly they were not of the mortal character which Dr. Northcote appears afterwards to have considered them to be. In the first place, it is an awkward thing for a young man who has a pass-key lent him for the night, to become a party with a number of other youngsters to the taking of a wax impression of that key, with the avowed purpose of going to the smith in the village and getting a key clandestinely made, which would afford these young fellows access to every room in the house, where they had no business to be. No doubt all of us have done a great many things for which we have deserved punishment, sometimes getting it, and at other times escaping it; but I must say that that was rather a bold and daring thing to do, and few of us would probably venture upon it. However, that he does; and then he gets into another scrape, and his privileges are taken away from him for three days. He was up after eleven o'clock, which was contrary to the regulations. It is all very well to make reflections on Mr. Stone; but I must say that I think there are certain things in an establishment of this kind which are so essential to the welfare of the institution, that discipline ought to be enforced with regard to them; and one of those things is, that in a large establishment where there are two hundred persons,—young people,—those who are youths should retire to their beds at night at a certain time, so that all lights and candles may be put out, and the danger of fire, which may be mortally destructive if it breaks out, to the utmost extent avoided. If a young man chooses to remain up till half-past eleven o'clock, when the regulations say that he shall go to bed at ten o'clock, I do not think there is any reason to complain if the Prefect of Discipline says: "You have violated a most important regulation, and you must suffer for it: I take away your privileges for three days."

Mr. Fitzgerald says afterwards he questioned the authority of the Prefect of Discipline, as such, to take away the privileges of this class, which was called "The Philosophers," of which he was at that time a member. But I do not find that Mr. Fitzgerald took the right course to bring that question to an issue, if he desired to do so—namely, by going to the President and asking the question whether Mr. Stone had the authority to do what he had done; but he takes upon himself the next day to go out; and inasmuch as they were always obliged to make up a party of three, and put their names down on paper and hand them in to the Prefect, he puts his own name down with the others and hands in his paper with his own name, which might have been done for the purpose of challenging the question whether Mr. Stone had the authority or not. However, Mr. Stone had not time to attend to the matter that day. But on the next day comes another escapade. In the mean time Mr. Fitzgerald had got into difficulty with Dr. Northcote, and I think Dr. Northcote had confined him to bounds; but he is found at a public-house drinking and playing at bagatelle, which was altogether contrary to the regulations.

Gentlemen, Mr. Coleridge has reminded you of your school-days; and one of you asked a very natural question, whether, if a young man is allowed to walk about the country, and happens to get thirsty, it is an intolerable offence to call at a public-house and ask for a draught of beer? Probably it is not; but you see, if you come to accumulate offences, any one of which may not of itself amount to sufficient to justify sending a young man away from such an establishment as this, each subsequent offence assumes a graver aspect from the fact of it having followed very speedily upon some other which went before it. If a young man has been confined to bounds for some other offence, and has not only broken bounds, but is found breaking some other important rule, and is discovered in a public-house playing at bagatelle, you will not wonder that the master, whose authority has been thus set at naught, treats the matter with some gravity, and as somewhat important. Although it is necessary to make such a regulation in a public school, even with regard to the upper boys—taking a more extended area than the others are limited to, giving to them liberty to go about the country, and so forth—there is nothing unreasonable in requiring that they shall subscribe to the general rules, which are necessary for the government of the establishment, and that they shall not frequent taverns, which is altogether inconsistent with the notion of boys at school, however advanced the ages of those boys may be. We may all agree that merely to stop at an inn and have a drop of something to refresh them, if they are really thirsty, would be a matter that the master might very naturally overlook; but it is nevertheless a breach of discipline; and if that breach of discipline comes to be cumulative upon former offences, and violations of rules and regulations imposed upon the young man, it assumes a graver aspect. I merely say that because remarks have been made upon the supposed hardship of Mr. Stone's proceedings in this very matter.

But unfortunately the matter does not stop there. He is confined to bounds, not only by Mr. Stone, but by the authority of the President; and notwithstanding that, he is found out of bounds, and he is doing that which it is quite clear no young man in the position of a scholar at school can be allowed to do —using fire-arms, which may be attended with danger to himself, and very probably be attended with danger to other persons, and which no master in any establishment can allow to be carried on within the precincts of the institution. He is found doing that, and there again unpleasantness arises. Mr. Stone hears the report of a pistol,—he sees the smoke,—he is aware that Mr. Fitzgerald is breaking the bounds,—he is aware that Mr. Fitzgerald is setting the authority of the President at naught, and naturally and most properly Mr. Stone goes up to inquire about the pistol; he would have been wholly wanting in his duty if he had not done so. He goes up and demands the pistol, and asks, "Where is it?" and then there is an unsatisfactory answer. No doubt, in one sense, if you have thrown a pistol into a hedge, you do not know where it is; but in another sense it is easy to say, "I have thrown it away; it is in the hedge; I daresay we can easily find it." But an unseemly altercation takes place; and there, I think, Mr. Stone was to blame. The word "lie" is a word which grates on every body's ear, whether it is applied to a man or a boy. But he goes a step further, and acknowledges that he lost his temper. Then this comes to the knowledge of Dr. Northcote. The boy goes to complain. He anticipates the complaint of Mr. Stone; but although Mr. Stone had forgotten himself when he threatened to box his ears, you will be satisfied that upon the whole young Fitzgerald had misconducted himself, knowing well that what he was doing was egregiously wrong. Being there, when confined to bounds, was a flagrant breach of discipline; and in point of fact, although he may not have laid himself open to the imputation of telling a lie in the direct and positive terms in which it had been imputed to him by Mr. Stone, yet nevertheless his answer to Mr. Stone's question, which he was perfectly justified in putting, had not been ingenuous and straightforward; and accordingly Dr. Northcote expressed himself in a manner as to this part of the matter which I think nobody can fairly or candidly find fault with. Then the young man is told, "Now you see you have been going on committing one offence after another; you will be obliged to leave if this conduct continues;" and I think it was on that occasion that Dr. Northcote said that matters had gone on so badly that he must write to his father giving him warning that the young man had gone beyond his control, and, in short, that it would be much better to take him away. I own I regret that some such warning was not given to Mr. Justice Fitzgerald. I think that the position the young man occupied was fatal to himself. He was conscious of being no longer in the position of the other boys,—he was something between a schoolboy and a University man; and I daresay he felt impatient at the restraint of the establishment, and the discipline and authority which were exercised towards him, the more so as he appeared to be somewhat mutinous. However, he begs off; and Dr. Northcote with kindness, if not with discretion, forgives it. If his discretion is to be blamed, certainly his good feeling is not to be blamed. He says, "I will give you another chance; but I am putting myself in a false position, because if any thing else happens, I am sure your father will think I have not acted with due consideration towards him; I am risking my character upon your honour: can I trust myself so to do?" The young man says, "Depend upon it I will not get myself into another scrape."

Then comes this unfortunate matter, into which so much inquiry has been made; and that is this story about the confederacy, or conspiracy, because that was the culminating point of this young man's delinquencies, connected with which they justify sending him away; and incidentally to sending him away, assaulting him and taking his pocket-book from him, and imprisoning him prior to his being sent away. Now, if the fact really was—and that is to be submitted for your consideration—that young Fitzgerald, after the ill feeling which had in former times existed between the lay students and the clerical students at that establishment, really did organise a confederacy among the boys and young men at that establishment, for the purpose of renewing that unhappy and discreditable feud, and for the purpose of making the condition of these students who formed the clerical part of the establishment—who were men of inferior birth, station, rank, and fortune to themselves—uncomfortable and unhappy, beyond all doubt that was a most unjustifiable, ungenerous, and improper proceeding, which, if it did in point of fact exist, would, on the part of the President and authorities of that institution, call for intervention, in some marked and conspicuous manner, in order to crush such an attempt before it had reached any thing like a head, and to prevent the peace and comfort and happiness of that institution being seriously affected, as it must have been if such a scheme had taken effect and been allowed to be carried into execution. It appears there is a great difference in point of social position between the greater number of the lay students and the clerical students, who come there to prepare themselves for the Roman Catholic priesthood. It appears that in former times there was a very considerable amount of bad feeling between these two portions of the school; and I think one can pretty well see why that should be, or at least why there should be a tendency towards that state of feeling. It seems that as soon as the clerical students have gone through the course of the school, those who are intended for the Church remain there, and are called by the denomination of "Divines:" and from these Divines many of the masters are taken. You know there always has been in all ages, and I suppose will continue to be to the end of the world, a sort of antagonism, more or less marked and defined, between the schoolmaster and the schoolboy; and if you suddenly convert a schoolboy into a schoolmaster, without much difference of age between the two,—and if the schoolmaster comes from amongst that class of scholars which is not the most distinguished in social position,—one can quite understand that there would spring up a certain amount of antagonism and uncomfortable feeling between the two elements of the institution.

Of course, that has at once to be kept down: so far from being allowed to exist, every thing should be done to keep it down and prevent it gaining a head; but I doubt whether the proper mode of doing that is by severity of discipline. You cannot by severity root out ill feeling: you may smother it, you may make it smoulder; but you cannot extinguish it. You may, by evoking generous sentiments and teaching men what constitutes the true aristocracy of life, induce them to give up any miserable, petty, dirty feelings, which are more or less rife amongst boys, and unfortunately exist sometimes in men, but which are never otherwise than discreditable to those who entertain them, and which are best got rid of by a high and noble training, and by instilling into the breasts and hearts of men the true sentiments of charity, love, and Christian virtue. Now, here it appears from this evidence, that it had—for a time, at all events—been demonstrated that these young men had associated on friendly terms, as schoolfellows should do, without any reference to unpleasant distinctions; but it certainly does appear, that about this time certain indications of a different feeling manifested themselves and gained ground, and the old dissensions came up; that is to say, one or two talked about this; and it certainly appears that a list was made out, by somebody or other, of the different students in the school; and marks were placed against the names of the different students, indicating that they belonged to the one class or the other; and then somebody said a list was made out of the aristocracy of the school; and upon this, it seems, Mr. Stone got alarmed. He saw this list, and somebody told him it was a list of the aristocracy of the college; and thereupon Mr. Stone thought that that meant that they were going to bring up the old uncomfortable feeling again, and that a system of persecution was about to be established against the clerical students. I must say that that appears to be a conclusion drawn from very narrow and limited premises indeed. He hears that there is a list, and he hears from somebody who comes and tells him—a Divine, I think—that there is an Anti-Bunker Club, or an Anti-Bunker Confederation, or something of that kind; and that somebody has got the list, and that Fitzgerald is at the bottom of it. Upon which Mr. Stone, instead of inquiring—which it seems to me would have been a wiser and more discreet course to pursue—whether, supposing any such society to exist, it had shown itself in any thing like practical results, in any thing like persecution of the clerical part of the students, or in annoyance exhibited towards them, the first thing he thinks of is to get hold of the paper, and to see the list; and he goes to the room of Mr. Fitzgerald, for the purpose of seeing if he can discover any document, or any list, from which he can form an opinion as to whether the society exists or not. Unfortunately, Mr. Fitzgerald had left his pocket-book upon the table; and I suppose, between the Master, the Prefect, and Divine, and the young man — who, although a young man, is a member of the Philosophers' class—there did not exist the honourable forbearance which tells you that you are not to open another man's pocket-book or read his letters. Mr. Stone opens his pocket-book, and there he finds what you have had read again and again, and which will be submitted for your own ocular inspection; and from this he is perfectly satisfied of the existence of this formidable conspiracy, which was to shake to its foundation and rend in twain the establishment—namely, this frightful confederation of Anti-Bunkers; and fearful of the efficacious power of this confederacy, he goes to the President. And there I do not blame him; I think it was a proper matter for inquiry to be made into, and that it should be ascertained whether these young men had formed any association amongst themselves for the purpose of doing any thing that would be annoying to any portion of the establishment, whatever portion it might be. Dr. Northcote having heard the complaint, tells Mr. Stone to summon young Fitzgerald, and at the same time to demand from him this book; and if he would not give it him, to take it by force. Accordingly Mr. Stone comes and asks him for the pocket-book. He takes the young man into his room, and shuts the door; and on Fitzgerald refusing to give it up, he takes it from him—I will not say by superior force, but still he takes it from him—against his will, by putting his hand in his pocket.

Gentlemen, the first question will be this: Had Dr. Northcote, in the position in which he was placed with reference to these young men, as the master of a scholastic establishment in which Mr. Fitzgerald was a pupil, having reason to believe that there was something on foot with regard to the organisation of a society amongst the boys for the purpose of putting themselves into a state of antagonism with other members of the school, which could only lead to discomfort and unhappiness in the institution,—had he a right to make such an inquiry as he could, under the circumstances, to ascertain how that matter stood? Now, the power and authority of a schoolmaster is for the time the same as a father would have under the same circumstances. You place your child in the hands of a schoolmaster, delegating to him all that is essential to the welfare and good conduct of the child, and all the authority which is incidental to you as a father. Suppose any one of you had reason to believe that a son of yours was doing something which you would consider improper, wrong, wicked; and you believed that evidence of that conduct was to be found in a pocket-book which he had on his person, would you or would you not think yourself authorised to insist upon having that book handed over to you, and, on his refusal to hand it over, to use that reasonable amount of force which a father is entitled to exercise towards a son who is still within the parental control, for the purpose of obtaining from him that which, as a father, exercising a father's authority, you might desire to see, with a view to the reasonable correction of the boy, or for the purpose of bringing him into the right path? I cannot help thinking that, so far as this part of the case is concerned, you will be of opinion, having heard what these authorities have done, that Dr. Northcote,—having been informed by his subordinate officers that there were in this pocket-book entries having reference to the organisation of a confederation or association, which, if it really did exist for the purpose supposed, could not be characterised as otherwise than mischievous and pernicious,—as head-master of that establishment, would be justified in insisting on seeing the pocket-book which was supposed to contain evidence throwing light on the question which he was so much interested in ascertaining, and which it was his duty to settle to the satisfaction of all. But then comes the question whether, when this pocket-book was seen, the contents were such as to justify any reasonable person in coming to a conclusion that it really had any serious object or meaning, or that there really was any association amongst these lads organised and existing for the purpose of putting down, annoying, or in any way molesting and offending these poor Bunkers, as they were called, that is to say, the clerical students of the establishment. That is a matter on which you must exercise your judgment. As I said before, it is incidental to the authority of the head of a scholastic establishment to expel and dismiss from the school over which he presides any student or scholar whose conduct is such that he can no longer be permitted to remain a member of the establishment without danger to the other boys, from the contamination of his example. On the other hand, when a schoolmaster or the head of a scholastic establishment—in my days, I recollect, we used to call the establishment "school," the head was "head-master," and the second the "second-master" or "under-master," and so on; but now they call them colleges, heads, and principals: it used to be the fourth, fifth, and sixth form, or the first, second, and third class, according to the mode of enumeration then adopted in the one school or the other; now they are poets, rhetoricians, and philosophers. People now have got to use larger and more grandiloquent expressions, as "head," "president," "divine;" but it is the same thing. The head undertakes the care of the schoolboys; and he is then to be in the relation of schoolmaster to schoolboys, and it is one of the incidents of that relation that if the schoolmaster takes your son to educate him for a given time, whatever may be the time, he is bound by the terms of that contract to keep your boy and educate him, unless the circumstances are such as reasonably to warrant him in breaking his contract with you in reference to that boy on account of his misconduct. I cannot at all go the length which Mr. Karslake contended, of saying that is a matter in the mere arbitrament of the master, that he may exercise a mere capricious discretion—that it is not to be questioned. I admit that it ought not to be questioned lightly. The due exercise of the great authority which a schoolmaster or the head of a scholastic establishment enjoys, with reference to the general welfare of all those committed to his charge, is of such immense importance that a very large latitude must be allowed him. We must assume that such a power will not be lightly, wantonly, causelessly, and arbitrarily exercised; in other words, we are entitled to expect that it will be exercised reasonably: and if you are of opinion that here there has been an unreasonable exercise of that authority, it is not because we ought in all cases to make a very great allowance for the difficult position in which the head-master is placed that the plaintiff is not entitled to obtain your verdict. I cannot go the length that Mr. Karslake went, but I am bound to tell you that I think you ought to make the greatest possible allowance for the head-master of such an institution; and that, unless you are of opinion that Dr. Northcote exercised it unreasonably, you ought not to say so by your verdict; because no doubt the master is called on to exercise his authority in such a matter with more or less rapidity of decision, —he cannot deliberate over it as we have done—but he must form an honest judgment under the circumstances, and exercise a reasonable discretion, and not be led away by any caprice or any imaginary fancies of danger when none exists.

Now, gentlemen, you will say for yourselves whether or not you think that the evidence before you leads to any thing like a reasonable conclusion that there was this association organised amongst these young men for the purpose which is relied on by the defendants. Now one thing I own that strikes me very forcibly in this case is, that I do not find that amongst the clerical students any one comes forward and says, "We have been subjected to any annoyance or any molestation of any kind;" and I must say that I cannot help thinking that, instead of being satisfied with the mere production of this pocket-book, Dr. Northcote would have done much more wisely and sensibly if he had extended his inquiry and given it a little wider scope, and examined some of the clerical students with a view to ascertain whether there had been any outward manifestation of the motives and purposes for which this society was supposed to have been organised or promoted by Mr. Fitzgerald. You know the way in which it is put on the part of the plaintiff is, that this was mere nonsense; that he had jotted down some names for the amusement of himself or of some of those who, with himself, did not quite like the Divines and the masters who belonged to that portion of the institution: in a fit of either spleen or anger against Mr. Stone, he had jotted down, in a mere spirit of wanton frolic, the names of some of those who, he supposed, would form a society—what he called the

"Anti-Bunker Society." If this had been merely done in a spirit of frolic and fun, and never intended to go any further; if it was something between himself and one or two more, done in a moment of idleness and thoughtlessness, and had never assumed any thing like a practical form, probably you will agree with me in thinking that the wiser course would have been for Dr. Northcote to say, "Young man, this is a very foolish business; you do not stand on the safest ground; you have been in several scrapes this season; I very much fear you have done this with a bad motive, but I will inquire farther about it." And if he had inquired farther about it, he would have found that it rested entirely upon theory; that the parties to the A. B. C. had gone no further than putting down these names; that no one had been molested, and that in fact the confederation had assumed no tangible form whatever; that young Fitzgerald had gone out with his companions about the country just the same as he did before, and that it had no meaning, no substance, but was a sort of thing that existed only in an aërial imagination, and dissipated in a moment if you attempted to grasp it. Then if Dr. Northcote had ascertained this, it would have been a monstrous thing to say, and he would not have said probably, "You shall have that stigma attached to your character, that you have been expelled from a public establishment like this, because your conduct was so unworthy of the character of a gentleman, that you were not fit to associate with gentlemen." I must say I think they were a little hasty, to say the least of it. You must judge whether, upon the information they received with respect to the pocket-book, there was any thing to warrant a really well-founded charge against this young man of being the promoter of a society which, if it existed and was organised for the purpose for which Dr. Northcote supposed it was founded, was certainly of the most mischievous and pernicious character. You must judge for yourselves, not only whether any such society was formed and existed, but also whether Dr. Northcote had fair and reasonable ground to believe in its existence. As I have said before, the expulsion is not a matter on which you can give any damages, because it is not the ground of complaint in this action; it is only necessary to consider that incidentally, for this further purpose: they imprisoned him in his room and kept him there for a couple of hours, upon the ground that his conduct had been so bad that it was necessary to expel him; and they felt it had been such that, inasmuch as it was necessary to expel him, in order that he might not be brought into contact with the other students, and so have an opportunity of contaminating them, it was also necessary that during the interval that elapsed between the sentence of expulsion and his being taken away (he had to pack up and so on), he should be kept isolated and separated from the rest of the scholars. If the circumstances were such as to call for his expulsion, then no doubt it would be a right thing to say, "You have sought to sow dissension and to do mischief and create an ill-will amongst your fellow students,—that is the reason why you shall not stay here; and it is also a reason why, during the time you must stay, you shall not be allowed to come into contact with them." But if the first falls, then the second falls also; and even upon the second question I am not sure whether you will be of opinion that, even if they were justified in sending him away, they were justified in isolating him to this extent, namely, that he should not be allowed to have communication with the rest of the students. Inasmuch as a command from the proper authority to the other students might have been perfectly effectual to keep them in their bounds or in their playground, and to prevent them holding communication with him, the question is, whether it was necessary to turn the lock and confine him to the room during that time? Mr. Stone says, that is the fashion of the establishment when a boy is expelled, that he shall be kept locked up before he is removed, and that he acted on that. "It did not occur to me," he says, "at the time, that there was any particular expediency in keeping him separated from the rest of the boys, but I acted from the custom of the school." Gentlemen, it is for you to say whether that custom is reasonable. It is not because they have done so on former occasions, that they are justified in doing so when they say, "We will have you no longer a member of this establishment; you are expelled from it; your name is erased from the list of members; you no longer stand in the position of scholar and pupil to us as masters; we have done with you." Whether, after that, they are entitled to lock him up is a very serious question. But, however, if you think they were not justified in expelling him, then they were not justified in putting him under lock and key. These are the matters which are for your consideration.

I will just read to you the questions which I have put on paper, for it is a matter so complicated that it is just as well to have them in a tangible shape. The first question is, Whether the facts alleged in the declaration are made out? Whether the plaintiff was assaulted by the defendants, or either of them? If by the defendant Stone, was the latter acting under the authority of the defendant Dr. Northcote? If so, both are liable, unless the assault be justified. The same question applies as to the imprisonment. The same question as to taking of pocket-book. Now, on the plea of justification. First, was the plaintiff a pupil under the tutelage and government of the defendant, and subject to the rules and discipline of the school? If he was not, he was not liable to be expelled, because he was not a member of the school, for the breach of its rules or discipline, because he was not subject to those rules. As to that, the evidence is all one way, and I cannot help thinking you ought to find that issue in favour of the defendant. Now comes this important question, Was a society or combination formed and organised among certain of the students, injurious to the school and to some of the pupils? If so, was the plaintiff a member and promoter of such society; or, fourthly, had the defendant Dr. Northcote reasonable ground to believe such a society or combination to exist, and that the plaintiff was a a member of it? Fifthly, was it necessary, with a view to maintain the good order and discipline of the school, that the defendant Dr. Northcote should be made acquainted with the constitution and objects of the society, and who were its members? If so, was it necessary, for this purpose, that the plaintiff's pocket-book should be examined, or had the defendant Dr. Northcote reasonable ground to believe that such examination was necessary? If so, I direct you that if the plaintiff was subject to the authority of the defendant Dr. Northcote as master, the plea of justification, so far as the taking of the pocket-book is concerned, is made out, and also as to the assault committed in order to obtain it, unless more violence was used than was necessary. Then as to the imprisonment, were the circumstances such as to justify Dr. Northcote, in the reasonable exercise of his authority, in expelling the plaintiff? I put that to you not with a view to damages, because you cannot give damages. If so, was it necessary, for the purpose of preserving the discipline of the school, that the plaintiff should be prevented from communicating with the other pupils? Again, if so, was it necessary that he should be confined in his own room? Had the defendant Dr. Northcote reasonable grounds for believing that the course pursued was necessary for preserving the discipline and interests of the school? As you find the answers to those questions which I have put to you, we will enter the verdict for the defendant or for the plaintiff.

There still remains one question, as to the detention of the pocket-book. After the necessary purpose and object of taking it had been fully accomplished and satisfied, certainly the pocket-book might as well have been returned to him before he left; but it was not; and in respect of its detention, the plaintiff would be entitled to your verdict. But the defendants meet that by paying a shilling into Court for the detention of that, as nominal damages. It was no inconvenience not to have that old pocket-book with the manuscript, and therefore they say, "We pay a shilling into Court, and we say that will abundantly meet the justice of the case." If that is so, the defendant will be entitled to your verdict in respect of that detention. That leaves the real matter open.

Gentlemen, there was some manifestation of opinion elicited from you in the course of the case yesterday. One or two gentlemen were very anxious to stop the case in its outset. I cannot help thinking you will be satisfied now that the case was one which it was desirable on all accounts you should hear out from its commencement to the end, and that you will feel that there was more in it for your decision than may at first sight have appeared. It is a question of great importance on the one hand and on the other. It is for the general benefit of society, and especially of the younger portion of it, that the authority on the part of those who are at the head of our scholastic institutions shall be maintained, and on the other hand it is equally important that the authority shall not arbitrarily, capriciously, and unreasonably be exercised; and as you think it has been exercised here reasonably or unreasonably (we cannot doubt that it has been exercised honestly), so you will find your verdict for the plaintiff or for the defendant. If your verdict should be for the plaintiff, I do not apprehend that you would desire to give any thing like vindictive damages. The distinguished individual who represents the plaintiff here can have but one object, which is to perfectly rehabilitate his son, and to restore him to that position in society which he is entitled to occupy, without any stigma or stain attaching to him in respect of his conduct at this institution. On the other hand, however desirable that may be, if you think the plaintiff is not fairly entitled to your verdict, you will not, in order to effect that very desirable object, give him your verdict, whatever may be your sympathies for the boy.

With these observations I leave the case entirely in your hands, and by your answers to those questions I shall be guided in directing the verdict.

Mr. Karslake: Will your Lordship let us have a copy of the questions?

Lord Chief-Justice Cockburn: Certainly.

[The Jury retire to consider their verdict at 4·15. At 5·40 the Jury return into Court.]

The Associate: Gentlemen, are you agreed upon your verdict?

The Foreman of the Jury: We are (*handing in a paper*).

Lord Chief-Justice Cockburn: You find for the plaintiff, on the ground that he was imprisoned and assaulted, with damages, 5*l*.

The Foreman of the Jury: Yes, my Lord.

Lord Chief-Justice Cockburn: Hand in my paper. (*It was handed in to his Lordship.*) Your answers in detail to these questions are: That the plaintiff was assaulted by Stone, by the authority of Dr. Northcote; that he was imprisoned; that his pocket-book was taken from him. You find that he was a pupil subject to the discipline of the school; that there was not a society or combination organised; that the circumstances were not such as to justify Dr. Northcote, in the reasonable exercise of his authority, in expelling the plaintiff; nor had he reasonable ground for believing that the course pursued was necessary for the purpose of preserving the discipline of the school. Then you find upon the whole for the plaintiff: damages, *5l.* And as regards the detention of the pocket-book, that one shilling is sufficient. That is a verdict for the plaintiff: damages, *5l.*

Mr. V. Harcourt: There are in this case certain questions of law which may properly and fairly be raised; and under those circumstances, I hope your Lordship will put us in a position of raising those questions.

Lord Chief-Justice Cockburn: What questions of law?

Mr. V. Harcourt: I would of course much rather not go into a detail of them; but there are questions of law.

Lord Chief-Justice Cockburn: I must see that there are some grounds on which I ought to stay execution. Neither of you have suggested any question to the jury, other than those I have put.

Mr. V. Harcourt: I might state, as a single question, the question of the existence of a contract between the father of the pupil and the schoolmaster with reference to the expulsion, and the character of that contract. That is clearly a question of law.

Lord Chief-Justice Cockburn: Yes; but it is one on which I entertain no doubt whatever, and therefore I do not think I ought to stay execution.

Mr. V. Harcourt: Again, your Lordship will see, even though there were such a contract, this is not a person who was a party to that contract.

Lord Chief-Justice Cockburn: And I have told the jury that they ought not to give any damages in respect of the expulsion; but inasmuch as it was necessary to determine whether they were right in sending this young man away, with a view to the question of imprisonment, it was necessary to look at that part of the case.

Mr. V. Harcourt: I do not wish to persevere against your Lordship's opinion; but of course, without prejudicing our right to move, I only make the application.

Lord Chief-Justice Cockburn: You do not want any leave on my part for moving in the matter. On the contrary, I should be very glad that you should do so, if you think, on reflection, that there is any thing that ought to be reviewed or reconsidered. But I own I entertain such a confident view of the doctrine I have laid down, that I do not think I ought to give any sanction.

Mr. V. Harcourt: This is out of Term, your Lordship sees; and it is not a question of money in any way, but a question of merely discussing these points.

Lord Chief-Justice Cockburn: I quite agree; but I think the Judge implies some doubt when he does any thing to stay the execution.

Mr. V. Harcourt: Your Lordship has said enough to remove that impression.

Mr. Coleridge: Will your Lordship certify for a special jury?

Lord Chief-Justice Cockburn: Yes.

Mr. Coleridge: And further, that it is a proper case to have been tried here?

Lord Chief-Justice Cockburn: Yes, certainly.

Mr. V. Harcourt: Will your Lordship allow us to have a copy of the findings and the answers of the jury?

Lord Chief-Justice Cockburn: Yes, certainly; I will take care you have them. On the trover count there will be a verdict for the defendant.

Mr. Coleridge: Certainly.

THE END.

www.ingramcontent.com/pod-product-compliance
Lightning Source LLC
Chambersburg PA
CBHW030346270326
41926CB00009B/983
9783741139925